38.X

5.99

Ezra Pound, Popular Genres,
and the
Discourse of Culture

Michael Coyle

Ezra Pound, Popular Genres, and the Discourse of Culture

The Pennsylvania State University Press
University Park, Pennsylvania

Library of Congress Cataloging-in-Publication Data

Coyle, Michael, 1957–
    Ezra Pound, popular genres, and the discourse of culture / Michael Coyle.
        p.   cm.
    Includes bibliographical references and index.
    ISBN 0-271-01421-0 (acid-free paper)
    1. Pound, Ezra, 1885–1972—Criticism and interpretation.
2. Pound, Ezra, 1885–1972—Knowledge and learning.   3. Influence (Literary, artistic, etc.)   4. Popular culture in literature.
5. Language and culture.   6. Literary form.   I. Title.
PS3531.O82Z565   1995
811'.52—dc20   94-31113
                                                                                         CIP

Copyright © 1995 The Pennsylvania State University
All rights reserved
Printed in the United States of America

Published by The Pennsylvania State University Press,
University Park, PA 16802-1003

It is the policy of The Pennsylvania State University Press to use acid-free paper for the first printing of all clothbound books. Publications on uncoated stock satisfy the minimum requirements of American National Standard for Information Sciences—Permanence of Paper for Printed Library Materials, ANSI Z39.48–1984.

The diseased periphery of letters is now howling that literature and poetry in especial, should keep within bounds. I find this limitation entitled "respect itself," which phrase is perverted to mean that literature should eschew the major field by omitting and leaving untackled a great deal of the subject matter that interested such diverse writers as Propertius, Dante and Lope de Vega.
—Ezra Pound, "The Individual in His Milieu" (1935)

Contents

Acknowledgments ix
Abbreviations xi
Introduction 1

1 The Frontiers of Criticism and the Circumscription of Ol' Ez

    Retrospective Selection/Definitive Edition 11
    "The Setting of Bounds" 18
    "An Illusion Fostered by Academic Authorities" 26

2 "A Profounder Didacticism": Ruskin, Orage, and Pound's Vision of Cultural Totality

    "Pound at His Most Old-Fashioned" 35
    Aestheticizing "the Aesthete's Critique" 45
    A. R. Orage and the Eclectic *New Age* 54
    The Symptomatic and Pound's "Aggregation of Particulars" 64

3 Epic Inclusiveness and the Innovations of *Eleven New Cantos*

    The Pressure of the Literary 79
    Narrative in Epic and Epic Narrative 86
    The Prose of the *Pagany* Cantos of 1931 99
    "Litterae Nihil Sanantes" 113

4 Popularizing Primers and the Discourse of Culture

    The Popularizers of Romance 121
    A Proliferation of Alphabets 127
    The Impact of Fact, or History as Table Talk 134
    Frobenius and the Constructions of *Guide to Kulchur* 140

5 Unpacking Münch's Satchel:
  Musical Notation and the Defiance of *Pisan Cantos*

    "The Poetry Breaks Off"   149
    The Legacy of Pater: Eliot, Lewis, and the Idea of Music   153
    "Gettin Round to a Few Formulations"   162
    Making "Sense" of Pound's Musical Notation   168

6 "These are the Histories, OR": Narrative in the Benton
  Cantos of *Section: Rock-Drill*

    The History That Is in the *Cantos*   183
    The Underpinnings of Benton's *View*   187
    "Whole Slabs of the Record": Pound's Poetics of Inclusion   192
    View and Vortex   198

7 "Nummulary Moving Toward Prosody":
  The Del Mar Cantos of *Thrones*

    "The Main Interest Is Not in Aesthetics"   211
    Numismatics and the Discourse of Cultural Totality   215
    Prophet and Profit   222

8 *E Basta*   241

Index   247

Acknowledgments

No reading is immediate; no acknowledgments can ever be complete. While working on this project I realized more than ever that, as Michel Foucault first suggested, the idea of the individual author is merely a convention. Many people have contributed to my work here, and their contributions took many forms. This project originated ten years ago in the doctoral seminars of Ralph Cohen, whose work on genre has long pioneered a new literary history capable of exploring the interactions of text and context, and of demonstrating how the latter is a constituent of the former without depending on historicist totalization. Professor Cohen often insists that the place to begin in the study of any text is with those parts of it that seem least to belong: the impress of that teaching is obvious in what follows.

To other scholars I owe other debts. The work of the late Raymond Williams in crucial ways made this study imaginable, both in its historicizing of some of our most enabling critical premises, and in its demonstration of what Williams called "our tradition." That I am more skeptical of the tradition he first identified as such makes me no wiser, but undoubtedly sadder. Jerome McGann quickened my awareness of how much the development of this tradition in Britain and America owed to Coleridge. Exchanges with Herbert C. Tucker enriched my sense of nineteenth-century conceptions of epic and their relation to the discourse of culture. Early on in my work, Robert Langbaum encouraged me to pursue Pound's relations with Ruskin. Ron Bush proposed further readings on that theme and was generous with his time and attention. Kenneth Elzinga, at the University of Virginia, and Michael Haines, at Colgate University, both offered different kinds of guidance through what was for me unfamiliar terrain in economic theory and history. David Radcliffe, of Virginia Polytechnic Institute and State University, provided invaluable encouragement by keeping me always mindful of how strange modern notions of "culture" would have seemed to the seventeenth- and eighteenth-century subjects of his own study. Patricia O'Neill, of Hamilton College, struggled against insuperable odds to protect the nineteenth century from my reconstructions and reread certain chapters a no-longer-ascertainable number of times. This book owes much to the conversation and patience of my colleagues and friends, particularly to Lea

Baechler, Peter Balakian, Linck Johnson, Margaret Maurer, and Edward Tomarken. It owes something more, however, to the patience and curiosity of my daughter, Deirdre; her delighted transformation of canceled drafts into drawing paper reaffirmed daily the importance of making things new and reminded me that learning should be a labor of love.

I thank New Directions Publishing Corporation and Faber and Faber Ltd. for permission to quote from the poetry and prose of Ezra Pound. The Division of Humanities at Colgate University supplied lengthy support for research, and for a near constant flow of interlibrary loans. In fact, Jane Pinchin has been the perfect dream of a division director, taking time off from her own work to foster an academic atmosphere of industry and community exchange. To the interlibrary loan office, and the reference office, at Case Library I offer slightly embarrassed thanks and marvel that I have yet to wear out their good will and patience. The Colgate University Research Council and Faculty Development Committee have supplied funds for study and travel. Parts of this book have appeared in different form in *ELH, Modern Language Quarterly*, and *Paideuma*.

Abbreviations

ABCE   Ezra Pound, *ABC of Economics* (London: Faber & Faber, 1933); rpt. *Selected Prose* (New York: New Directions, 1973), 233–64.

ABCR   Ezra Pound, *ABC of Reading* (New York: New Directions, 1934).

EPM   R. Murray Schafer, ed., *Ezra Pound and Music: The Complete Criticism* (New York: New Directions, 1977).

GK   Ezra Pound, *Guide to Kulchur* (London: Faber & Faber, 1938); originally published in America as *Culture* (New York: New Directions, 1938).

LE   T. S. Eliot, ed., *Literary Essays of Ezra Pound* (New York: New Directions, 1954).

NA   *New Age* (London), 1907–1922.

NEW   *New English Weekly* (London), 1931–1933.

OPAP   T. S. Eliot, *On Poetry and Poets* (New York: Farrar, Straus and Cudahy, 1957).

SE   T. S. Eliot, *Selected Essays*, 2d American ed. (New York: Harcourt, Brace & Co., 1950).

SL   D. D. Paige, ed., *Selected Letters of Ezra Pound, 1907–1941* (New York: New Directions, 1971).

SP   William Cookson, ed., *Ezra Pound: Selected Prose, 1909–1965* (New York: New Directions, 1973).

SR   Ezra Pound, *The Spirit of Romance*, New American Edition (New York: New Directions, 1968).

Introduction

> Kinds are the very life of literature, and truths and strengths come from the complete recognition of them.
> —Henry James, preface to *The Awkward Age*,
> vol. 9 of *The Novels and Tales of Henry James* (1908)

During his London years Pound occasionally delighted in excerpting snippets from the mass-circulation dailies and reprinting them in the more "highbrow" weeklies and monthlies with which he was variously associated. Giving the excerpts sarcastic titles like "Revolutionary Maxims," "Revelations," or—less playfully—"Inconsiderable Imbecilities," he sought to embarrass popular opinion by placing it into elite context. In retrospect, these cuttings often preciously imitated the politically topical "Current Cant" or "Press Cuttings" columns that A. R. Orage ran in the *New Age*, but methodologically they exemplify that mixing of genres Pound would later call the new historical method. By that time he was involved in the wholesale inclusion of texts and parts of other texts into his own. As he described it in *Guide to Kulchur* (1938), this "new historical method" was to be distinguished from more orthodox post-Enlightenment practice by its inclusion of "whole slabs of the record." By "history" Pound meant actual historical texts—not just academic commentaries on them, and not just histories but texts of all kinds—the "concrete" evidence of legal codes and poems alike. By "including" he meant neither paraphrase nor allusion, but the transposition of the language of his sources onto his page. He expected that this procedure would ensure historical integrity. Pound himself did not consider that he was introducing change of any kind, but only revealing latent significance; nevertheless, this kind of inclusion meant changing the meaning of words by changing their context. This revealing worked, in other words, as had his satiric "Revelations," on the basis of generic transformation.

My study of Pound proceeds on the same basis: I endeavor to change our sense of his work by reasserting the pressure of its contemporaneous contexts and by examining the implications of its generic intersections. Pound's generic experiments were programmatic and purposive, even where they failed or were superseded by subsequent and different experiments. I propose, moreover, the value of generic inquiry even where Pound had been thinking in other terms, reconstructing generic matrices whose force has been lost to scholarly explanation. But if like Pound I alter context, I do not do so to embarrass other readings of his work, but to foreground the assumptions on which critical constructions rest. If we cannot read Pound in the manner he intended (a manner that changed over time), we can clarify why not, even as we consider whether to continue reading him at all.

The most characteristic feature of the *Cantos*, as well as of such prose works as *Guide to Kulchur*, is its inclusiveness. After once sustaining work on the *Cantos*, and throughout frequently shifting thematic interests, Pound worked continuously to expand poetry's "proper" domain. What resulted was so wildly heterogeneous that some critics concluded that questions of genre had been rendered irrelevant.[1] For the most part, critics preferred to follow Hugh Kenner's often dazzling lead and explained Pound's work in terms of Pound's own metaphors of "patterned energy" and "self-interfering patterns." In the mid-eighties, however, the debate between Michael André Bernstein and Max Nänny reasserted the value of genre study, with Bernstein defending his perception of the *Cantos* as an epic against Nänny's

---

1. Consider the three very different examples of Allen Tate, Hugh Kenner, and Jean-Michel Rabaté. Tate's "Ezra Pound's Golden Ass," *Nation*, 10 June 1931, argues for the singular simplicity of Pound's form—*conversation*. In *The Pound Era* (Berkeley and Los Angeles: University of California Press, 1971), particularly 168–71, Hugh Kenner develops several alternatives to the language of genre. Borrowing on the one hand from science and on the other from myth, Kenner elaborates on Buckminster Fuller's notion of the "self-interfering pattern" (145) and relates that notion to an understanding of "homeomorphic" transformation wherein "poems cohere, as do fish, and yet are derivable from other poems." Further on, Kenner aphoristically details the process of metamorphosis, in which "coherence remains, forms alter" (367–69). In *Language, Sexuality, and Ideology in Ezra Pound's "Cantos"* (Albany: State University of New York Press, 1986), a book whose very title suggests its many interests, Jean-Michel Rabaté submits that "to pose the question of genres in this necessarily rapid discussion seems a little idle, since Pound himself, who repeatedly alluded to his *Cantos* as an 'epic poem,' nevertheless discredited the relevance of such traditional and Aristotelian categories. Since no 'Aquinas map' is valid, it would be rash to superimpose an Aristotelian map" (292). If genre were indeed but a "category," even an "Aristotelian category," such impatience would be justified, but the work of recent genre theorists has liberated genre study from such clumsy models and disassociated it from the activity of classification.

revisionist identification of it as Menippean satire.[2] Nänny's case was compounded on his properly keen sense of the importance of Pound's mixture of prose and poetry, on Pound's having so widely "poached" on other genres, and on Pound's injunction in *The Spirit of Romance* that "an epic cannot be written against the grain of its time." "What the *Cantos* obviously do *not* do," Nänny maintained, "is to voice the general heart." Bernstein countered that Nänny's thesis, "instead of offering a more sharply focused view of the poem," only succeeded "in collapsing quite distinct literary forms into one another, thereby confusing the essential features of two separate genres to their mutual detriment." Bernstein's defense of his position rested on claims about the nature of genre itself: "Literary terms, it is useful to recognize, do not exist in isolation: they are parts of a classificatory system whose elements derive meaning from their place within an articulated structure." And because, he cautioned, "forms do change with each exemplary work," definitions "must be sufficiently well defined to be usable within the system of classification." I share Bernstein's conviction of the importance of genre study, but I do not agree that genre study is about classification or that generic features "derive their meaning from their place within an articulated structure."[3] In this book, and in general, I understand genre more dynamically, without reference to a prior model of a static, essentialized and closed system. Such a system can neither define its terms nor their interrelationships adequately because it finds in the heterogeneous a violation of normal practice.

If, with recent genre critics like Ralph Cohen or Clifford Siskin, we begin by assuming that the heterogeneous is itself normal, then it becomes surprising that so shrewd a thinker as Derrida should discern a "law" of genre that

---

2. The debate was inaugurated by Bernstein's *Tale of the Tribe: Ezra Pound and the Modern Verse Epic* (Princeton: Princeton University Press, 1980). Nänny published his "Ezra Pound and the Menippean Tradition" in *Paideuma* 11 (winter 1982). Bernstein's defense, "Distinguendum est inter et inter: A Defense of Calliope," appeared in *Paideuma* 12 (fall and winter 1983). Nänny's rebuttal, "More Menippus than Callipe: A Reply," appeared in *Paideuma* 13 (fall 1984).

3. Bernstein is not, of course, alone in conceiving of genre in this way. The notion that genres constitute a "system" has been central to the work of several recent theorists. Besides, for instance, Gary Saul Morson's *Boundaries of Genre* (Austin: University of Texas Press, 1981), to which Bernstein himself refers, there is the work of Ann Freadman, of which Tony Bennett has recently made use. Freadman proposes that genres are not "defineable in terms of a set of inherent characteristics," rather, "what are posited as inherent generic characteristics can only be so posited 'because they are correlated with places in a system of contrasts.' Constituted as a system of differences (not-statements), genres are inherently relational constructs." Freadman, "Untitled: (on genre)," *Cultural Studies* 2, no. 1 (1988): 79; quoted in Tony Bennett, *Outside Literature* (London: Routledge, 1990), 92.

calls for deconstruction.⁴ As Cohen explains, "genre concepts in theory and practice arise, change, and decline for historical reasons. And since each genre is composed of texts that accrue, the grouping is a process, not a determinate category. Genres are open categories. Each member alters the genre by adding, contradicting, or changing constituents, especially those of members most closely related to it."⁵ The strength of the idea that genres form a system lies in the attention it calls to the relations between genres and in its resistance to the narrowly formalist expectation that the individual text can generate the significance of generic features. The weakness of the idea that genres form a "system" lies in the encouragement such a conception gives to the impulse to codify. Here Derrida is right: any "law" engenders its own violation. But we can recognize that in any particular time, the relations among genres are hierarchical, both within and between related groups of genres.

The idea of "literature" itself involves shifting relations among genres, and the valorization of new groups of genres as uniquely expressive of imagination.⁶ The phrase Pound quoted from John Adams quoting Seneca the Younger, "litterae nihil sanantes," suggests the crucial question of how the *Cantos* relates to the various discourses which it mixes. Like many of Pound's most resonant phrases, it has a long history, and in the *Cantos* acquires multivalent function. In its most obvious sense it is a declaration for action over writing. Several critics have emphasized this aspect of Pound's rhetoric, but doing so does not explain why he then continued to invest his most passionate aspirations in writing. In its two appearances in the *Cantos* "litterae nihil sanantes" (literature that heals nothing) refers directly to men who wrote much, with the best intentions, but to little significant effect. In neither of these appearances does the word *litterae* refer to "literature" in its modern, exclusive sense; yet such a reference is finally inevitable, since other elements in the *Cantos* do ask to be judged according to the highest "literary" standards, and since critical response to the work has from the beginning turned on the issue of its "literary" merit. I identify many of Pound's experiments in genre in order to explain some of the strategies by which he hoped to make his writing enduring and effective.

---

4. See Jacques Derrida, "The Law of Genre," *Critical Inquiry* 7 (autumn 1980), and Ralph Cohen's critique of Derrida's notion of that "law," "History and Genre," *New Literary History* 17 (winter 1986). See also Siskin's account of Cohen's critique in *The Historicity of Romantic Discourse* (New York: Oxford University Press, 1988), 22.
5. Cohen, "History and Genre," 204.
6. In *Literary Theory: An Introduction* (Minneapolis: University of Minnesota Press, 1983), 9–11, Terry Eagleton makes an argument related to that which I advance here and in Chapter 3.

Pound did not believe, as Auden put it, that "poetry makes nothing happen"—although he understood and eventually rejected the nineteenth-century ideology of "culture" in which that "nothing" is valuable in and of itself. In this phrase Auden—appropriately enough since he was elegizing Yeats—reinscribes the romantic valorization of imagination and reaffirms the view of the mechanical world as hostile domain. Thus Auden's line was not as despondent as it is sometimes taken to be. But Pound's conception of the contest was entirely different and, in comparison with that of Auden or of almost anyone else, radical. Before 1920 he came to believe that "literature," romanticized and rarefied, could and would indeed change nothing. But for Pound "nothing" was not a charged word. He took his argument to be a historical one, and poetic anemia a merely modern condition. So long as poets and critics struggle to maintain for literature a privileged position, just so long would poetry remain enervated and etiolated. Pound pursued his attack on exclusive views of poetry both in his critical and poetic writing, but his broadest ambition was to create a work more inclusive than anything since Homer. He wanted a poetry of the agora, a poetry that could include the transactions of economic and political power.

As I explain in Chapter 2, Pound's was an extreme version of aestheticism: he wanted both to politicize the aesthetic and—more disturbingly—aestheticize the political. In examining the interaction between these two impulses, I represent Pound's career in a manner out of keeping with several stimulating recent studies. Philip Furia's *Pound's Cantos Declassified* (1984), for example, emphasizes the importance of the nonliterary elements included in the *Cantos*.[7] Although an important step, Furia's notion of "declassifying" "documents" discounts the dynamics of textual transformation and suggests that Pound's combinatory procedures are straightforward and transparent. As Dominick LaCapra has argued, this assumption is in general problematic.[8] It is particularly so in Pound's case, as I submit in Chapters 6 and 7. On the other hand, Kathryne Lindberg's *Reading Pound Reading* (1987) presents concerns antithetical to Furia's interest in the extraliterary.[9] Lindberg maintains that "literature never ceased being [Pound's] privileged category, if only by exceeding all categories" (47). Lindberg is not, of course,

---

7. Philip Furia, *Pound's Cantos Declassified* (University Park: Pennsylvania State University Press, 1984).

8. See Dominick LaCapra's *Rethinking Intellectual History: Texts, Contexts, Language* (Ithaca: Cornell University Press, 1983), esp. 23–71.

9. Kathryne V. Lindberg, *Reading Pound Reading: Modernism after Nietzsche* (New York: Oxford University Press, 1987).

concerned with genre, and so it is neither surprising that she should conceive of literature as a "category" nor that she should find Pound's practice in excess of categorical limits: again, any law engenders its own violation. Because I am interested in articulating how it is that different discourses interact, I describe Pound's project in terms of what it includes and not in term of what (norms) it exceeds or violates. Lindberg invokes a categorical generic model to insist that "Pound challenges the categories and hierarchies of canonical criticism and linguistics," presenting Pound as a sort of proto-Derridean. This makes for a provoking argument, but the "categories and hierarchies" that it requires Pound to have challenged simply were not in place during the early decades of the twentieth century. Certainly Pound's work challenged hierarchies; but if we conflate his responses to critics like Arnold Bennett, Edmund Gosse, William Gardner Hale, or Charles Whibley with poststructuralist critiques of formalism, we risk naturalizing those hierarchies and sacrificing important opportunities to study Pound's historical singularity, and our own. Lindberg's substantial contribution lies in her discussion of Pound's debts to Nietzsche. But we must not forget the extraliterary and popularized character of that debt. Pound indisputably absorbed a good deal of Nietzsche, but he did so through the mediation of A. R. Orage and such of his circle as J. M. Kennedy.[10] That Pound should have acquired the better part of his familiarity with Nietzsche through the *New Age* meant that the "Nietzsche" he picked up came already mixed with a stiff dose of Ruskinian cultural organicism.

Other recent studies have invoked theoretical models to establish the radical difference between Pound's writing and conventional humanistic models. The most severe argument has been made by Robert Casillo, whose *The Genealogy of Demons* asserts that "Pound's anti-Semitism and fascism, far from being adventitious, aberrant, or marginal features of his mind and work, are inseparable from his linguistic strategies and personal psychology."[11] Casillo's study in this way subsumes other interpretative claims about the *Cantos* under a new totality, argued for in terms of "ideology" and "deep structure." His approach is to "elucidate systematically the connection between Pound's work and the historical ideologies he embraces." Here, I present Pound very differently, not because I believe Pound was free of fascism—he was not—but because I proceed on the basis of different

10. For a study of Nietzsche's reception in English that has much to say about Orage and the *New Age*, see David Thatcher's *Nietzsche in England, 1890–1914: The Growth of a Reputation* (Toronto: University of Toronto Press, 1970), esp. chap. 8.

11. Robert Casillo, *The Genealogy of Demons: Anti-Semitism, Fascism, and the Myths of Ezra Pound* (Evanston: Northwestern University Press, 1988), viii, see also 16.

theoretical assumptions. The genre-based history I develop, by anticipating partial intersections—mixtures rather than essences—avoids reifying Pound's combinatory procedures into deep structures that somehow reproduce ideological totalities.

Like "culture," "ideology" is a nineteenth-century invention that is, in its very conception, inherently totalizing. As Raymond Williams explained (at the very time Pound was completing *Thrones*), both terms refer not so much to ideas as to ways of thinking. Terry Eagleton, who in the last decades of the twentieth century has been the most prominent advocate of ideology critique, envisions the critic's task as the striving to reveal how, within "the 'imaginary' of ideology, or of aesthetic taste, reality comes to seem totalized and purposive."[12] "Ideology," Eagleton argues, "aims to disclose something of a relation between an utterance and its material conditions of possibility, when those conditions of possibility are viewed in the light of certain power-struggles central to the reproduction (or also, for some theories, contestation) of a whole form of social life."[13] My historicization of "culture" complicates such explanations in two ways.

First, the expectation that a critic might articulate a "whole form of social life" underneath history is misdirected. In Pound's case, such thinking participates in the very totalizing dreams that remain the most important dimension of his work yet to be understood. We might, using one of the subsidiary understandings of the word that Eagleton isolates in *Ideology: An Introduction*, say that Pound's strivings for a totalizing vision were ideological; but it does not follow that those strivings were systematic or even consistent. As a descriptive term, "ideology" is unexceptional, but insofar as it anticipates "a whole social life" it is incapable of carrying explanatory weight. I would extend what the "post-Marxists" Ernesto Laclau and Chantal Mouffe have observed about the Marxist notions of "class" or "revolution" to the concept of "ideology" itself: it is "a myth," capable as such of power, but obstructionist in explaining the concrete relations among different kinds of discursive praxis.[14]

Second, I resist invoking notions of ideology because the totality that they posit is to be understood as anterior and external to the literary productions they supposedly underlie. In *Outside Literature*, Tony Bennett objects that "Eagleton's central contention in [*Criticism and Ideology*] is that works of

---

12. Terry Eagleton, *The Ideology of the Aesthetic* (London: Basil Blackwell, 1990), 87.
13. Terry Eagleton, *Ideology: An Introduction* (London: Verso, 1991), 223.
14. See Ernesto Laclau and Chantal Mouffe, *Hegemony and Socialist Strategy: Towards a Radical Democratic Politics* (New York: Verso, 1985), or Bennett, *Outside Literature*.

literature signify history indirectly via the ways in which they signify the ideologies which mediate their relations to history." In so doing, Bennett proposes, Eagleton merely displaces Marx's model of base/superstructure with the new equivalent terms of history/literature. Both oppositions depend on a larger, profound, totality. Pound's work too grew out of and refers to a vision of historical totality. In his case, he understood it and pursued it in terms of "culture," and it led him to deliberately antisystematic writing. It also led him into fascism; but instead of investigating whether or not Pound "was" a fascist and seeking another kind of explanatory purity and essence, genre-based history asks how fascism enters the discursive mixtures of Pound's writing—what kinds of changes does it introduce into that mixture and how.

I do not attempt to systematize Pound's work. I neither explain his vision of one totality in terms of another nor his enduring fascination with one of the most enduring myths of the nineteenth century, "culture," in terms of another, "ideology." When I refer to "the discourse of culture," I use the word "discourse" to post a semiotic tradition without having "postulat[ed] from the outset that the utterance discourse forms a whole."[15] I use the word "discourse" rather than "idea" to emphasize the materiality of this tradition and to focus on its implications for ways of writing or, in other words, generic practices. Ideas about "culture" created new genres and superannuated others, but not all at once or in the same way. I historicize "culture" to explore not the history of an idea but how certain assumptions and arguments about human relations alter the generic configurations of a period, by which I mean both particular genres and the relations among genres. There are large and complex histories to be written here, and in writing a generic history of Pound's poetic experiments and the relation of those experiments to "culture," I hope to suggest what kinds of problems such histories must confront.

Because it involves a heuristic model that does not depend on the assertion of positive identity, genre-based history can negotiate not only between "literary" forms, but also between "literary" and nonliterary discursive forms. In this capacity, it has enabled my representation of Pound's activity in a way that relies less on grand notions of "modernism" and the figures most "central" to it, and more on the often, to us, secondary figures through and with whom Pound acquired his sense of where and how he ought to do battle.[16] I return repeatedly to Pound's extended contacts with "popular"

15. A. J. Greimas and J. Courtés, *Semiotics and Language: An Analytical Dictionary* (Bloomington: Indiana University Press, 1982), 82.
16. For informative analysis studying the dissemination of ideas from serious philosophy, see

genres and traditions. Most often, where Pound seems to us to have embarked on exotic or idiosyncratic projects, there we will find him in contact with what were then relatively "vulgar" topics. But if these interests of Pound's attracted notice only to be dismissed as "old-fashioned," they have since typically attracted little notice at all, proving invisible to readers looking back to "modernism" as the source of the still-unassimilated "new."

This is not a book about popular culture so much as Pound's borrowings from and forays into extraliterary genres. In it I examine what happens to heteroclite elements once they are included in Pound's text, as well as how they alter the materials with which they are combined. I aim less to provide "close readings" than to read closely in order to understand how and why Pound combines different genres and includes different texts within his own. Generally, I conceive my subject as Pound's writing in relation to the changing features of critical discourse. As a study of Pound's combinatory procedures, it is then a study of historically specific relations: of "modernism" at its most elite with popular genres that carried over distinctly Victorian norms, of "literature" with didactic and utilitarian writings, and of poetry with prose; of a past become stranger than we ordinarily recognize that yet continues to mediate the more distant past.

I begin by reflecting on a salient instance of this mediation: Eliot's *Literary Essays of Ezra Pound*, in which Eliot endeavors quite overtly to establish a new context wherein a part of Pound's work might be taken for the whole. The book constitutes, in other words, another instance of generic transformation, and one to which Pound objected. Chapter 2 then turns to precisely that element of Pound's work which Eliot with the best of intentions strove to elide or at least subordinate. As an archaeology of Pound's conception of cultural totality, this chapter serves as a basis for the subsequent consideration of his determination to develop a radically inclusive poetics. That inclusiveness is then the subject of Chapter 3, in which I focus on *Eleven New Cantos XXXI–XLI* (1934): the first section of the *Cantos* to include prose without even gesturing toward the usual rhythms and textures of Pound's poetic line—particularly Canto 33, which after nine short lines, appears entirely in justified prose. Chapter 4 continues this attention to Pound's work with prose by turning to his didactic primers. I argue here that works like *ABC of Economics* or *Guide to Kulchur* are neither glosses on the *Cantos* nor irrelevant

---

Sanford Schwartz, *The Matrix of Modernism: Pound, Eliot, and Early Twentieth-Century Thought* (Princeton: Princeton University Press, 1985).

to it. These primers are rather extensions of the *Cantos*, and products of the same combinatory procedures, as well as of Pound's "ideogrammic" method.

Yet while I seek to alter our sense of the relation between Pound's prose and poetry, I want also to restore to its historical context our perception of Pound's activity as a popularizer. To this end I offer in Chapter 4 an account of that activity in terms of the characteristically nineteenth-century tradition of popularized scholarship. This concern with popularization then leads me in Chapter 5 to what might seem an unlikely place—the *Pisan Cantos*, and within it to a still more unlikely place, Canto 75. Pound's inclusion of the curious "bird-song" canto, which consists of seven lines of poetry and then a page and a half of musical notation, owes directly to his didactic ambitions, but the separation of sound from sense in Canto 75 prompts us to ask whether Pound's combinatory procedures create sense or resist the sense of his sources. These questions return us to the role played by critical activity and carry my study forward into its final two chapters. In Chapter 6 I examine what happens to Thomas Hart Benton's nineteenth-century prose narrative history once incorporated into the poetic line of *Section: Rock-Drill de los Cantares* 85–95. This section of Canto 88 is an important moment in the *Cantos*—Pound's last extended engagement of modern history, as well as his only sustained attempt to reproduce a narrative within his own programatically antinarrative work. The very nature of his attempt generated such internal resistance that Benton's material becomes, in narrative terms, unreadable. Nevertheless, that straining of intelligibility grew still more pronounced in Pound's last completed volume, which provides the site for Chapter 7. *Thrones* too turns to a nineteenth-century narrative history—but in this case Pound strove to reproduce, not so much its story, but its method. The narrative history was Alexander Del Mar's *History of Monetary Systems*, and Pound's use of it pleased few readers; time and again critics objected that this material failed to achieve the status of "art." Within the terms of their evaluations, those judgments were sound. There is, yet, an instructive irony to them, for the writing in *Thrones* exemplifies the extent to which Pound's pursuit of the extraliterary remained heavily aestheticized.

In this book I establish the presence of a variety of period materials in the generic mixtures of specific Pound texts. I have embedded my arguments in historical detail in order to escape shopworn metanarratives about either "the course" of the nineteenth century or of "the genesis" of modernism. This book develops on the basis of genre study because the dynamics of generic transformation offer a supple and powerful model for articulating the dynamics of "cultural" transformation.

1
The Frontiers of Criticism and the Circumscription of Ol' Ez

Retrospective Selection/Definitive Edition

Selection and order represent a criticism, the
imposition of a critical taste upon the reader.
—T. S. Eliot, "John Donne" (1923)

Few examples of literary collaboration have been so celebrated as that of Pound and Eliot upon the manuscripts and typescripts of *The Waste Land*, in part because few present so vivid an opportunity to examine the interaction between such distinct poetics. As various critics have observed, Pound's consistent objections to certain kinds of material and writing point to substantial aesthetic differences between himself and Eliot.[1] The poets disagreed about what subject matter was most appropriate to serious poetry, how that subject matter ought to be ordered, and how that ordering ought to be presented.[2] Thus Pound cut such things as Eliot's pastiches, insisted that Eliot should retain his five-part structure (that is, that Eliot neither add "Gerontion" nor delete "Death by Water"), and relentlessly attempted to pare down Eliot's language. Pound and Eliot disagreed, in other words, over the generic features most appropriate to the modern poem.

---

1. See, for example, the essays by Richard Ellmann, Helen Gardner, Hugh Kenner, and A. Walton Litz, in *Eliot in His Time*, ed. Litz (Princeton: Princeton University Press, 1973). For an essay that discerns greater changes arising from Pound's editorial work, see Marshall McLuhan, "Pound, Eliot, and the Rhetoric of *The Waste Land*," *New Literary History* 10 (Spring 1979): 557–80.

2. I am drawing here on the new model of genre developed by Ralph Cohen. See especially his articles: "Historical Knowledge and Literary Understanding," *Papers on Language and Literature* 14 (Summer 1978): 227–48; "A Propaedeutic for Literary Change," *Critical Exchange* 13 (Spring 1983): 1–17; and "History and Genre," *New Literary History* 17 (Winter 1986): 203–18.

Critics dispute why it was that Pound was able to close the poem that Eliot could not, but few would claim that Pound's contributions stemmed from any simple consonance of poetic or critical aims. Indeed, it may well have been the very disjunction between their work that enabled Pound to discover the coherence that eluded Eliot. Eliot's own appreciation that Pound "tried first to understand what one was attempting to do, and then tried to help one do it in one's own way," certainly presupposes important differences between them.[3] But for the most part, literary historians have been less interested in how Pound's principles altered the generic mixture of Eliot's poem than they have been in remarking the unusual success of that collaboration. In general, it might be said that there is a scholarly willingness to assume that Pound and Eliot understood one another even where they disagreed. But this assumption overlooks a project that, in several crucial ways, constituted an ironic corollary to Pound's work on *The Waste Land*—the *Literary Essays of Ezra Pound*, which Eliot edited for Faber and Faber late in 1953. Eliot's apparently innocuous edition had far-reaching consequences, and its impact on the academic reception of Pound's work compares with the influence of Pound's more famous editing on the shape of Eliot's reputation. If it was the publication of *The Waste Land* that prepared the way for Eliot's eventual establishment as a literary institution, it was the publication of *Literary Essays* that facilitated the institutional study of Pound. We must take seriously the promise of the jacket advertisement that Eliot's collection would be "definitive" if we are to recognize the importance of *Literary Essays* as a historical milestone in the institutionalization of modernism.

Since its first publication, when most reviewers rejected Eliot's praise for this material as "literary essays," only Donald Davie has commented on the apparent irony of Eliot's presentation.[4] That is, although by 1953 Eliot had experienced some thirty years of Pound's decidedly extra-aesthetic tirades, his introduction yet asserted that "the limitation of Pound's kind [of criticism] is in its concentration upon the craft of letters, and of poetry especially." Davie recognized that in using the term "craft" instead of "art" Eliot was executing "a contraction or diminution," just as he recognized how Pound's attention to "craft" rested on an assumption of organic integrity

---

3. From "Ezra Pound," *Poetry* 68 (September 1946): 326–38; reprinted in *Ezra Pound: A Collection of Critical Essays*, ed. Walter Sutton (Englewood Cliffs, N.J.: Prentice-Hall, 1963), 17–25, see esp. 23.

4. Donald Davie, "The Critics Who Made Us: Ezra Pound," *Sewanee Review*, 92 (July–September 1984): 421–32.

between artistic and socioeconomic production. But Davie's focus fell on the indefensibility of Pound's critical assumptions, without at the same time attending to the equally troubling assumptions implicit in Eliot's critical frame. In what follows I identify Eliot's assumptions and consider how they informed the constitution of "modernism" as a cultural triumph, and as culture triumphant. I do so by considering *Literary Essays* in the context of his other work of the same period and with reference to Pound's own uneasy combination of aesthetic and meliorative principles.

Eliot's edition is indeed "definitive" in its very design, but this recognition need not lead us to suspect his motives. Rather, insofar as *Literary Essays* works to re-form an existing body of work, it participates in familiar modernist praxis. Henry James, for instance, had used the occasion of the New York edition of his works (1907–1909) as an opportunity to re-present his career, to revise and select a part of his work to stand thereafter for the whole. James's project itself observed the romantic precedent set by the likes of Scott and Balzac, but with an emphasis shaped by a century of reification of romantic aesthetic. It was not simply a collected edition, but a concerted effort to transform the historically heterogeneous into the perfect artistic whole of an *oeuvre*. Eliot's interest in this idea, evident as early as his 1917 review of Edward Garnett's *Turgenev*, was well-established by the late twenties. At this time Eliot wrote two important essays on the nature of a poet's lifework: his introduction to his selection of Pound's poetry (1928), which maintained that "Pound's work . . . represents a continuous development,"[5] and his introduction to G. Wilson Knight's *Wheel of Fire* (1930), which praised Knight's attempt "to take Shakespeare's work as a whole."[6] Like James, Yeats, or Joyce, Eliot was concerned to leave to the future a perfected past. The same principle of wholeness informs *Literary Essays*, where even the ordering of the essays reveals Eliot's concern to demonstrate the internal coherence of Pound's work. He subordinates issues of chronology or development to those of sensibility, grouping essays together under the three general headings of "The Art of Poetry," "The Tradition," and "Contemporaries" in order to distinguish purportedly persistent qualities of imagination.

This attempt to isolate the historical individual from his aesthetic productions had particular value in the difficult case of Ezra Pound, then entering

---

5. *Ezra Pound: Selected Poems*, ed. T. S. Eliot (1928; rpt. London: Faber & Faber, 1959), 7.
6. *The Wheel of Fire: Essays in Interpretation of Shakespeare's Sombre Tragedies* (London: Oxford University Press, 1930), xvii.

his eighth year of incarceration at St. Elizabeths. But at no point in his introduction does Eliot mention Pound's distress, and we must be careful not to confuse the critical and aesthetic aims of Eliot's edition with the more immediate and limited appeal of other generic reformations, like the excerpts from Pound's radio speeches that Olga Rudge had assembled in 1948 under the title *If This Be Treason. . . .* Although Eliot elsewhere voiced concern over the conditions of Pound's incarceration, his attention to Pound's position more fundamentally focused on, not strictly political or humanitarian, but aesthetic principles. Eliot seemed to feel, as C. David Heymann has put it, that Pound's "was not just the trial of a modern-day poet—or even of a man who had remade poetry—but of the stuff, of the genre of poetry itself."[7] In this respect, Eliot's work on *Literary Essays* reflects his then prevailing critical and aesthetic concerns and the crucial difference of those concerns from those of the work he here sought to represent.

Certainly the radical inclusiveness of Pound's experiments with genre, not only in the *Cantos* but in his critical writings as well, implies a sweeping attempt to reform tradition. His combinations of heterogeneous discourses attempted to generate power by incorporating apparently distinct forms of human exchange. But where Pound was inclusive, Eliot strained to establish and maintain defensible frontiers. Eliot's work on *Literary Essays* suggests that he regarded Pound's promiscuous generic experiments as a failure that threatened the freedom of poetic and cultural activity. The book *Literary Essays* was in itself a trial "of the stuff, of the genre of poetry," in that it worked to contain and to reorder the relations among the diverse elements of Pound's critical work. That object was not to be accomplished by the republication of such titles as *Make It New* (for which Eliot expressed dislike) or *Polite Essays*.[8] Eliot's own comments serve to locate the crucial issue

---

7. C. David Heymann, *Ezra Pound: The Last Rower, a Political Profile* (New York: Viking Press, 1976), 194.

8. It is interesting that both *Make It New* and *Polite Essays* were Faber collections, put together by Frank Morley. For a brief account of those negotiations, see Humphrey Carpenter, *A Serious Character: The Life of Ezra Pound* (Boston: Houghton Mifflin, 1988), 542. In his 1946 essay on Pound, Eliot wrote that "on the whole, I prefer the collected papers as one finds them in the two volumes published in New York [*Pavannes and Divisions* and *Instigations*], to the later book, *Make It New*, published in London. For me, at least, the former volumes recall the first appearance of several items, in periodicals, and so have the savor of their original timeliness which they cannot have for those who know only the collected criticism." Of the contents of *Make It New*, Eliot went on to find the essay on French poets dated, found the essay on James still "of value, though the study of the subject has reached a different phase," and submitted that the essay on Rémy de Gourmont was mistaken in the importance it attaches to its subject. On the other hand, he believed that "the

within a broader debate about the proper formal or generic characteristics of criticism:

> Being a retrospective selection, this book differs from the four books of critical papers from which the bulk of the material has been taken, and to the publishers of which I make acknowledgement: *Pavannes and Divisions* (A. A. Knopf, New York, 1918), *Instigations* (Boni & Liveright, New York, 1920), *Make It New* (Faber & Faber, London, and the Yale University Press, 1934), and *Polite Essays* (Faber & Faber, London, 1937). These collections were assembled in a form which does not seem to me permanently satisfactory: they have served their purpose in prolonging the effect at which the various papers were aimed on their original publication in periodicals. . . . There remain two books from which I have taken nothing: *Guide to Kulchur* (Faber & Faber, 1938) and the early but very important *The Spirit of Romance* (Dent, London, 1910). Both these books have been out of print, but have recently been republished by New Directions: they should both be read entire.
>
> The present book is designed differently from any previous collection of Pound's essays; so I believe there is justification for its having been entrusted to another hand than that of the author. (*LE*, ix)

Notice that the inadequacies which Eliot detected in Pound's earlier collections had to do with their "design" and "form." That Eliot was not here taking issue with Pound's social criticism per se is clear from his recommendation that *Guide to Kulchur* "should be read entire." Rather, Eliot was objecting to the mingling of sociocultural and literary criticism.

Eliot's edition has proven a quite successful redaction: for thirty-five years now *Literary Essays* has been the only one of Pound's critical books to remain consistently in print, and between 1953 and 1968 it was the only serious collection still in print in either Britain or America.[9] Eliot's framing of

---

observations on the troubadours, on Arnaut Daniel, and on the Elizabethan and other early translators, are as good as they ever were. And the short papers at the beginning and end, 'Date Line' and 'A Stray Document,' are just as necessary for the beginner in the art of verse as they were when they were written." Here again, especially in this last praise, is Davie's "contraction or diminution." Given Eliot's ability to discern the "form" of a collection of essays, it is striking that he reserved comment on the force of "Date Line" and "A Stray Document" as papers that "framed" Pound's call to "make it new."

9. According to *Books in Print, British Books in Print,* and *The Reference Catalogue of Current*

Pound's essays was characteristically shrewd, even to the point that we hardly notice how he qualifies his most ringing phrases—his judgment, for example, that Pound's "literary criticism is the most important contemporary criticism of its kind." As Cyril Connolly noted, "this is a high claim which, coming from the other most important critic of his time, must be carefully considered."[10] But so too does the fact that in his introduction Eliot refers three times to the existence of different "kinds" of criticism, and does not do so casually. By "kind" Eliot meant "genre" or "tradition," and he recognized that Pound's critical prose was empowered by conventions quite different from those of academic writing. Eliot distinguished Pound's kind of criticism on the basis of three accomplishments, the final two being that it was attuned to "the needs of the time" and that it opened up for criticism "whole areas of poetry." But it was the first accomplishment that most informed Eliot's edition: "If this selection succeeds in its purpose it will show . . . that Pound has said much about the art of writing and of writing poetry in particular, that is permanently valid and useful" (*LE*, x).

Eliot's praise tells us several things: that he considered the aim of Pound's critical work to be distinctly different from his own, a distinction that will become clearer as we go on; that Pound's critical accomplishments are permanent and so by implication to be distinguished from his other prose writings; and finally, and more implicitly still, that whatever immediate needs Eliot's collection was designed to serve, his estimation of Pound's critical work remained unchanged by all that had transpired during the war. Eliot's introductory comments about the value of Pound's "kind" of criticism remained substantially unchanged from, for instance, his *Criterion* "Commentary" of July 1937: "The only poet and critic who survived Imagism to develop in a larger way was Mr. Pound, who, as literary critic alone, has been probably the greatest literary influence of this century up to the present time. The central importance of Mr. Pound's criticism has not yet been fully recognized. The most recent period, up to the present day, seems to be one of a less lively interest in the actual problems of good writing, and has been more concerned with aesthetics in general and with psychology." Eliot believed that the value of Pound's early criticism lay in its attention to

---

Literature. The word "serious" here excludes *Pavannes and Divagations*, an enlarged edition of *Pavannes and Divisions* (1918), which New Directions had initially intended to publish under the title "Frivolities."

10. "Ezra Pound as Critic," in *Previous Convictions: Selected Writings of a Decade* (New York: Harper & Row, 1963), 255.

practical aesthetic problems, and that such criticism had performed a necessary historical function. This perception, that the importance of Pound's criticism issues from its focus on the practical, is the "diminution" observed by Davie and derives from Eliot's belief that the critical needs of his own day were different, "more concerned with aesthetics in general and with psychology." By the mid-forties this incipient tendency would become quite pronounced, but in retrospect the direction is evident even in this "Commentary" of 1937. Eliot's emphasis on Pound "as literary critic alone," like his claim that "the central importance of Mr. Pound's criticism has not yet been fully recognized," works to isolate those features of Pound's work that most resembled the emphases of postwar formalism, the professionally aggressive "New Criticism" of John Crowe Ransom and others.

But however sustained, Eliot's attention to differences in *kind* was overlooked by contemporary reviewers, who seized instead on the familiarity and universality of Eliot's claims about Pound's value as "literary" critic. To understand this is to recognize that many of the negative responses that Eliot's collection elicited arose from frustrated generic expectations. The response of the anonymous reviewer for the *New Yorker* is a case in point: "Mr. Eliot's introduction assures us that Pound's criticism constitutes 'the least dispensible body of critical writing in our time,' but a surprising amount of it fails to hold up—is now, indeed, visibly half-baked (Shaw is 'a ninth-rate coward'), rhetorically irresponsible ('Milton is the worst sort of poison'), or hopelessly limited (Jane Austen's books are about 'a dull, stupid, hemmed-in sort of life, by a person who has lived it')."[11] Phrases such as "visibly half-baked" or "rhetorically irresponsible" suggest, much more than a rejection of conclusions, a refusal to accept Pound's writing (or even Pound's sort of writing) as proper criticism. Charles Tomlinson made the point directly, submitting in his review that Pound's comments often "point us to the absence of the discipline of an organic literary-critical approach." Donald Davie reacted in a similar fashion: "Instigations to experiment with, or at any rate examine, some novel or neglected procedure—that is the most charitable description of most of the things printed here. Pound hardly ever even offers to give considered literary judgements." Other reviewers took similar lines, as indeed they had reason to do, since Eliot was offering Pound's work as "literary criticism."[12]

11. Anonymous review published in the *New Yorker*, 27 March 1954, 134–35.
12. Charles Tomlinson's review appeared in *Spectator*, 19 February 1954. Donald Davie's review was published in *New Statesman and Nation*, 27 February 1954.

Having himself distinguished between Pound's critical work and academic models, Eliot might have anticipated the objections of these reviewers. But Eliot was caught in a way he probably had not foreseen between contradictory tasks: on the one hand to celebrate Pound's criticism in what he took to be its own terms, and on the other to separate in the public mind Pound's literary criticism from his political criticism. Eliot sensed the value for what in 1948 Charles Norman had called "the case of Ezra Pound" of a deft redaction of Pound's career: a judicious presentation that emphasized the "literary" concerns that Pound's criticism often included but subordinated to other concerns. Eliot would not have seen this as portending any reformation or transformation of Pound's work. He did not expect or recognize that his frame would have such transformative power. Eliot no doubt saw in his work nothing more intrusive than the kind of editorial check that Pound had once provided him: an attempt to free a friend's work from impertinences and irrelevancies. There is an irony here in that Pound had long hoped to reach a broad, nonacademic audience. But by the 1950s, the very success of modernism had so altered the nature of the poetry-reading public that Pound's ability to find a larger audience depended on his first being able to meet academic expectations. Ironically, the populist—"the village explainer" as Gertrude Stein would have it—came to require the assent of the professors about whose narrowness he had, in good Carlylean fashion, for so long complained. *Literary Essays* accomplished a highly attractive redaction with unprecedented agility, with a touch so light and familiar that thirty-five years later we still hardly notice its pressure. We do not notice because the frame of *Literary Essays* has in large part become, as Eliot must have hoped it would, the frame through which we view the sprawling and heterogeneous body of Pound's prose.

"The Setting of Bounds"

The illusion that in poetry we come nearer to
a purely aesthetic experience makes poetry the
most convenient *genre* of literature to keep in
mind when we are discussing literary criticism
itself.
    —T. S. Eliot, "The Frontiers of Criticism"
        (1956)

Eliot's framing of *Literary Essays* did not follow from merely personal or idiosyncratic motives. He had himself been singed by the conflagration that consumed Pound's credibility; his concern, evident from the war through the mid-fifties, to outline a purely literary criticism represented a deliberate withdrawal—a "diminution." It was not simply the sociopolitical ugliness of his own *After Strange Gods* (1934) that he repudiated but the very advisability of criticism that mixes the analysis of poetic texts with social prescription.

Shortly after writing the essays published in *After Strange Gods*, Eliot declared that: "at the present time I am not very interested in the only subject which I am supposed to be qualified to write about: that is, one kind of literary criticism. I am not very interested in literature, except dramatic literature; and I am largely interested in subjects which I do not yet know very much about: theology, politics, economics, and education."[13] Here again distinguishing different *kinds* of literary criticism, Eliot's implicit renunciation of that kind which attends strictly to *literary* issues would later cause the regret that motivated his editing of *Literary Essays*. But the uncharacteristic excess into which his interest in "theology, politics, economics, and education" led him did not produce sudden theoretical reversal. One year later he could still praise A. R. Orage as "that necessary and rare person, the moralist in criticism; not the inquisitor who tries to impose (his) morals upon literature, but the critic who perceives the morals *of* literature."[14] Five years later, in *The Idea of a Christian Society*, he avowed that the "decay" of the arts "may always be taken as a symptom of some social ailment to be investigated" and argued against Christopher Dawson that "in isolating culture from religion, politics and philosophy we seem to be left with something no more apprehensible than the scent of last year's roses."[15] But with the progress of the war Eliot's emphasis shifted more rapidly; and although he would maintain that a "culture" was the "incarnation" of a people's religion, Eliot himself would soon be concerned to dissociate culture from the pressures of politics and economics (106). In the serial essay "Notes Towards a Definition of Culture" (January–February 1943), Eliot deplored the disintegration of culture into "specialized groups" before "the progress in civilization." He indicated the direction of these essays more boldly in 1948, when republishing them with other essays of the war years, with two apparently slight modifications: he changed his title to "Notes Towards *the* Definition of Culture," and as an epigraph to the whole of the book cited

13. T. S. Eliot, "The Problem of Education," *Harvard Advocate* 121, no. 1 (1934): 11–12.
14. See Eliot's *Criterion* "Commentary" for January, 1935.
15. Reprinted in T. S. Eliot, *Christianity and Culture* (New York: Harcourt Brace Jovanovich, 1960), 31 and 60.

from the *Oxford English Dictionary* the primary definition of "definition": "the setting of bounds." The addition of the definite article and epigraph foregrounds definition as an activity, what would be Eliot's major critical activity for several years to come. Eliot's *Notes* work at "setting bounds" both when disclaiming any attempt "to determine the frontier between the meanings of these two words [culture and civilization]"(85), and when announcing three pages later its "attempt to disentangle culture from politics and education"(88). These statements are contradictory: one evades what the other assumes. But both statements associate the idea of culture with the determining of frontiers, and that association bore immediately on Eliot's notions of literature, and of the territory appropriate for its critics.

This retrenchment marks a quite specific juncture in Eliot's career; his criticism during this time is dramatically unlike not only his more expansive work of the twenties and thirties but his pronouncements of the later fifties as well. Especially instructive is the difference between the position represented by *Notes* and the positions Eliot outlined in "To Criticize the Critic" (1961) and "The Frontiers of Criticism" (1956). In "To Criticize the Critic" Eliot insisted that "it is impossible to fence off *literary* criticism from criticism on other grounds, and that moral, religious and social judgements cannot be wholly excluded." In this formulation Eliot allows that a "literary" criticism will involve special considerations, but ultimately, as a subgenre of the larger activity of "criticism," it must engage broader responsibilities. This late position marks no unprecedented moment in Eliot's career; it was instead a return, with differences, to Eliot's less reserved critical theorizations of the twenties and thirties, which we might characterize with the position developed in "The Function of Criticism" (1923):

> When I say criticism, I mean of course in this place the commentation and exposition of works of art by means of written words. . . . No exponent of criticism (in this limited sense) has, I presume, ever made the preposterous assumption that criticism is an autotelic activity. I do not deny that art may be affirmed to serve ends beyond itself; but art is not required to be aware of these ends, and indeed performs its function, whatever that may be, according to various theories of value, much better by indifference to them. Criticism, on the other hand, must always profess an end in view, which, roughly speaking, appears to be the elucidation of works of art and the correction of taste. (*SE*, 13)

Although Eliot elsewhere placed criticism at the service of art, he contrasted the two here for reasons similar to Matthew Arnold's in "The Function of Criticism at the Present Time."[16] Eliot sought to establish the high seriousness of critical activity.

Eliot's indirection in "The Function of Criticism" aimed to make his assertion of the moral responsibility of the critic more palatable to an audience grown used to critical abrogations. That is, Eliot's allowance that "art is not required to be aware of these ends" was a prolepsis that repeated the Paterian creed without permitting its usual extension: he proposed the distinct function of criticism by denying to it the special privilege of art. Eliot first established what criticism does not do in an effort to leave his view of what it should do inescapable. It is in his concern with "the correction of taste" that this formulation is most aggressive, since such a change implies the inclusion of moral, religious, and social judgments within the discourse of a literary criticism. This was a view of critical activity very different from that which guided Eliot during his work on Pound's *Literary Essays*.

"The Frontiers of Criticism," a lecture Eliot delivered in a University of Minnesota gymnasium to over thirteen thousand listeners, challenged his own insistence that "criticism must always have some end in view."[17] This time Eliot submitted that "every critic may have his eye on a definite goal, may be engaged on a task which needs no justification, and yet criticism may be lost as to its aims" (*OPAP*, 116).[18] Consequently, Eliot proposed the ongoing necessity of determining when criticism is "not literary criticism but something else" (*OPAP*, 117). Eliot's emphasis in "Frontiers" fell on the importance of seeing how it was that different genres require different critical approaches, and even how individual works inevitably defeat the objectifying activity of critical explanation: "But as for the meaning of the poem as a whole, it is not exhausted by any explanation, for the meaning is what the poem means to different sensitive readers" (126). Eliot's aim here was not to link aesthetic experience to other experiential paradigms but to consider how it was that criticism could help us approach an understanding of "purely aesthetic experience."

Much of the criticism Eliot wrote during the 1950s exhibits a similar

16. First published in *Essays in Criticism* (London: Macmillan, 1865).
17. On Eliot's address, see James Breslin, *From Modern to Contemporary: American Poetry 1945–1965* (Chicago: University of Chicago Press, 1983), 14.
18. See also Breslin, *From Modern to Contemporary*, 1–22.

interest in sundering the aesthetic work from its contextual origins, and in isolating and insulating aesthetic experience. In "The Three Voices of Poetry" (1953), to cite an instance contemporaneous with Eliot's work on Pound's *Literary Essays*, Eliot was exercised to differentiate between poetry and mere verse, which he described as lacking in intensity. In "Goethe as the Sage" (1955) Eliot ran through a series of circumscriptions and definitions, proposing at one point that there are "three important phases . . . in the development of taste and critical judgement in literature," and later trying to determine "what part of the work of Dante, Shakespeare or Goethe can we isolate and say that it gives us the essential Dante, Shakespeare or Goethe?"[19] The position Eliot developed during the years surrounding *Literary Essays* and "Frontiers" was perhaps a retreat to his symbolist heritage; but the crucial point here is to recognize the extent to which Eliot's essays of this period subordinated critical principles that guided his activity both earlier and later in his career.

For this brief but distinct period "The Frontiers of Criticism" stands as Eliot's most important critical work. Its principal argument is that in order "to save ourselves from being overwhelmed by our own critical activity" we must continually question "when is criticism not literary criticism but something else" (*OPAP*, 117). Answering such a question can never be merely descriptive, and in Eliot's case it meant driving a wedge between "literary" criticism and criticism that strays over the proper frontiers: "The thesis of this paper is that there are limits, exceeding which in one direction literary criticism ceases to be literary, and exceeding which in another it ceases to be criticism" (113). The parallelism of this construction lends a kind of "natural," commonsensical tone to Eliot's argument, when it was in fact a matter of particular historical concern. Indeed, Eliot's predilection for determining frontiers was nearly coincident with the retrenchment that is our concern here—although earlier work sometimes raised the issue. In "Experiment in Criticism" (1929), for instance, he observed not only that different ages mark "the edges" of criticism in different ways, but also worried that the modern consciousness of such history "has obscured the frontiers between literature and everything else." But metaphors of boundary are noticeably absent a year later in "Poetry and Propaganda" and remain so for another ten years, the period of his most active attention to socioeconomic reform. Metaphors of boundary reappear when Eliot's reforming energies turn inward, recon-

---

19. "Goethe as the Sage," *OPAP*, 241 and 248.

ceptualizing their subject in the more ideal notions of Church and Culture.[20]

So, in his *Criterion* "Commentary" of 27 April 1939, Eliot warned that "poetry, if it is not to be a lifeless repetition of forms, must be constantly exploring 'the frontiers of spirit.'" Nevertheless, he then explained, the idea of frontiers inescapably presents questions of authority even as it invites the exploration and testing of limits: "These frontiers are not like the surveys of geographical explorers, conquered once for all and settled. The frontiers of spirit are more like the jungle which, unless continuously kept under control, is always ready to encroach, and eventually obliterate the cultivated area." This concern with the consolidation of authority represents a marked change in emphasis from the otherwise similar claim of "Experiment of Criticism" ten years earlier—that the task of criticism in the modern world will be "not only to expand its borders but to clarify its center." His emphasis in 1939 was more defensive. It called, not for expansion or even "clarification," but for the preservation of the already cultivated.

This later agenda was predicated on a Kantian basis eventually elaborated in "Reflections on the Unity of European Culture" (May–August 1946). Identifying "culture" with the "spiritual *organism* of Europe" as opposed to its "material *organisation*," Eliot's notion of "frontiers" tied the vitality of the center to that of the periphery. It meant an identification of a further kind, one which made the concern with frontiers necessary and central. To understand this is to recover the sense of Eliot's contrary claims in "The Responsibility of the Man of Letters in the Cultural Restoration of Europe," that "the man of letters is not concerned with the political or economic map of Europe," but also that "I should not like to give the impression that I assume there to be a definite frontier, between the matters of direct and those of indirect concern to the man of letters."[21] Eliot's notion of "frontiers" was itself, like the arguments in which it figured, idealist; it turned on a valorization of essentially romantic ideas about "culture." But (as I explain in Chapter 2) where Pound's conception of culture led him to pursue an overtly totalizing enterprise, Eliot's eventually fostered a more defensive posture. In order to determine "the frontiers of criticism" Eliot had necessarily to posit discriminatory criteria, which in turn exert their own determining force—as they did in the framing of *Literary Essays*.

20. T. S. Eliot, "Experiment in Criticism," *Bookman* 70, no. 3 (November 1929): 225–33; and idem, "Poetry and Propaganda," *Bookman* 70, no. 6 (February 1930): 595–602.
21. T. S. Eliot, "The Responsibility of the Man of Letters in the Cultural Restoration of Europe," *Norseman* 2, no. 4 (July–August 1944): 243–48.

But Eliot did not see this project as prescriptive. Rather, he considered that he was coming to terms with practical problems posed by a long tradition. Just as he had often before blamed the weakness of modern poetry on the romantics, Eliot here attributed the trouble with modern criticism to the same source, albeit in an inverse formulation. Whereas he had argued that the main tradition of English verse had little to do with the romantics, Eliot found that "the criticism of to-day, indeed, may be said to be in direct descent from Coleridge" (*OPAP*, 115). He distinguished this tradition from such Enlightenment criticism as Samuel Johnson's *Lives of the Poets* (which Eliot praised) on the basis of "the scope and variety of the interests which Coleridge brought to bear on his discussion of poetry. He established the relevance of philosophy, aesthetics and psychology" (115). Similarly, in "Goethe as the Sage" Eliot confessed that Coleridge was the only English romantic whom he still enjoyed, and here "rather as philosopher and theologian and social thinker than poet" (243). Were Coleridge alive today, Eliot speculated, he would probably "take the same interest in the social sciences and in the study of language and semantics, that he took in the sciences available to him" (115).

But even in this measured praise, Eliot was careful to prefer Coleridge as a "social thinker" and not as a literary critic. What criticism owed to Coleridge, Eliot believed, was the importation of extrinsic and systematizing techniques into the analysis of aesthetic experience. This development in turn helped foster the institutionalization of literary study, and Eliot understood these related processes to be "the two main causes of the transformation of literary criticism in our time." While anxious not to deride the new critical sophistication which had done so much to promote his own work, Eliot worried about how the institutionalization of criticism would alter its relation with the reading public: "The critic to-day may have a somewhat different contact with the world, and be writing for a somewhat different audience from that of his predecessors. I have the impression that serious criticism now is being written for a different, a more limited though not necessarily a smaller public than was that of the nineteenth century" (115). The context of Eliot's address, delivered in the academy itself, could only have made his observations more pointed. But Eliot's reservations stopped short of any resolute indictment. He generally approved of the New Criticism, and in this essay was happy enough to identify himself with it. Eliot was no Luddite; he had no wish to surrender sophisticated tools of analysis by objecting to important elements of critical writing. He did, however, wish to readjust the relations among these elements and to reaffirm the importance of the critical object—be it poem, play, or piece of prose. To put it another way, and so return to the seminal phrase of "Frontiers," Eliot's critical object was to explore the nature of "purely aesthetic experience."

Eliot's attempt to define the limits of critical activity had important consequences for his preparation of *Literary Essays*. His valorization of "purely aesthetic experience" amplified his interest in presenting Pound as an essentially "literary" critic and lent weighty sanction to the already growing disjunction between critical appraisals of "Pound the poet" and "Pound the political monster." That disjunction, already hardened during the controversy over Pound's receipt of the Bollingen prize in 1948, needs no reenactment here.[22] But although it once facilitated academic study of Pound's work, thirty-five years later the artificial circumscription of Pound's "literary" criticism no longer serves either the reputation of his work or our understanding of it. My purpose is then not to fault Eliot, but only to foreground the differences between the problems he set out to solve in 1953 and those that confront Pound's readers today. Eliot's circumscription by design encourages readers to consider Pound's work in terms of familiar and respected artistic categories, the very categories Pound held responsible for the pettiness of modern poetry. For this reason the readiness of interested parties to debate Pound's merit across the dichotomy of "art" and "politics" may ultimately suggest his greatest failure. Eliot's emphasis on the strictly "literary" interest of Pound's criticism exemplifies this circumscription: a reordering of the elements that characteristically make up Pound's writing in order to relocate his work within a generic tradition that Pound himself regarded as inadequate.

As I discuss later, Pound attempted to perpetuate the Carlylean or Ruskinian tradition of treating cultural endeavor in all its aspects as an organic whole. This tradition provides an alternative heuristic model, grounded in Pound's historical practice, to Eliot's notion of "literary" criticism. While Eliot showed the shrewder understanding of contemporary critical praxis, his willingness to facilitate and exploit the institutionalization of literary study conflicted with Pound's Ruskinian resistance to the compartmentalization

22. Cookson inveighed against this false distinction in the introduction to his *Selected Prose* (73), but his argument is fundamentally different from the one that I am making here. Whereas Cookson argues that Pound's nonliterary prose reflects many of the thematic concerns of the *Cantos*, and so deserves our attention just as much as his "literary essays," my point is not a thematic one, but concerns how Pound made his arguments. Except in a superficial way, Pound would not have recognized in his own critical work the categorical distinction that the separate publication of *Literary Essays* and *Selected Prose* continues to respect.

of experience. What resulted was no mere critical disagreement, for Delmore Schwartz scarcely exaggerated when he said that Eliot had by 1945 become America's "literary dictator."[23] His strategic frame has since remained persuasive for much the same reason that his notion of the "literary essay" has continued to seem a natural rather than historical category. Critical discourse is itself a "kind" of writing with its own generic continuities.[24] Since the Second World War critical discourse has been predicated on ideas of literariness. The problem here is that Pound, Eliot, and contemporary critical discourse all invoke many of the same terms, but employ them in different ways. Eliot's use of the term "Literary," for example, differed radically from Pound's. Eliot's understanding of it was consonant with the more "advanced" critical thinking of his time, the so-called New Criticism; by contrast Pound's use of the term was, in the middle decades of our century, almost anachronistic. And yet Pound was not blind; he was simply dead set against the more professional and precise uses of the term that Eliot and other critics were developing with such enthusiasm.

Eliot's notion of "literary" criticism exerted a transformative force on Pound's critical prose, but not all of the changes he introduced were conscious or deliberate. Eliot, in his qualified way, believed in the value of Pound's "kind" of criticism, and undoubtedly believed that he was presenting that work in the best possible light. Nevertheless, any collection or anthology constitutes an act of criticism; the best possible light that Eliot turned on Pound's criticism changed how we see it, and so changed what we see.

"An Illusion Fostered by Academic Authorities"

Mr ElYuTT HAS stuck the narsty title of
"LITerary essays" on his whatever yu call
it/Ezpurgation of Ez. or Possumation or
wotNOT.
—Ezra Pound, Letter to Huntington Cairns

23. Breslin, *From Modern to Contemporary*, 14.
24. On this issue, see Ralph Cohen's "History and Genre," *New Literary History* (winter 1986), or his "On a Shift in the Concept of Interpretation," in *The New Criticism and After*, ed. Thomas Daniel Young (Charlottesville: University of Virginia Press, 1976); Clifford Siskin's *Historicity of Romantic Discourse* (New York: Oxford University Press, 1988); or Breslin, *From Modern to Contemporary*, chap. 2.

In the introduction to *Literary Essays* Eliot divulges that he had omitted a number of works that Pound believed important because they struck him "as being outside the frame of a volume entitled 'Literary Essays.'" In identifying some of these, Eliot was most particular to name the essays concerned with such nonliterary arts as "music, painting and sculpture." It was conducive to his recuperative project, his formalist recasting of Pound, to mention these essays. What he passed over silently was the vast body of material that combined the evaluation of literary works with attacks on the "status rerum"—economic, intellectual, social, or political. Concerning this dimension of Pound's work, the presuppositions of cultural organism that Eliot needed as it were to anatomize, Eliot said nothing directly. He did, however, after mentioning a half-dozen authors about whom Pound wrote nothing, react against the narrowing institutionalization to which his editing of *Literary Essays* had necessarily to submit. He cited a particularly telling example of the kind of material that his collection could not include: "I mention these omissions, not as cautious reservations in my admiration for Pound's criticism, but the better to praise it for what it is. You can't ask everything of anybody; and it is an illusion fostered by academic authorities on literature, that there is only one kind of criticism, the kind that is delivered on academic foundations, to be printed afterwards in the 'proceedings' or as a brochure in a series. . . . Mr. Pound regrets the omission (for which the editor is responsible) of an essay on René Crevel" (*LE*, xiv). Having published the essay in *Criterion* in January 1939, Eliot had particular knowledge of the incompatability of "René Crevel" with "academic foundations." That Pound had requested the inclusion of "René Crevel," and that Eliot mentioned his own denial of that request, suggests the self-conscious negotiation that accompanied the preparation of *Literary Essays*—even how this project effected a kind of re-formation of Pound's career. Eliot's exclusion of the essay from *Literary Essays* was no oversight.

Consider then, "René Crevel" as a paradigmatic instance of Pound's prodigious body of criticism: a body of work too vast to characterize neatly, except to observe that most of it would resist inclusion in an ostensibly "literary" collection like Eliot's. "René Crevel" is neither better than the material Eliot selected nor superior to academic critical models, but it is different in kind. Understanding the generic mixture of this excluded essay will enable us to reconstruct Eliot's exclusionary principles and allow us to determine more clearly the shaping influence of Eliot's frame on those essays that were included.

"René Crevel" typifies Pound's critical writings precisely to the extent that it attempts to remake the genre of critical writing—to alter relations among its constituent features, often by introducing features from nonacademic and noncritical genres. In its very digressiveness, in its unusual use of the word "literary," in its political references, and even in its taking as subject an extracanonical author, this essay is characteristic of Pound's deliberate violation of the frontiers that Eliot helped to establish and institutionalize. The initial sentences of "René Crevel" deliver the thrust of Pound's ambitious project without hesitation: "A Nation which does not feed its best writers is a mere barbarian dung heap. The social function of writers is to keep the nation's language living and capable of precise registration. Laws set down in ambiguous phrases are a paradise for shyster attorneys and a boil on the neck of the people." Pound's "social function of writers" is anything but "purely aesthetic," and in deliberately paratactic writing he went on to submit that there is an ineluctable tie between "TEXNE" [technique] and "a discussion of its where and amid what." Or rather, Pound did not so much submit the presence of such a tie as he assumed it. The description of Crevel's prose—precisely the kind of place we might expect literary analysis—offers a striking example:

> The "copia," the long bustling sentence, "un-french"?, no, not unfrench, sentences like a bon père de famille carrying 43 parcels, piled to chin, held in both hands, tied with string one to another with the large loaf spiked on his umbrella's point, but OF, imperatively OF the time, the god damned bourgeois, loan-capitalist supernumerary, footing footless, ineffably modified time. Post-Proust, and goodbye to it. Post the damn lot of 'em and good BYE to it, 1929.[25]

Pound simply assumes that economic conditions equate with moral horizons, and therefore determine stylistic possibilities for any given age. This notion was hardly new to Pound's work: it is visible in his essays for the *New Age* (1911–21); it was an important element of *Guide to Kulchur*, published the year before "René Crevel"; and in subsequent years it became still more explicit. In a radio broadcast of 1942, for example, Pound imagined that "future art criticism will be able to tell the component of usury tolerance.

25. See *Criterion* (January 1939), 231; 1929—the year in which Crevel published *Etes-vous fous?* as well as, of course, the year of the great crash—was for Pound a convenient marker of the demise of the "bourgeois, loan-capitalist" age.

How far the TOLERANCE of usury prevailed, or did not prevail when a given picture was painted."[26]

This vulgar historicism had the immediate effect of deprivileging aesthetic concerns, and no other part of Pound's critical practice was less compatible with Eliot's interest in fostering a "literary" criticism. Although that especially "knowing" tone appeared more prominently after Robert Graves's *Goodbye to All That* (1929), Pound had, by 1939, written "goodbye" to aestheticism many times: as early as "On Technique" (January 1912), and most dramatically in "Hugh Selwyn Mauberley" (1920).[27] In this case Pound's parody of the Proustian sentence, a parody of aestheticism in general, leads angrily to its indictment. Early twentieth-century aestheticism was "sick," Pound insisted, because the age was sick: a condition Pound claimed to understand on the basis of his survival into the age of "the Italian awakening" and "the time of [Silvio] Gesell." From this vantage, Pound identified the sickness that had debilitated the "bourgeois, loan-capitalist" period as not only economic but moral.[28] The art of this time he found "footing footless," for the same reasons he would later write that "the lot of 'em, Yeats, Possum, Old Wyndham / had no ground to stand on": it was an art kept in the wilderness, apart from the fullness of modern life, because of its ignorance of economic law.[29]

In his historicist equation of artistic with economic production, his belief that discussion of the work "may almost require a discussion of its where and amid what," we can locate the fundamentally Ruskinian underpinnings of Pound's critical practice. For all his renowned concern with "the axes of TEXNE," Pound had come to regard purely intrinsic analysis with indignant exasperation—although he could always be provoked by those critics who

---

26. The transcript of this radio broadcast has been reproduced in *Ezra Pound Speaking: Radio Speeches of World War II*, ed. Leonard W. Doob (Westport, Conn.: Greenwood Press, 1978), 191–94.

27. "On Technique" was the ninth installment of "I Gather the Limbs of Osiris," which was published serially in A. R. Orage's socialist weekly the *New Age*. Here we find Pound not only dissatisfied with aestheticism but also forging principles that critics often assume he developed only after his 1919 "conversion" to Social Credit economics. Pound's essay is on technique, but its approach to that question shows that he was paying a good deal of attention to Orage's "Guild Socialism": a movement which itself developed from the principles of Ruskin and Morris. Pound's argument mixes considerations of poetic technique with proposals about money and trade.

28. This identification repeats Pound's fulminations in *Guide to Kulchur* that "we know that history as it was written the day before yesterday is unwittingly partial; full of fatal lacunae; and that it tells next to nothing of causes. We know that these causes were economic and moral; we know that at whichever end we begin we will, if clear headed and thorough, work out to the other" (*GK*, 31).

29. See Canto 102/742.

moralize over art with no understanding of those axes. Clearly, there are important distinctions to be made between Ruskin and Pound. Not least, Pound exhibited Ruskin's religious fervor without the religion that had fired his critique of political economy. Nonetheless, Pound's growing tendency to conceive of all aspects of culture as a single organism was profoundly Ruskinian and marks his most significant difference from the more analytical Eliot. Like Ruskin, too, Pound sought to resist modern tendencies to isolate artistic activity. He could hope that changes in the arts might initiate broader cultural improvements; but he certainly believed that cultural degradation inevitably depraved the arts. For this reason, Pound saw the task of his criticism as inseparable from his poetic ambitions.

Although Eliot knew this much, he chose to emphasize, perhaps even dislocate, Pound's concern with craft from his broader analyses. His presentation of certain of Pound's essays as "literary" establishes a criterion whereby the apology for Pound's "concentration upon the craft of letters" acknowledges the failing that becomes at last ground for his canonization. In Eliot's conception, "limitation" is strength; in Pound's it is simply limitation. So it was that Pound brought "René Crevel" to a close with a ringing denunciation of attempts to limit critical activity to properly "literary" writing, and to respect as literature only the ostensibly artistic: "Young writers now . . . must first recognize a new orientation. The live brains are not now in la vie littéraire, they are in la vie même, including all those verbal manifestations and processes which went into the codes of Constantine and Justinian, which filled the reading matter of John Adams and Jefferson, and which had for centuries been part of the 'clerc's' existence and nutriment. It was only in the grovelling age of usura and usuriocracy that letters were lowered to mean merely 'belles lettres' and that the subject matter was gradually reduced to personal titillations." To understand fully Pound's position we must remember that modernist art has been most widely characterized as dismissing the importance of subject matter in favor of presentation. Like Yeats before him, Pound steadfastly refused to make any such sacrifice—either in his "creative" or his "critical" writings, a distinction that Pound did not respect.

Of course neither Eliot's short introduction nor his selections and exclusions can account entirely for the academic reception of Pound's writing. Eliot's treatment is symptomatic as well as transformative, participating in those broader cultural changes which it helped authorize. Nevertheless, by presenting Pound's critical prose in the terms he did, Eliot encouraged a broader public—unfamiliar with most of Pound's work—to evaluate Pound's work according to criteria only incompletely relevant. This means not only that Pound's writing has been misunderstood because, as a result of a continuing pattern of editorial selection, it has been misrepresented; it also means that because we read it according to a frame that changes the emphasis of what it encloses, we misunderstand what does stay in print. Indeed, as many reviewers such as Davie or Tomlinson recognized, Pound's prose writings are generally unacceptable as "literary essays": unacceptable not so much because of his opinions as for the inclusiveness of his generic mixtures.

So much is evident to even a cursory glance. In Eliot's first section, "The Art of Poetry," where we might expect materials relatively amenable to his generic revision, Pound's essays reveal a stubborn recalcitrance. "How to Read" (1929) develops its much-repeated exposition of the categories of "melopoeia," "phanopoeia," and "logopoeia" within the context of a fundamental challenge to the institutional isolation of "literary" study, with its expectation that art should somehow be distinct from public life. "Date Line" (1934) presents more serious problems still. Having originally served to introduce *Make It New*, here it served to conclude Eliot's section "The Art of Poetry." Inexplicably, Eliot preserved Pound's heading, in which Pound dated the essay according to the fascist calendar in order to underscore his quite specific and extraliterary sense of the "new." Pound's essay itself then insists that the superiority of language, and so of criticism, derives from the fact that other means of communication "are all narrowly zoned to their specific departments." Even "The Serious Artist" (1913), among the earliest pieces Eliot selected, develops its celebrated insistence on the importance of technique within an ambitious attempt "to rewrite Sidney's *Defense of Poesy*" (*LE*, 41). Pound's strategy in this task might be paraphrased with a quotation from "René Crevel": "The social function of writers is to keep the nation's language living and capable of precise registration." In 1913, and in language that recalls the third volume of *Modern Painters* or *Unto This Last*, Pound wrote:

> The arts, literature, poesy, are a science, just as chemistry is a science. Their subject is man, mankind and the individual. The subject of chemistry is matter considered as to its composition.
>
> The arts give us a great precentage of the lasting and unassailable data regarding the nature of man, of immaterial man, of man considered as a thinking and sentient creature. They begin where the science of medicine leaves off or rather they overlap that science. The borders of the two arts overcross. (*LE*, 42)

The subsequent two sections of *Literary Essays*, "The Tradition" and "Contemporaries," reveal similar incompatabilities. When attacking Edmund Gosse's *Life of Algernon Charles Swinburne* (1918), for example, Pound praises Swinburne for his recognition of "poetry as an art," but ultimately faults him for having "neglected the value of words as words" in favor of "their value as sound" (292). Yet Pound concludes that "there is, underneath all the writing, a magnificent passion for liberty—a passion dead as mutton in most of his contemporaries, and immeasurably deader than mutton in a people who allow their literature to be blanketed by a Comstock and his successors; for liberty is not merely a catchword of politics, nor a right to shove little slips of paper through a hole. The passion not merely for political, but also for personal, liberty is the bedrock of Swinburne's writing" (294). Such conclusions reveal how distant Pound's concerns were, even in 1918, from an obsessive "concentration upon the craft of letters, and of poetry especially." His 1922 review of *Ulysses*, which Eliot included in the third part of *Literary Essays*, develops a similar emphasis. Celebrating Joyce's having "taken up the art of writing where Flaubert left it" (403), Pound again joins the question of craft to the question of cultural vision. For, the issue of *le mot juste* aside, the Flaubert that mattered most to Pound was not *Madame Bovary* but *Bouvard et Pécuchet*, which Pound understood as a profound exercise in what a contemporary critic might call "demystification." Pricking the same vein from which flowed his praise for Swinburne, Pound asserted that "Messrs Bouvard and Pécuchet are the basis of democracy; Bloom also is the basis of democracy; he is the man in the street, the next man, the public, not our public, but Mr Wells' public; for Mr Wells he is Hocking's public, he is *l'homme moyen sensuel*; he is also Shakespeare, Ulysses, The Wandering Jew, the Daily Mail reader, the man who believes what he sees in the papers, Everyman" (403). Pound thus praised *Ulysses* for its "general sense of civilization" (408). And in an argument that Ruskin or even Mill might have made a century before, he went on to use *Ulysses* as an opportunity to displace a tired opposition, insisting upon the utility of culture: "A Fabian milk report is of less use to a legislator than the knowledge contained in L'Education Sentimentale, or in Bovary"—or of course in *Ulysses*.

Eliot's highly selective anthology did not deliberately misrepresent Pound. But his editorial work changes how we read Pound's critical prose by altering the often volatile relations among its heterogeneous constituent features. It does so moreover in a most polite fashion, "acknowledging" the difference (and so creating it) between Pound's "literary" essays and such books as *The Spirit of Romance, Guide to Kulchur*, or *ABC of Reading*. The point is not that Pound had no concern with technique, or that Eliot saw things in Pound that were never there. Generic models are normative and hierarchical, suggesting ways of ordering our experience of texts and groups of texts. We know those models to be inadequate or ill adjusted when they prove incapable of assimilating prominent elements to our expectations; and what we then do is change or readjust our model. It is this kind of change that I propose. We have let the term "modernist" beguile us into expecting that the major figures of the period should fight the same battles and pursue the same ends. Thus in 1954 Harry Levin professed that "to us 'the tradition' means largely Eliot and Pound, the poets they rediscovered and the critics who make criticism new by accepting and applying their criteria."[30] Nearly thirty years later, Harold Bloom identifies Pound with Joyce and Eliot as the precursors of the New Criticism, as if all modernists must necessarily have preferred intrinsic and institutional criticism.[31]

But such transformations of Pound's work will not be corrected by a simple reversal of the relations I have just described; we need rather to consider how in Pound's case the concern for craft and the vision of culture as a single organism interact. More generally, Eliot's editing of Pound's critical prose raises questions about the relations between historically specific ways of reading and the processes of canonization. To paraphrase and appropriate Eliot, we might say that *Literary Essays* was a collection assembled in a form that is no longer satisfactory. Although Eliot's emphasis once helped rehabilitate Pound's poetic reputation, Donald Davie's perception of the damage wrought by such separation of Pound's poetry and politics seems increasingly perceptive.[32] Having watched the breakup of New Critical positivism, we can predict that no selected essays, however organized, can be for long "definitive." Late-twentieth-century debates about the postmodern have helped demonstrate the extent to which the subject of modernism is inseparable from the history of its receptions. Considered in terms of its

30. See "Unfrocked Professor," a review of *Literary Essays of Ezra Pound, Yale Review* (summer 1954): 602–3.
31. Harold Bloom, introduction to the "Prophets of Sensibility" edition of Thomas Carlyle's *Sartor Resartus* (New York: Confucian Press, 1981), v.
32. See *Ezra Pound: The Poet as Sculptor* (New York: Oxford University Press, 1964), 242–43: "What [the award of the first Bollingen prize to *Pisan Cantos*] meant in effect was that American society accepted and recognized an absolute discontinuity between the life of the poet and the life of the man. Ever since, in British and American society alike, this absolute distinction has been sustained, and upheld as the basic assumption on which society must proceed in dealing with the artists who live in its midst. . . . Pound has made it impossible for any one any longer to exalt the poet into a seer."

generic strategies, *Literary Essays* remains for this demonstration as crucial as Pound's own collections through the 1930s. Yet our ideas both about "modernism" and about the "literary" are not isolated examples of conceptual change; the study of Pound's writing is beset by the reification of crucial terms.

Eliot's editorial work of the early fifties, both of Pound's writing and his own, underscores the extent to which our picture of modernism is a carefully constructed retrospective. As a young man with the epic *The Waste Land* just behind him, Eliot had described his task as "making the modern world possible for art";[33] as a survivor of the political pandemonium of the thirties, and the holocaust of the Second World War, Eliot was satisfied to examine the nature of aesthetic experience in isolation. Whether or not we choose to respect that later project, we should recognize that it contradicted the impulses of many of those writers whom we have learned to call modernist. In the manner in which it undermines its own premises, *Literary Essays of Ezra Pound* restages modernist ambivalence over choosing an intractable political world over a potentially perfectable aesthetic one. While Eliot never entirely relinquished his reformist hopes, he did withdraw them from the arena of immediate political contest. By contrast, Pound's ideas about stimulating political or economic reform grew increasingly direct; he came to challenge romantic conceptions of "literature" as a mediation of the most stultifying and disabling kind. Although he liked to imagine "the city of Dioce whose terraces are the colour of stars" (Canto 74/439), Pound rarely longed for anything like Yeats's Byzantium. He wanted instead to reground the arts, and pursued his bid to do so as long as he continued writing. He clung to his hopes that his work could effect change even after he was resigned that "literature," in its received forms, could not. This was not egotism, but a hope that grew from his most fundamental convictions—and these derived in ways he never recognized from the Victorian sages. Ironically, the impulse to free poetry from romantic mediations came to him much mediated.

---

33. T. S. Eliot, "Ulysses, Order, and Myth," *Dial* 75 (November 1923); reprinted in *Selected Prose of T. S. Eliot,* ed. Frank Kermode (London: Faber & Faber, 1975), 175–78.

2
"A Profounder Didacticism": Ruskin, Orage, and Pound's Vision of Cultural Totality

> Under these circumstances . . . no designing or any other development of beautiful art will be possible.
> —John Ruskin,
> *The Two Paths* (1859)

> So long as the system of competition in the production and exchange of the means of life goes on, the degradation of the arts will go on.
> —William Morris,
> "Art under Plutocracy" (1884)

> The literature and art of today are the parallels of the economic situation of today.
> —A. R. Orage,
> "Profiteering in Literature" (1912)

> With usura hath no man a house of good stone
> each block cut smooth and well fitting
> that design might cover their face
> —Ezra Pound
> Canto 45 (1936)

"Pound at His Most Old-Fashioned"

The success of Eliot's recuperative project followed precisely from its emphasis on the "literary"—a term whose residual explanatory force informs both the reading and, at least in the last century and a half, the writing of poetry and fiction. But the strictures of literariness are nowhere more deforming than in the case of Ezra Pound. Quite simply, Pound militated against romantic and aesthetic notions of the properly "poetic" or "literary" for most of his working life, and so "literary" explanations of his work must necessarily do what Eliot did in his editions of Pound: ignore many elements of Pound's work, or treat them as incidental to his "true" art, or recast or reframe such elements as might resist literary attention.

By the end of the First World War, Pound's work, not just in the *Cantos* but in his criticism, historical writing, and popularizing guides as well, came to two distinctive innovations: the use of problematic and even unstable generic combinations, and the inclusion of (in Pound's phrase) "whole chunks" of other texts in his own. But neither of these innovations can be understood in terms of an obsessive "concentration upon the craft of letters." Such an understanding requires rather that we examine what could be gained by the importation into poetic discourse of the language of commerce, law, history, or even of divergent literary models. Ultimately, Pound aimed to reestablish poetry at the center of public discourse: in the agora—in the way of the temples, the houses of government, the academy, the halls of commerce. Indeed, by the time he began at last to make headway on the *Cantos* Pound was willing to use the heterogeneous energies of the agora synonymously with his idea of the "vortex." In his "Paris Letter" of January 1922, Pound insisted that

> if the term "letter" at the head of this rubric is to be anything but a mockery it should imply not only communication but answer. To form any sort of porch, vortex, academia, agora there must be at least five or six people sufficiently interested in one another's ideas to wish, one need not say, to correct, but to bring them into some sort of focus; to establish not a foot-rule but some sort of means of communication, and some understanding of how a given idea, emitted from the left side of the table (Rome, Paris) may strike someone seated at the other end or opposite side of the board (Denver, London, Rio de Janeiro).[1]

Pound's language here is in itself already the language of the agora, for it is about exchange and community; his insistence is less the curmudgeonly complaining of the Ruskin of *Fors Clavigera* (of which more shortly) than it

---

1. *Dial* 72, no. 1 (January 1922): 73–78.

is an expression of his desire that literature resume an active role in the establishment of value.

Despite the obvious benefits such an aggrandizement of writing might bring to authors and poets, it rests uneasily with "literary" concerns, at least insofar as those ideas have been handed down from the late Enlightenment. The concept of "literature" that Pound inherited unconsciously from the romantics functioned to circumscribe certain groups of texts and was part of a broader attempt to define "culture" apart from the activities of "merely" material civilization. It was Coleridge who had first set out this opposition in England. In *The Constitution of Church and State* (1830), while attempting to "ascertain the end, or national purpose" of the Church, Coleridge proposed that both the aristocracy and middle class

> depend on a continuing and progressive civilization. But civilization is itself but a mixed good, if not far more a corrupting influence, the hectic of disease, not the bloom of health, and a nation so distinguished more fitly to be called a varnished than a polished people; where this civilization is not grounded in *cultivation*, in the harmonious development of those qualities and faculties that characterise our *humanity*. We must be men in order to be citizens.
>
> The Nationality, therefore, was reserved for the support and maintenance of a permanent class or order, with the following duties. A certain smaller number were to remain at the fountain heads of the humanities, in cultivating and enlarging the knowledge already possessed, and in watching over the interests of physical and moral science; being, likewise, the instructors of such as constituted, or were to constitute, the remaining more numerous classes of the order.[2]

In effect, Coleridge would here legitimate an elite priestly class, pronouncing it the guardian of culture, of true well-being as opposed to wealth. His identification of civilization as "a mixed good" had precedent not only in German idealism but in Rousseau, whose First Discourse (1750) warned that "our souls have been corrupted in proportion to the advancement of our sciences and arts toward perfection" and that civilization propagates "the

---

2. *On the Constitution of the Church and State*, ed. John Colmar, vol. 10 of *The Collected Works of Samuel Taylor Coleridge*, ed. Kathleen Coburn (Princeton: Princeton University Press, 1976), 42–43.

semblance of all the virtues without the possession of any."[3] However, Coleridge's concern with "a certain smaller number" suggests the conservative nature of his project, a project whose "literary" implications are manifest in poems like "Kubla Khan." The elaborate preface and complex myth-making of this "fragment," this "vision in a dream," provide multiple frames about the lyric itself that work in ways analogous to the walls of Kubla Khan's pleasure dome, or the magic circles we are warned to weave around the visionary poet, with "his flashing eyes, his floating hair": they function to isolate and insulate the realm of the "imagination," of the soul, from the increasingly pervasive quantifications of deterministic Enlightenment science and its utilitarian attempts to create "social science." In this way, Coleridge helped to set the terms for discussion that, a century and a half later, still continues. The historicity of the idea of culture has received much attention.[4] But it remains difficult all the same to discuss these developments precisely because their origins and subsequent courses were so various, if interrelated. I will therefore offer here a most schematic synopsis, one that by design looks forward to the discursive practices we ordinarily understand as "modernist."

Allan Bloom has complained that "we all know with some degree of precision what commerce is, while I, at least, have no understanding of what 'culture' is, and it is a word I never use. 'Culture' somehow refers to the 'higher' things, to 'spirituality,' and shares the vagueness and contentlessness of those terms. It belongs in the family of other amorphous notions like 'genius,' 'personality,' 'intellectual,' and 'creativity,' all of which have a noble, if flawed, intention and have inevitably been debased over the two centuries of their currency."[5] Raymond Williams arrives at a different verbal

---

3. *The First and Second Discourses of Jean-Jacques Rousseau*, ed. Roger D. Masters, trans. Roger D. Masters and Judith R. Masters (New York: St. Martin's Press, 1964), 36 and 39.

4. See Allan Bloom, "Commerce and Culture," *This World*, no. 3 (fall 1982): 5–20, rpt. in *Giants and Dwarfs: Essays 1960–1990* (London: Simon & Schuster, 1990), 277–94; David DeLaura, "Ruskin, Arnold and Browning's Grammarian: 'Crowded with Culture,'" in *Victorian Perspectives: Six Essays*, ed. John Clubbe and Jerome Meckier (London: Macmillan, 1989), 68–119; Terry Eagleton, *Literary Theory: An Introduction* (Minneapolis: University of Minnesota Press, 1983), esp. 1–53; E. H. Gombrich, "In Search of Cultural History," in *Ideals and Idols* (Oxford: Phaidon Press, 1979), 24–59; Robert Langbaum, "The Victorian Idea of Culture," in *The Word from Below: Essays on Modern Literature and Culture* (Madison: University of Wisconsin Press, 1987), 78–88; Harry Levin, "Semantics of Culture," in *Daedalus* (winter 1965); Douglas Lane Patey, "The Eighteenth Century Invents the Canon," *Modern Language Studies* 18, no. 1 (1988): 17–37; Karl J. Weintraub, *Visions of Culture* (Chicago: University of Chicago Press, 1966); Raymond Williams, *Keywords: A Vocabulary of Culture and Society* (Oxford: Oxford University Press, 1976).

5. Allan Bloom, "Commerce and Culture," 277.

configuration, but really, despite his obvious political differences from Bloom, to much the same effect. The terms "culture," "literature," "aesthetic," the idea of "zeitgeist" or "spirit of the age"—with its attendant assumptions of cultural organism and totality—all of these terms acquired their modern senses during or immediately after the putative failure of the Enlightenment. It is not that all of these terms "arose" at the same "moment," but that in the nineteenth century they are always already reconfigured as related.

Culture and its related terms thus constituted for nineteenth-century writers an idealist removal, and a mystification of the problem of value in a deterministic universe. Pound's ambitions were finally extraliterary precisely to the extent that he regarded the by his time vaguely spiritual promise of totality as literally and materially demonstrable. He turned, as it were, the romantic religion of art on its head by insisting on its importance within, rather than above, the totality of "cultural" relations. To put it another way, Pound aestheticized the notion of utility, and then turned that notion against the Paterian valorization of the aesthetic. This is the move that Alan Megill—in his discussion of Nietzsche, Heidegger, Foucault, and Derrida—has described as the extreme form of romantic epistemology:

> As it is usually employed, the word "aestheticism" denotes an enclosure within a self-contained realm of aesthetic objects and sensations, and hence also denotes a separation from the "real world" of non-aesthetic objects. Here, however, I am using the word in a sense that is almost diametrically opposed to its usual sense. I am using it to refer not to the condition of being enclosed within the limited territory of the aesthetic, but rather to an attempt to expand the aesthetic to embrace the whole of reality. To put it in another way, I am using it to refer to a tendency to see "art" or "language" or "discourse" or "text" as constituting the primary realm of human experience.[6]

Kathryne Lindberg, in her book *Reading Pound Reading*, addresses the analogies between Pound and Nietzsche directly—although, true to her poststructuralist orientation, she denies that their texts "delineate a tradition or an orderly genealogy of works and ideas either":

> We must recognize that the disorganization, the maddening inter- (and intra-) textuality of Pound's criticism, is not wholly fortuitous. His use

---

6. *Prophets of Extremity: Nietzsche, Heidegger, Foucault, Derrida* (Berkeley and Los Angeles: University of California Press, 1985), 2.

of fragments and his attention to irreducible—if "luminous"—details appear to the contrary a critical or textual strategy. His criticism, part of a lengthy, heated polemic against all takers, is not merely *a*systematic. While I do not mean to reverse the usual devaluation of his prose in relation to his poetry, one must recognize that his notion of reading is often stunningly *anti*systematic. At first blush it might seem odd to treat Pound's works with those of a German philosopher (or, to use Pound's word, "flyosopher," letter to T. S. Eliot, January 1940). But who more than Nietzsche explored the modern desire to comprehend all culture in a totalized reading, condemning in the same gesture the very tactics he was forced to employ.[7]

Lindberg's understanding, that Pound's criticism is indeed *anti*systematic, and that his resistance to the systematic is ineluctably tied to his preoccupation with "totality," does indeed carry us to the crux of Pound's interpretive activity. What makes Pound's project extra- or even antiliterary is not that he had economic and political interests that were sometimes reflected in his "art," but that for him the idea of cultural totality denoted an integrity in which economics, aesthetics, and politics were all vitally interrelated. It was not the Victorian arguments about culture which Pound regarded as stultifying but what he saw as their spiritless twentieth-century repetitions. He saw "culture" as a vital process, not an aggregate of museum pieces—not, as he wrote in "Mauberley," "two gross of broken statues" and "a few thousand battered books." But to rejuvenate culture, to regain for poetry its ancient centrality, Pound found it necessary to attack at one and the same time contemporary notions of "literature" or "art" and "economics" or "history."

Pound's experiments in genre can be understood only in terms of these

---

7. Kathryne Lindberg, *Reading Pound Reading: Modernism after Nietzsche* (New York: Oxford University Press, 1987), 4–5. In the previous year, Jean-Michel Rabaté published his *Language, Sexuality, and Ideology in Ezra Pound's "Cantos"* (Albany: State University of New York Press, 1986), a study which proposes relations between Pound and another of Megill's prophets of extremity: Martin Heidegger. Working from similar theoretical warrants, Rabaté justifies his comparison in similar ways: "Placing the names of Pound and Heidegger side by side generally calls up a monstrous image of two difficult writers, who have little in common apart from a highly specific and idiomatic command of language. . . . My belief is that only a detour through Heidegger can permit one to understand the 'foundational' position of Pound as poet, and to understand its imbrication in a general historical perspective. . . . Pound and Heidegger have both attempted a general survey of the question of language in its relation to 'metaphysics' at large, without eschewing the problems of politics, art and even changes in the modern way of life" (2).

larger purposes. It is only in terms of these purposes that Pound's extraliterary ambitions do anything but enforce his marginality. Pound's concern to infect "purely aesthetic experience" with the germ of history and economics identifies his perpetuation of a tradition in English writing sustained over two centuries, and which in the nineteenth century included among others Coleridge, Carlyle, Ruskin, Arnold, Morris, and Bosanquet. Pound's tragedy was really that he sought to conserve that which was already lost—that he went to war with obsolete equipment and tactics, opposing the armor of Sherman tanks with Ruskin's armour of St. George. Carlyle and Ruskin had battled the claims of determinism with claims for the freedom of "imagination"; they had insisted on the supremacy of will over causation and opposed to promises of universal progress the enduring importance of history and the changelessness of the human heart. Where Bentham or the elder Mill recognized only the claims of self-interest, Carlyle or Ruskin insisted on the totality of human relations and respect for the organism of its collective inner life.

Pound's affinities, at least with Ruskin, have not gone unnoticed. Guy Davenport, for instance, has broadly proposed "that almost all of Ruskin is taken up by Pound," a position that Michael Alexander articulates somewhat more narrowly when describing "the radical integrity Pound finds between economics, the life of the arts, craft, nature, procreation and religion"; it is, Alexander finds, "both a critique of and a jeremiad against the modern industrial world," and as such is the "logical development of the Ruskinian tradition."[8] But Donald Davie has observed not only the extent of Pound's affinities with Ruskin, but also their comparatively anachronistic character. In Davie's phrase, when Pound assumes that "the level of craftsmanship . . . registers the good or ill health of a period or society," we then see him "at his most old-fashioned."[9] That human beings are given to imagining the future in terms of the familiar past is itself a familiar spectacle. Nevertheless, Davie's identification of Ruskin as "the last considerable figure before Pound" to maintain the principle of cultural integrity makes it difficult to explain why Pound should have taken up neglected assumptions. In fact, this way of thinking had proven so successful, though not without contest, that it had

---

8. See Michael Alexander, *The Poetic Achievement of Ezra Pound* (Berkeley and Los Angeles: University of California Press, 1979), 179; Guy Davenport, *Cities on Hills: A Study of I–XXX of Ezra Pound's Cantos* (Ann Arbor: UMI Research Press, 1983), 21; see also Louis B. Salomon, "The Pound-Ruskin Axis," *College English* 16 (February 1955): 270–76.

9. Donald Davie, "The Critics Who Made Us: Ezra Pound," *The Sewanee Review* 92 (July–September 1984): 426.

largely ceased to be a matter of intellectual debate and had become the stuff of popular journalism. It is there that Pound absorbed it. In other words, Davie's estimation of Ruskin as "the last considerable figure" to assume an integrity between art and the society in which it is produced is correct, but largely beside the historical point. For the issue here is not the kind of priestly "tradition" of great men for whom Eliot, Leavis, and others taught respect, but the broad dissemination of a way of thinking and of writing. The notion of cultural integrity pervaded many of the middle-class journals of the day. Pound's experience of this idea amid the *New Age* circle of A. R. Orage was less exceptional than it was a kind of socialist catechism.

All of this helps to explain a common critical puzzle: Ruskin is widely conceded to have been important to Pound, but Pound rarely refers to him explicitly. What references there are come and go quickly, without calling attention to themselves. Consider Canto 89, the second of the "Benton" cantos of *Section: Rock-Drill*:

> "What he meant to *us* in those days"
> said old Image (Selwyn) referring to Ruskin.
>
>   Canto 89/615

Selwyn Image was a minor aesthete who had, thirty-five years before, figured in Pound's composite persona "Hugh Selwyn Mauberley." What "old Image" remembered was a time when embattled artists found in Ruskin a fervent champion. But although Pound's construction memorializes Ruskin, it also declares him out of date: Ruskin could matter "in those days," but is today as dated as the old aesthete who remembers not even the man so much as his reputation. Pound's preservation of Image's emphatic "us" suggests as well that Ruskin's work was itself too aesthetic.[10] Pound's references to Ruskin typically temper such slight praise with condescension: in "The

10. It should nevertheless be noted that Ruskin figures in Canto 89 as a bit of oral history. As I explain in Chapter 4, oral history was Pound's preferred model because he saw it as the transmission of the impact of facts — the residuum of ideas in the sensibility of a people — rather than the mechanical transmission of acquired knowledge, which he associated with academically written history. In Canto 89, Pound's reference to Ruskin forms part of a series of quotations from speech, punctuated halfway through (and only two lines above the quotation from Image) by Pound's didactic reminder, "This section is labeled: Rock Drill." Because Pound's emphasis on oral transmission is complexly related to his assumptions about cultural totality, the condescension to Ruskin in Canto 89 is itself thus made on a Ruskinian basis. Moreover, the line that immediately follows, "Tasso, Kidd, Raleigh, all jailed," associates Ruskin (whom Pound thought of as driven mad by a country imperturbable in its smugness — see his review "Swinburne's Letters," published

Drama as a Means of Education" (16 April 1920) Pound suggested that Ruskin was suitable reading only for "the suburban wife";[11] "in "The City" (Autumn 1928) he allowed only that "Ruskin was well-meaning but a goose"; and in "A Place for English Writers: Definition of a Usurer" (18 June 1938), Pound placed Ruskin in a tradition of failed reformers:

> Then the Empire started expanding and mercantilism was made very attractive. Opportunity for the hard working non-thinking go-getter was preached to the simple-hearted. And for a long time very few people recovered. There were a few cranks like Shelley and Godwin and Ruskin and Wm. Morris, but if they ever got down to brass tacks the public was not let into the secret. The mercantilist, God hellup us, "virtues" of thrift alias greed, of diligence alias keeping your eye off all consequences except those in the immediate foreground, spread from commerce into all parts of the English mind. And letters languished.[12]

And yet even this dismissal of Ruskin invokes the quintessentially Ruskinian assumption of cultural totality: as usury corrupted economic relations it violated human relations, "and letters languished." This conviction came to Pound not so much as an idea but as a way of receiving ideas; it was not something that Pound "thought" but a way of thinking that informed his poetic, scholarly, and political activities alike.

This is to suggest a rather different explanation for Charles Tomlinson's stimulating description of Ruskin as the ubiquitous absence in Pound's work.[13] Pound did not actively seek to bury his debts to Ruskin because he was largely unconscious of them—they were already buried. Pound's relations to Ruskin are no idle matter of "influence," for to understand how Pound's thinking was informed by the long post-Enlightenment debate over "culture" is to recognize that, for all its striking modernity, the *Cantos* was a determined working-out of principles that remained as incompletely assimilable for most readers in Pound's time as they did in Ruskin's—or as they

---

in *Future*, February 1919) with authors jailed for their political actions, a group among whose company Pound would have inevitably numbered himself.

11. "The Drama as a Means of Education," *Athenaeum* 94, no. 4694 (16 April 1920): 520.
12. "A Place for English Writers: Definition of 'Usurer,'" *Action* 122 (18 June 1938): 13.
13. Tomlinson offered this description in "Ruskin's Relevance to the Twentieth Century," a public lecture delivered in the Hall of Presidents, Colgate University, 27 April 1987.

remain in our own. The problem was (and is) that as the idea had grown familiar it ceased to threaten. Yet Pound took to it with a fire and zeal which he never lost. From the first he wrote as if reminding his readers of something they already knew, but had faithlessly forgotten, in a tone that owed less to his own sense of having "been born / in a half savage country, out of date" than it did to a posture inherent in the role of jeremiad.[14] But however much he miscalculated his public, Pound recognized that the organic (or in Pound's term—"totalitarian") social vision which he saw in Douglas's economics, or in the criticism of de Gourmont, Orage, or Upward, would not permit business as usual. The *Cantos* would either succeed in reorganizing human relations, or they would fail as Shelley, Godwin, and Ruskin had failed.

Pound did not perpetuate the arguments of "culture" in ignorance of historical change, but in the idealist confidence that material change did not alter essentials. Pound's moral failures thus resulted, not merely from moral idiosyncracy, but from the end effects of a broad heritage. Thus, as Davie proposes, Pound's fascism cannot be separated from his poetry because it "represents a disastrously false judgment made in the course of following through a conviction *not* self-evidently false—about there being a connection between the health of letters and the health of the commonweal."[15] Davie's judiciousness in speaking of convictions that are "not self-evidently false" is well taken. Although the terms of the argument have shifted, the question of cultural integrity continues to be a subject of debate late into the twentieth century. For most critics, especially those who turn to Marx, or to Foucault or Kristeva, for their warrants, the issue is not whether culture constitutes a totality, but how it does so. The question of Pound's relation to Ruskin involves much more than "similarities in personality, interests, and convictions." It involves a historically specific vision of human productivity which shaped profoundly how both writers ordered their subject matter and presented that ordering.[16] To say then with Davie that Pound's "disasterously false judgement [was] made in the course of following through a conviction *not* self-evidently false" is not to excuse Pound, but to observe how he kept a very literal faith with promises that may have been, as he wrote in "Mauberley," "wrong from the start." As more contemporary arguments

14. The authoritative discussion of the qualities characteristic here remains Sacvan Bercovitch, *The American Jeremiad* (Madison: University of Wisconsin Press, 1978).
15. Davie, "Critics Who Made Us," 427.
16. The "similarities in personality, interests, and convictions" are the subject of Louis B. Salomon's uncannily titled "Pound-Ruskin Axis" (see note 6).

about the ideas of "epistēmē" or "discourse" illustrate, these promises of totality retain for us their fascination.

Aestheticizing "the Aesthete's Critique"

"HEALTH is MORE interesting than disease. Health is TOTAL."
—Ezra Pound, "Continuity," a radio broadcast (1942)

What effect could a serious and continued reading of those fellows ["the Ruskins and Carlyles and Holman Hunts"] have had but 1914? And 193-?
—Ford Madox Ford, *Portraits from Life* (1937)

In considering Ruskin's ordering of his subject matter, and then his presentation of that ordering, we raise generic questions that can lead to an understanding of how it was that Ruskin could be so important to Pound and yet so conspicuously absent. As we shall see, the principal generic features of Ruskin's didactic prose were developed from his totalizing conception of "culture." This faith in cultural totality proved more persuasive than any of Ruskin's particular arguments and amplified romantic assumptions about the organic integrity of form and of the relations among forms. Ruskin's model proved seminal, so that by the turn of the century his opponents identified its pervasiveness as being in itself cause for renewed resistance. Between Ruskin and Pound there flourished a variety of writers, such as William Morris, Bernard Bosanquet, J. A. Hobson, or A. R. Orage, whose work reaffirmed, perpetuated, and disseminated the principles of organicism and cultural totality. As they did so, these writers gradually transformed the controversial into the conventional and brought what had been a fairly rarefied critique of the modern state into something approaching a standard socialist attitude. Morris concerned himself with Ruskin's ideas about the relation of the worker to his work; Bosanquet the aesthetician, with "the criticism passed by popular writers upon Mr. Ruskin that he turns aesthetic into ethic"—finding the "connection between the content of ethic and that of aesthetic" to be "essential," and that "it is a worse error to neglect, than to state with technical incorrectness" this connection. Hobson the economist attacked attempts to dissociate questions of wealth from those of human welfare and celebrated Ruskin as a serious reformer. Orage included Ruskin in his eclectic program to aestheticize socialist attempts at reform. That the work of these figures was generally unrelated says much about the broad and varied ways in which Ruskin's work was received and assimilated. Much of Ruskin's influence can be measured in the broader dissemination of the idea of cultural totality. As Robert Langbaum has said, "The word 'culture' was from the beginning charged with a world-view,"[17] and in the first third of the nineteenth century it resounded as "a battle cry"; but by the same period of the twentieth century the word was entirely orthodox, institutionalized in *The Oxford Universal Dictionary* (1933), and though possessed of a proliferating number of uses, defined, in its "absolute" sense, as "the intellectual side of civilization." The battle cry had been reified into a quality. Carlyle opened his essay "Signs of the Times" (1829) by observing that "it is no very good symptom either of nations or individuals, that they deal much in vaticination," apologized for so doing, and offered his very need to do so as another sign of the times. Two years later John Stuart Mill began his serialized meditation on "the spirit of the age" by noting that the expression is "in some measure novel," and not "to be met with in any work exceeding fifty years in antiquity." By contrast, early twentieth-century writers such as Spengler, Yeats, Pound, or Eliot accepted the idea as a given—accepted it as in the nature of things that each age should have its own spirit or culture, and worried instead over the relations between historical epochs.[18] When in 1910 Pound published the series of public lectures he had given under the title "On the Development of the Literature of Southern Europe," he called it *The Spirit of Romance*, with no more self-consciousness than a prefatory allusion to Carlyle: "The study of literature is hero-worship."

In a certain sense, Pound's work prior to the twenties recapitulates the

17. Robert Langbaum, "The Victorian Idea of Culture," in *The Word from Below: Essays on Modern Literature and Culture* (Madison: University of Wisconsin Press, 1987), 84.
18. Mill's "Spirit of the Age," in five parts and seven installments, can be found in volume 12 of the *Collected Works*, ed. Ann P. Robson and John M. Robson (Toronto: University of Toronto Press, 1986). Oswald Spengler's *Untergang des Abendlande* (1918–22), translated into English as *The Decline of the West* in 1926–28, in many respects presents the ultimate version of the theory of culture, since Spengler's cultural morphology depends on organic metaphors, and since in his writing the idea of organism presumes a totality so complete that any culture must necessarily remain impervious to heterogeneous influences. Yeats's *Vision* (1925), for all its arcana, is predicated on a similar historicism, although Yeats's model allows for more heterogeneity within a dominant phase.

broad historical transmission wherein that cluster of related ideas—culture, the totality of collective life, zeitgeist—moved from prophetic critique to popular catchword. As James Longenbach has shown, Pound's work through the middle of the war was aggressively elitist, sometimes more Yeatsian than Yeats.[19] Pound's vorticist manifesto of September 1914, for instance, affirmed both that "one does not want to be called a symbolist, because symbolism has usually been associated with mushy technique," but also that a "belief in a sort of permanent metaphor is, as I understand it, 'symbolism' in its profounder sense. It is not necessarily a belief in a permanent world, but it is a belief in that direction."[20] Having taken Pound's relations to Yeats and the occult more seriously than anyone else before him, Longenbach is able to demonstrate Pound's adherence to a belief in "the artist's visionary power." But this elitist strain was invariably met by a contrary popularizing impulse. The impulse was there even in early work like *The Spirit of Romance*. But by 1922, a long eight years after the formulations of "Vorticism," Pound's symbolist and didactic impulses had assumed a new relation. In July of that year he wrote to Felix Schelling, one of his professors at the University of Pennsylvania, allowing that "I am perhaps didactic; so in a sense, or in different senses are Homer, Dante, Villon, and Omar, and Fitzgerald's trans. of Omar is the only good poem of Vict. era that has got beyond fame de cénacle. It's all rubbish to pretend that art isn't didactic. A revelation is always didactic. Only the aesthetes since 1800 have pretended the contrary, and they aren't a very sturdy lot. Art can't offer a patent medicine. A failure to distinguish that from a profounder didacticism has led to the errors of 'aesthete's critique'" (*SL*, 180). The letter indicates Pound's growing resolution about the direction of his work. It does not, however, signal a break from his earlier orientation. For constant between his ideas of "'symbolism' in its profounder sense" and of "a profounder didacticism," is the expectation that a visionary unity belies surface appearances. Indeed, as the rhetoric of the "profounder" level remains unchanged, it suggests the binary oppositions that characteristically inform the discourse of "culture": Carlyle, for instance, expounding in "Characteristics" (1831) on

---

19. *Stone Cottage: Pound, Yeats, and Modernism* (New York: Oxford University Press, 1988), see especially part 1. For a different account of the early years of modernist writing, but one that also emphasizes the close interaction of a few key figures, see Michael Levenson's *Genealogy of Modernism: A Study of English Literary Doctrine 1908–1922* (Cambridge: Cambridge University Press, 1984).

20. See Longenbach, *Stone Cottage*, 78–79; Pound's essay "Vorticism" is reprinted in *A Memoir of Gaudier-Brzeska* (New York: New Directions, 1970), 84–85.

the difference between symptom and disease, or between the "upper surface" of mere argument and the "depths" of "vital force." For Pound, the implicit promise of the "profounder" forms was the transcendence of fruitless oppositions—between "symbolism" and "realism," between imagination and didacticism: an aestheticizing, in Alan Megill's sense, of the very activity of writing.

The impulse to attempt "a profounder didacticism" was sparked during Pound's lengthy interaction with them who were for him the most important mediators of both Ruskin's legacy and the gospel of culture in general: Orage and such of his regular contributors to the *New Age* as Allen Upward.[21] But before we turn to Orage, we should consider how expectations of cultural totality inform Ruskin's most fiercely didactic work. Although Ruskin everywhere insisted on the integrity of aesthetic, economic, and moral issues, we can get a sense of how his work provided Pound with generic models by quickly considering his *Fors Clavigera: Letters to the Workmen and Labourers of Great Britain* (1871–78, 1880–84). These models certainly inform not only such of Pound's late work as *Section: Rock-Drill* (1955), the very title of which reproduces the metaphor of hammering, but also many of the cantos published after *A Draft of Cantos 17–27* (1930). But more striking still is the extent to which these models are reproduced in Pound's critical writing of the decade immediately preceding his steady work on the *Cantos*. There too Pound often returned to the Ruskinian trope of "the hammer that hits the nail on the head"—itself, in such a context, a strangely rarefied use of a popular cliché. Consider this example from "Affirmations VI": "For when words cease to cling close to things, kingdoms fall, empires wane and diminish. Rome went because it was no longer the fashion to hit the nail on the head. They desired orators."[22] Pound's subject here is verbal

---

21. The title of the *New Age* is of interest, especially given its short but complicated history. Having originally been founded in 1894, by Frederick A. Atkins, as "a weekly record of Christian culture, social service, and literary life," it was purchased in 1895 by the socialist A. E. Fletcher, who reconceived it as "a journal for thinkers and workers." It would have two more editors before Orage assumed the task, and called it "an independent Socialist review of politics, literature, and art." But throughout these various changes of subtitle, the title remained constant. As such, it suggests popular interest (popular indeed, since Atkins claimed to have a circulation of 56,000) in "the spirit of the age" and the popular expectation that history segmented into "ages" each of which had its own "spirit." See John L. Finlay, *Social Credit: The English Origins* (Montreal: McGill-Queen's University Press, 1972), 63.

22. Ezra Pound, "Affirmations VI: Analysis of this Decade," *New Age* 16, no. 15 (11 February 1915): 409–11; reprinted in *Gaudier-Brzeska: A Memoir* (New York: New Directions, 1961), 133–41.

precision, although it is not verbal precision per se, but rather the total network of human relations that ties verbal exchange with all other forms of human relation.

Despite its magnificent condescension, its patronizing and shaming tone (a misfire that would characterize Pound's attempts at popular exposition as well), Ruskin's *Fors* was intended for a popular audience. It was addressed, as its subtitle indicates, to Britain's working classes. Written in the form of letters (even though after Letter 35 Ruskin, in high dudgeon, ceased to include opening or closing salutations), its development is both digressive and dialogic. Ruskin gave much space to correspondence with his readers. But most important here are the premises of Ruskin's analysis, of his conviction that an apparently random and digressive ordering could still accomplish his explicit didactic purposes. The title, as Ruskin insisted, was an attempt "shortly to mark my chief purpose": "fors" meant "chance, guided by the hidden hand of fate. Clavigera meant that chance carried a club, or nail or a key." While Ruskin allowed that his title might have other connotations, he himself "interpreted" it to mean "Chance, the fate that hits the nail on the head."[23] There was a serious concern behind this apparent whimsy. What Ruskin was proposing was that even the most happenstance occurrences can be made to reveal the essential condition of an entire culture. In effect, Ruskin's thinking here and elsewhere attributed to culture a unified organic life analogous to that which romantic aestheticians discerned in individual works of art. This way of thinking about culture characterized Pound's work as well. His enthusiasm for Remy de Gourmont, which—because Gourmont played so crucial a role in Pound's thoughts about method—is no random example, partly derived from his perception that Gourmont shared this way of thinking: "You could . . . have said to De Gourmont anything that came into your head, you could have sent him anything you had written with a reasonable assurance that he would have known what you were driving at."[24]

Fors, and others of Ruskin's jeremiads like *Munera Pulveris* or *The Ethics of the Dust,* can begin to suggest how a strict belief in cultural integrity shapes and alters the generic features of didactic work—as well as how such a belief can inspire authorial confidence in projects of nearly boundless scope. In-

---

23. Quoted in Robert Hewison, *John Ruskin: The Argument of the Eye* (Princeton: Princeton University Press, 1976), 180.
24. See Richard Sieburth, *Instigations: Ezra Pound and Remy de Gourmont* (Cambridge: Harvard University Press, 1978), 42.

deed, the evidence of such pressure is evident in Carlyle's earliest work half a century earlier. The frustrated efforts of the "editor" of *Sartor Resartus* to establish a biographical narrative out of Teufelsdröckh's many unsorted sacks of notes and papers, all of which are labeled only with signs of the zodiac, provide a comic case in point. Carlyle develops his position in the interplay between the overly rational and the wildly romantic: the efforts of the editor to make sense of that which is beyond "sense" in any rationalist conception become, repeatedly, Carlyle's foregrounded subject. The "whole" of his vision is available in any of its parts. Carlyle's didacticism does not aim to impart a particular sequence of reasoning, or even to submit facts hitherto not accounted for; it aims, as romantic truism would have it, to change not "what" we see but "how" we see. In and of themselves, particular details matter little; the issue is not utilitarian analysis but coherent vision.

To explain Carlyle or Ruskin in this way is to return us to the familiar and overfamiliar premises of romanticism: it is finally in their overfamiliarity that they become of importance here, for insofar as they are overfamiliar we no longer see them. As critics like Jerome McGann or Clifford Siskin have noted, the romantics have shaped the way we read.[25] But the spectacle of Carlyle's political development, or Ruskin's or Pound's, invites us to reconsider the basis for any claims about cultural totality. Here again, Ruskin's *Fors* provides convenient illustration. We have already seen that Ruskin's title treated "chance" and "fate" equivocally, and that that equivocation owed much to his sense of cultural organism. Confident that wherever he might begin, the essential condition of modernity would prove manifest, Ruskin expanded in Letter 13 on the relations between luck and his sense of purpose: "These letters will put before you so much of the past history of the world, in an intelligible manner, as may enable you to see the laws of Fortune or Destiny, 'Clavigera,' Nail bearing; driving the iron home with hammer stroke, so that nothing shall be moved; and fastening each of us at last to the Cross we have chosen to carry."[26] But "driving the iron home with hammer stroke," as the machismo of its metaphor suggests, was a matter not of relentless, rationalist pounding away, but of the single serendipitous stroke. Ruskin felt that the presentation of his purpose required no rigorous logic-chopping. Rather, he expected that "chance" would put in his way the

---

25. See Jerome McGann's *Romantic Ideology* (Chicago: University of Chicago Press, 1983), or Clifford Siskin's *Historicity of Romantic Discourse* (New York: Oxford University Press, 1988).

26. John Ruskin, "Every Man His Due," Letter 13 of *Fors Clavigera*, vol. 27 of the Library Edition of the *Works of John Ruskin*, ed., E. T. Cook and Alexander Wedderburn (London: George Allen; New York: Longmans, Green and Co., 1907), 229–42, ref. on 230–31.

needful materials; typically, the needful materials were supplied by the day's periodicals, by the day's mail, or by his own reading. Although Ruskin's descriptions allow that he had a prior sense of what he was looking for, he was confident that his success did not depend on how he put together his total picture: "Of the many things I have to say to you it matters little which comes first; indeed, I rather like the Third Fors [meaning the principle of Chance] to take the order of them into her hands, out of mine" (Letter 19). Elsewhere in *Fors* this argument took even stronger form, Ruskin protesting that "it is impossible, either in history or biography, to arrange what one wants to insist upon wholly by time, or wholly by rational connection" (Letter 33). But as his perception of the totality of culture left him "entirely sure of [his] main ground, and entirely honest in purpose," Ruskin affirmed that "I know I cannot make any mistake which will invalidate my work" (Letter 32).

Even Ruskin's explanations of his method in *Fors* resonate with Pound's practice. Compare, for instance, Ruskin's statements in Letter 14 with Pound's dictum from *Guide to Kulchur* that all historical causes are "economic and moral" and "that at whichever end we begin we will, if clearheaded and thorough, work out to the other" (*GK*, 31). Ruskin expresses his belief that his readers would find the reading of "a few words of true history" restful after the "unexpectedly attenuated conditions" of "modern thought": "In laying them before you, I begin to give these letters the completed character I intend for them; first, as it may seem to me needful commenting on what is passing at the time, with reference always to the principles and plans of economy I have set before you; and then collecting out of past literature, and in occasional frontispieces or woodcuts, out of past art, what may confirm or illustrate things that are forever true." Ruskin's activity of "making reference always to [economic] principles and plans" anticipated directly Pound's determination to establish the "economic and moral" causation of history. It was only sixty years after the serialization of *Fors* that Pound's "Prolegomena" insisted on the "connecting or correlating" of "any act or thought" with some "main" principle. But in those sixty years Ruskin's vision of cultural totality had become Pound's "totalitarian" vision, and what had begun as a call for moral regeneration had been appropriated by the most destructive forces of modern history.

Pound's fall was then precipitated by the very beliefs which empowered his art; the principles that provided the basis for much of his finest work ultimately undermined his most fundamental project. His handling of discursive forms—"discursive" because in Pound's case questions of form and genre extend beyond the "literary"—responded both to notions about the removal of poetry from the quotidian and to initially less conscious convictions about cultural totality. It is only after the twenties that the friction between these two convictions becomes a serious issue in Pound's work, and then only because he had grown intolerant of the limitations of aesthetic circumscriptions.

In fact, the contradictions he then determined to resolve had been implicit in the idea of culture from its earliest articulations. The idea of "culture," for Coleridge, Carlyle, or Ruskin had always implied a kind of removal, a privileging of certain kinds of human activity over others. Nineteenth-century affirmations of cultural totality were typically predicated on the elevation and isolation of the arts. The insistence that a bad society could not produce good art was a damning charge precisely because the arts were at the same time valorized as the highest and most perfect expression of humanity. If the various aspects of a culture are integral as the various parts of a plant are integral, the arts correspond to that plant's flower. And yet, although the widely reproduced opposition of vision and analysis, of imagination and science, had initially served to establish the place of art in an increasingly positivist world, it eventually came to undermine its own originating aspirations. The very argument for the transcendent value of the aesthetic, and for the superiority of imagination and vision, necessarily interfered with claims for the interrelatedness of all things human: claims for transcendence led to enthronement of the arts on that marginalized Helicon, where so many writers by the early twentieth century found the arts languishing and neglected.

The idea of "culture," in its Coleridgean distinction from civilization, usually charges society with an essentially religious obligation to protect poets from the men of Porlock, or Teufelsdröckhs from the busy impertinences of editors. More than this, the discourse of "culture" typically excluded the legitimacy of utilitarian analysis even in its own ostensibly proper sphere. So the initial ironies of *Sartor Resartus* unsettle the dependability of "utility" as a criterion in the understanding of even so apparently practical a thing as clothing; Arnold demonstrates that the organization of human relations on a quantifiable, material basis produces—not order—but anarchy; or Ruskin's *Seven Lamps of Architecture* begins by dissociating "architecture" from all utilitarian questions of "shelter." Moreover, of course, Ruskin's notion of "lamps" brings into question the moral basis of his principles, since they "reflect" no material principles of science or nature but "shine" outward onto the totality of human relations. Elsewhere, Ruskin maintained the ability of the arts to inculcate special kinds of truth, insisting in *Fors* that in "the discussion of every such question [regarding human relations] the main use of works of fiction, and of the drama, is to supply, as far as possible, the defect of imagination in common minds" (Letter 36). On this basis Ruskin assumed the importance of poetry to be self-evident in that, he wrote, "All truly imaginative account of man is poetic."

Nevertheless, later figures like Morris found it difficult to carry those assertions of totality which Ruskin so carefully grounded in discussions of the arts into their own literary endeavors. The programmatic drama of Shaw is a significant exception, and plays such as "Mrs. Warren's Profession" sounded the very Ruskinian warning that "the same taint" infected both "the Gospel of Art" and "the Gospel of Getting On." But for Morris, the language of poetry and the language of social reform remained separate—even though both his poetic work and his critical work are informed by a vision of cultural totality.[27] When at work as a poet, the erstwhile fiery socialist left his politics at the door. He protested in the Apology to "The Earthly Paradise" that

> The heavy trouble, the bewildering care
> That weighs us down who live and earn our bread,
> These idle verses have no power to bear;

and gave advance notice that

> Not for my words shall ye forget your tears,
> Or hope again for aught that I can say,
> The idle singer of an empty day.[28]

This repudiation of artistic utility nonetheless is an assertion of artistic value, as well as of the value of art in its isolation. In its separation of imaginative and meliorative work, it represents an impulse that has since been amplified by critical practice, as we have seen with regard to Eliot's edition of Pound's *Literary Essays*. In Orage's case too, critical attention has hoped to amplify the interest of his work by presenting it in such purified generic or thematic selections as we have with Herbert Read's *Selected Essays and Critical Writings*

---

27. See, for example, William Morris, "Art under Plutocracy," reprinted in *Political Writings* (New York: International Publishers, 1973), 57–85; or the title poem from *The Defence of Guenevere and Other Poems* (London: Bell and Daldy, 1858).

28. William Morris, "The Earthly Paradise: A Poem" (London: F. S. Ellis; Boston: Roberts Brothers, 1868).

(1935), Montgomery Butchart's *Political and Economic Writings* (1936), or Wallace Martin's *Orage as Critic* (1974).²⁹ Pound's work resisted such separation of genres, and agitated to replace Morris's persona of the "idle" singer with an emphatic insistence on activity, as in Pound's *Active Anthology* (1933). Although he too was often disposed to regard the artistic production of a society as the crucial symptom of its vitality or decline, Pound ultimately sought to revitalize poetry by exploding the realm of the aesthetic: aestheticizing the sociopolitical and politicizing the aesthetic.

A. R. Orage and the Eclectic *New Age*

Literature affects life for better or worse.
—A. R. Orage, "Readers and Writers"
(1913)

It is my emphatic opinion that art as we
know it today has no power over the conscience of mankind.
—A. R. Orage, "An Editor's Progress"
(1926)

Of the figures mediating between Ruskin and Pound, none was more important than A. R. Orage. Pound first met him in the fall of 1911 in the Frith Street salon where T. E. Hulme was lecturing on Bergson's concept of "the image." By this time, Orage had already entertained a number of intellectual enthusiasms. During the nineties he had found no contradiction in simultaneous participation in the Independent Labour Party and the Theosophical Society. Between 1893 and 1900 he devoted as well seven years to the study of Plato, but abruptly punctuated that study to plunge into seven years of Nietzsche. Still restless, he began organizing a "Gilds Resto-

---

29. With the important exception of William Cookson's *Selected Prose* (1973), this same impulse distinguishes those collections of Pound's work published after *Literary Essays*—like *Translations* (1953), *Ezra Pound and Music* (1977), or *Ezra Pound and the Visual Arts* (1980), from those he shaped himself. Pound's *Impact: Essays on Ignorance and the Decline of American Civilization,* is also an exception, although less so than it might seem. While it preserves Pound's heterogeneous generic mixture, it was edited by Noel Stock to "present his [Pound's] mature view as it was, say, in 1940" [xvii]. That Stock should have found it difficult to represent Pound's "mature view as it was, say, in 1940"—that 1940 should have seemed so very long ago—offers further testimony to the success of Eliot's *Literary Essays,* and the consequences, as Davie has observed (*Poet as Sculptor,* 242), of Pound's Bollingen prize.

ration League" with A. J. Penty, and founded a "Fabian Arts Group" with Holbrook Jackson, groups which renewed his commerce with the socialism of Ruskin and Morris.[30] Orage's public advocacy of the "Social Credit" economics of C. H. Douglas after 1918 constituted a deliberate departure from the medievalism of Guild Socialism, and a return to the "scientific applications" of socialism, which previously had led him to break with the Fabians. His conversion three years later to the mysticism of Gurdjieff was no "synthesis" of socialism and spiritualism, but an attempt to address material problems in a more fundamental way. Even then Orage's vacillations did not end. In 1931 he returned to London hoping to reassume his role as editor of the *New Age* and, when denied that hope, founded a new journal, through which he intended to pick up where he had left off a decade earlier. He called this venture the *New English Weekly* and announced its purpose to be the continuation of his earlier struggle to win an audience for Douglas's ideas. His death only two years later may well have given this last turn an unimagined finality, for according to Philip Mairet, Orage's philosophic and speculative interests "came oftener to the surface" in his last months. "Soon, he hoped, the cause of Social Credit would be won," and his commentaries might include "economics as only a secondary interest."[31]

Orage's vacillating orientation—between the idealist and even mystical, and the materialist and purportedly scientific—can be understood in terms of his Ruskinian valorization of culture. Orage wanted a means of articulating the relations among aesthetic and socioeconomic forms. He was not inclined merely to use aesthetic criteria as a bludgeon against a "philistine" public. Rather, he maintained that "it is not the fault of economics that it dominates, if it does, other aspects of society: but *their* fault. The predominance of economics, in short, is due to the poverty of spirit of the religious, the artistic, the humane, and so on."[32] Orage's difficulties in settling on a program had much to do with this determination to view culture as totality. Like Ruskin, he was given to playing on the language of Luke—so that he wrote, "A tree is known by its fruit; Columbus knew the social condition of America by the wood-carvings he found adrift off its coasts; and a society is known by its commodities." But Orage's sense of cultural totality led him

30. Penty, for example, paid explicit homage to Ruskin, and to Carlyle and Arnold, in his preface to *The Restoration of the Guild System* (London: S. Sonnenschein, 1906). See also Wallace Martin's history of Orage's activities during these years in *The New Age under Orage* (Manchester: University of Manchester Press, 1967).
31. Philip Mairet, *A. R. Orage: A Memoir* (London: J. M. Dent & Sons, 1936), 117–21.
32. A. R. Orage, *An Alphabet of Economics* (London: T. Fisher Unwin, 1917), 171.

still further, so that in writing of that very Ruskinian opposition of quality vs. quantity Orage mused: "It is not that society need be organised for qualitative production directly; for that is to subordinate human to economic values. It is simply that, as a consequence of a right ordering of Society, economic values reach their maximum. Economics as a test of social virtue!" Both of these quotations are from the same entry in Orage's economic primer, *An Alphabet of Economics* (1917), and it is telling that Orage should have included this lesson on cultural organism, or totality, in such a book. The interrelation of ethical and economic issues is for him the most primary lesson of all.

The address of his *Alphabet* underscored the aims of his fifteen years of editing the *New Age*; Orage aspired to reach a broad, middle-class audience, as opposed to the Fabian aspiration of reaching the elite and professional. He wanted a means to guarantee the vitality and superiority of "cultural" values over the material values imposed by the improvements of civilization. But in so reasserting ethical over economic relations, Orage left himself that old and nagging problem of how to heal the spirit of a public that will not hear. The generic heterogeneity of the *New Age* was itself an answer, mixing considerations of the arts, politics, philosophy, economics, psychology, and religion. Orage himself pointed to the importance of such heterogeneity, and admonished its critics in 1915 that "the sooner the whole of *The New Age* is regarded as more important than any of its parts the better." More particularly, the Guild Socialism for which he labored between 1907 and 1919 attempted to transform human relations by altering economic ones—by changing the conditions of work. Largely founded on Ruskin's critique of political economy, it carried on much of his longing for a "vital" and spiritually integrated "culture." Orage's editorial eclecticism had of course many motivations; but one useful way of understanding it is in terms of his various enthusiasms, in terms of his attempt to find a way of understanding art and economics alike as not only manifestations of a larger spirit, but as a means of acting on that spirit to ensure its total health.

Guild Socialism developed from and further nurtured this eclecticism. Historians have remembered it, when at all, with little sympathy, and few would quarrel with Samuel Hynes's description of it as an "untidy mixture" that reflected "Orage's untidy thought." Hynes's description is fair enough. And yet it was just the "untidiness," the obvious heterogeneity of Orage's economics that, I believe, most appealed to Pound, and most deeply affected him. It is no accident that Orage's work presents us with a confluence of recognizably nineteenth- and twentieth-century ideals much like that we encounter with Pound. What Hynes calls an "untidy mixture," and Martin an "ingenious synthesis of political Socialism and industrial Syndicalism," might well be called both. But although Orage himself had much to do with setting the usually dismissive tone of subsequent commentators, it would be more valuable still to consider how its variously fortunate or failed intersections and divergences interacted with more enduring agendas. There is substance for both responses in the much-quoted account from Orage's autobiographical essay of 1926, "An Editor's Progress":

> Socialism was not then either the popular or unpopular vogue it has since become; but it was much more of a cult, with affiliations now quite disowned—with theosophy, arts and crafts, vegetarianism, the "simple life," and almost, one might say, the musical glasses. Morris had shed a mediaeval glamour over it with his stained-glass *News from Nowhere*. Edward Carpenter had put it into sandals. Cunninghame Graham had mounted it on an Arab steed to which he was always saying a romantic farewell. Keir Hardie had clothed it in a cloth cap and a red tie. And Bernard Shaw, on behalf of the Fabian Society, had hung it with innumerable jingling epigrammatic bells—and cap. My brand of socialism was, therefore, a blend or, let us say, an anthology of all these, to which from my personal predilections and experience I added a good practical knowledge of the working classes, a professional interest in economics which led me to master Marx's Das Kapital, and an idealism fed at the source—namely, Plato.[33]

The lightness of tone here is in keeping with so eclectic and antisystematic a program. But Orage's reference to his "brand" of socialism as an "anthology" is not as offhand as it might seem. Much of his description attends to the aesthetic dimension of this avowedly political phenomenon: Morris's writing functioned like stained glass to change the way humanity saw itself; others, like Graham with his "romantic" posturings, Hardie with his cap and tie, or Shaw with his epigrams tended rather to change the look or presentation of the thing only. From Orage's perspective in 1926, it all looked far too literary, far too aesthetic, and more comical than critical.

But this perspective depended also on the postwar collapse of that whole socialist milieu. The man who so impressed Pound in 1911 was the editor of

---

33. A. R. Orage, "The New Age," part 1 of "An Editor's Progress," *Commonweal*, 10 February 1926, 376.

the *New Age*, which as Orage himself said was "the first Socialist weekly of London literary distinction." Orage was a prominent figure in London intellectual life. Indeed, within the heterogenous group meeting at Frith Street, Orage was known as Hulme's most stubborn contestant. Shaw would later call him "a desperado of genius, in whose capacities there was neither beginning, middle nor end." And Gorham Munson would even describe him as not only "the best talker I have ever listened to," but a veritable "fisher of men."[34] One can only imagine that Pound, then much the connoisseur of intellectual acquaintance, was quick to seek Orage's approval, and Orage ready enough to give it; for by that November Pound was publishing in the *New Age*.[35]

Nevertheless, it remains difficult to summarize Orage's mediation of Ruskin for Pound neatly. It was at last his editorial ideals, rather than his actual example, that helped shape Pound's determination to modernize his prose style. And although Orage's example reinforced Pound's inclinations to pursue a critical discourse that mixed aesthetic with political and economic concerns, Orage's own confidence that "literature affects life for better or worse" faltered after his own attempts to promote Douglas's proposals met with public indifference or even ridicule: this precisely when Pound was discovering that confidence which carried him through the Malatesta sequence (1923), *A Draft of XVI Cantos* (1925) and beyond. By contrast, Orage concluded that "art cannot save art; and still less, when artists have failed art, can critics save it."[36] Yet Orage was in this regard less the skeptic than the idealist, and between the two comments endures a fundamental concern with the relation of art to society.

The "editor's progress" that Orage described eventually led him not only away from editorship, but even from practical life—Orage having by that

---

34. Shaw offered his description in "Orage: Memories," a collection of eulogies by literary figures that appeared in the *New English Weekly* for 15 November 1934. Munson's comment is from his book *The Awakening Twenties: A Memoir-History of a Literary Period* (Baton Rouge: Louisiana State University Press, 1985), 258.

35. Dermot Robert McCarthy, in "A Pound of Cure" (Ph.D. diss., Queens University, Kingston, Ontario, 1975), 137, identifies two appearances by Pound in the *New Age* prior to his meeting Orage: the first was the poem "To Anthea's Bosom" (24 February 1910); the second was a letter to the editor under the caption "Materialism and Crime" (18 August 1910). In a letter to the author, A. Walton Litz, on examining these pieces—both of which are signed "E.P."—has identified their author as the popular novelist Eden Philpotts. Neither of these submissions is recognized in Donald Gallup's bibliography.

36. The remark is from "New Standards in Art and Literature," *Atlantic Monthly*, February 1925, 205.

time become a disciple of Gurdjieff. "I know," he wrote, that "this is heretical according to the gospel of Ruskin and Morris; and blasphemous in the ears of the modern dilettantes of art. But it is my emphatic opinion that art as we know it today has no power over the conscience of mankind." Orage's heresy, as is so often the case with heresy, was implied in the gospel. In this variation and fugue on Luke 8, bad soil will never produce good seed; good seed will take root and flourish only on good soil. The "gospel" depends at last on an inescapable circularity. Orage's determinations of the mid and late twenties reveal his frustration with the difficulty of establishing the foundations of reform—and from his sense of having gone at the problem the wrong way. Near exhaustion from fighting to win Douglas a hearing, he concluded, not so differently from Carlyle before him, that only a prior spiritual rejuvenation could make for healthy economic and material relations. It was a conclusion hard for a practical editor like Orage to make—one he reached only after the period of his most active acquaintance with Pound, and even then eventually gave over.

For fifteen years the *New Age* provided Orage with a versatile means wherewith to pursue his most radical attempts at reform. Again, as his not so ironic reference to "the gospel of Ruskin and Morris" might suggest, Orage admired Ruskin greatly, and Guild Socialism drew heavily on Ruskin's critique of political economy. But this debt has only tended to confirm the dismissals of economists and historians. John Finlay, the principal historian of the Social Credit movement that—under Orage's sponsorship—supplanted Guild Socialism, so finds that "the fact that guild socialism presented twin appeals, via economics and via morals, was not a source of strength but of weakness."[37] Yet Finlay's attitude about discursive mixtures, which refuses the heterogeneous enthusiasms that had prevailed within the *New Age* circle, derives from his aim to make a case for Social Credit as scientific analysis. But the eclectic policies of the *New Age* derived from a quite contrary impulse to carry the consideration of economic problems away from the analytical, utilitarian coolness of either Fabian socialism or of more conventional political economy. The lack of hard science, or hard-nosed dogmatism, to which Orage's detractors have always pointed, was precisely Orage's editorial ideal.

Wherever the investigation of human behavior was concerned, Orage was consistently suspicious of nothing so much as consistency. He recognized that the form of an argument helps create its content, that disciplinary

---

37. Finlay, *Social Credit,* 68 and 118.

method determines subject matter. Insofar as it aspired to scientific foundations, economics must necessarily present a narrowly materialist model. And so, just as he came to see the abstraction of "culture" in late-century socialism, Orage saw too that "economics, as an abstraction of certain human activities, regards man in a particular and partial way" (*Alphabet of Economics*, 77). He sought even as a young man to dislocate economic discourse from the direction that, with an ever deepening commitment, it has since taken. But by the time he was editing the *New English Weekly*, and battling again for Social Credit, that effort could take on a somewhat bitter tone: "We feel, in the presence of the orthodox economists and politicians of today, rather like Columbus in the presence of Isabella. Is it possible, we ask ourselves, that the news has not reached them or, having reached them, has not been realized, that the New World of Plenty actually exists, and that the psychology of Scarcity, together with the Economics and Sociology based upon it, is now only at best a superstitious survival and at worst of the order of devil-worship? The facts, if facts are allowed to speak, can speak eloquently for themselves."[38] Orage proceeded by denying to classical economics its most important premise: its status as a dispassionate science. It was bad psychology; it was, he maintained, dangerous nonsense.

Believing that facts can speak for themselves, Orage undertook to end expert occultation. In 1917 he published *An Alphabet of Economics*, which Finlay has called "a tribute to the 'sensible' Ruskin." It was explicitly a challenge to classical economics: an attempt to reverse the process whereby, Orage said, economics "must, in fact, become more and more detached as time goes on, and less and less, therefore, reconstructive." In another organicist metaphor, Orage claimed to be "laying the axe to the very root of the tree," which he did in the form of attacks on the definition of "Land, Capital, and Labour as the true factors of production." But the details of his arguments are less germane to our study than are their very nature, the peculiar ways in which he ordered and presented them. As a popular handbook, or "ABC," Orage's *Alphabet* exemplifies an important and heavily trafficked genre that had gathered considerable momentum in the Victorian period. More immediately, the book can help identify Orage's formal importance for Pound's very interest in economic argumentation. As Finlay proposes, in seeking to resolve the ethical contradictions inherent in contemporary economic practice, "Orage was led to a restatement of much of the Ruskinian

---

38. From the *New English Weekly* 2, no. 14 (1933); reprinted in *Political and Economic Writings*, ed. Montgomery Butchart (1936; reprint, Freeport, New York: Books for Libraries Press, 1967), 62.

tradition. But he went on to add points which the prophet had not mentioned. Thus where Ruskin attacked the senseless accumulation of profit, Orage went beyond this to attack the very notion of work. 'In economics,' he said, 'progress means the advance towards the idea of production without labour.'" Finlay's account affirms that Orage held a rather different view of Ruskin than that customarily taken by contemporary literary critics.[39] Orage did not regard Ruskin as a poetic visionary but as a "sensible" man committed to badly needed reforms. This was a perspective well familiar to Orage's contemporaries: J. A. Hobson, seeking in 1898 to perpetuate Ruskin's legacy, brought out a monograph titled *John Ruskin, Social Reformer*; Shaw, endeavoring in 1919 to make over that legacy, called his critique *Ruskin's Politics*. Pound's few explicit allusions to Ruskin situate his importance on this same contested ground. In, for instance, his review of Swinburne's *Letters*, published in *Future* and also in 1919, Pound wrote that when Swinburne's publishers and friends advised him to suppress *Atalanta in Calydon*, "poor old Ruskin accepted the work, and later went mad in a society that wouldn't." Pound's remark not only suggests that Ruskin went "mad" in a country incapable of appreciating Swinburne's work, but also that Ruskin went "mad" in a society blind to its own moral outrage. Continuing in this way, Pound then grouped Swinburne and Ruskin together—along with Shelley, Byron, and Landor—as victims of a "Platonic res publica" that has "no place for disturbing authors." In other words, Ruskin was for Pound, as for Orage, not primarily a critic of "art" but of the culture that produced it.

While introducing *An Alphabet of Economics*, Orage explained that although it "grew out of an attempt to compile a glossary of economic and political terms," it "developed into a more or less systematic attempt to define economics in terms of the wage system, and, at the same time, to suggest an alternative to it." Orage himself does not in this book so much as mention Ruskin, let alone so identify his alternative. But that omission, more than anything else, suggests the extent to which both this book and

---

39. Finlay, *Social Credit*, 78. Also see, for example, Harold Bloom's introduction to *The Literary Criticism of John Ruskin* (Gloucester, Mass.: Peter Smith, 1969). Bloom is primarily interested in Ruskin "the aesthetic visionary, fascinated by the world of form and color." My point is not that Bloom and contemporary critics are wrong to be concerned with an "aesthetic" or "visionary" Ruskin, nor is it that nineteenth century responses were more interesting. Rather, in this changing response to an author of continuing importance we can recover an important perspective on an aspect of Pound's career that has come to be seen as anomalous. Pound's work resembles Ruskin's precisely to the extent that it lends itself to both aesthetic and meliorative responses, and one of the greatest tasks facing Pound's critics at this time is to understand in more than thematic terms how he combined economic and poetic discourses.

Orage's career up to that point had become, as Finlay says, a kind of tribute. Notice how the passive constructions of the exposition below allude to what Orage knew to be a long-familiar conflict:

> It has long been realised that modern industry depends for its main motive upon the desire for gain; and hence that "profiteering," or production for the sake of profit, is an accurate description of it. It has long also been realised that in thus permitting production to be carried on from an irrelevant motive we were admitting an ethical contradiction into the practices of the State. At the same time, since economists, by means of their analysis of the factors of production, found themselves unable to detect any intellectual defect in the system, the ethical defect was assumed to be either a passing phenomenon, to be remedied by education, or inherent in human nature. Nothing, they concluded, was wrong in the theory of economics; hence nothing could be wrong in the practice unless it were due to factors outside economic control. Economic theory, in short, was assumed to be able to leave the court, where it had been charged with the crimes of modern industry, without a stain upon its character.
> (*Alphabet of Economics*, vi)

The glossary that follows this polemic introduction works much like a more recent example of the same kind: Raymond Williams's glossary *Keywords*. Like Williams Orage endeavored to set out in more or less plain terms the mysteries of the high-falutin'. As Orage said in his entry for "Economic Terms": "Generalised or abstract terms facilitate discussion among persons technically interested in the theories of economics; but at the risk (or, rather, in the certainty) of confusing the lay mind." Orage's aim was to "reconcretise" such terms, "reducing them to their common and real meaning." Thus the entry for "Co-Partnership" begins by calling it "a fancy name for profit-sharing, invented to deceive wage-labourers into believing themselves a kind of partner with Capital." "Employment" is similarly dressed down as "a fancy name for the good old English word hiring."

For many of Orage's contemporaneous admirers, *An Alphabet of Economics* was shortly antiquated by his work with C. H. Douglas on *Economic Democracy* (serialized in the *New Age* between June and August of 1919). For us, however, Orage's *Alphabet* is important as a generic instance, because as such it proved an important model for Pound—although, for all his recurrent activity as a definer, Pound never produced a glossary of such length. But

Pound's economic writings characteristically display the same popularizing bent; moreover, they depend on and take for granted the same oppositions between ethics and economics, culture and capitalist civilization.

Wallace Martin has observed that Orage distinguished culture from civilization in terms "almost identical" to Coleridge's; but the evident historical difference between them is that Orage's fundamental critical aim was to reconcile flamboyantly romantic claims for the autonomy of literature with a Ruskinian devotion to social responsibility. Thus in 1915 Orage submitted that "art includes utility, but it also transcends utility."[40] This was not a platitudinous compromise; these two views of art were, in their traditional terms, irreconcilable, and Orage entered the argument by striving to transform the notion of utility. Five years later his approach became more direct. His interest, he wrote, was in a vigorous didactic prose, one which, in its perfection "will be anything but a sedative after a full meal of action. It will be not only action itself, but the cause of action; and its deliberate aim will be to intensify and refine action and to raise it to the level of a fine art. Anything less than a real effect upon real people is beneath the dignity even of common prose."[41] Significantly, since it reproduced the same disjunction found in Morris or in early Pound, Orage's manifesto exempted poetry from service in his cause. In the twenties Orage would exempt art in general, avowing that it is to be distinguished from "practical conduct" in its "substitution, as end, of the impossible and the unattainable for the possible and attainable," a formulation which supplants Ruskin with Arnold. Nevertheless, until the twenties it was Ruskin who informed his work. Indeed, in his vision of aestheticized action we find Orage's own singular version of Ruskin, a Ruskin filtered through seven years of Nietzsche.[42] Orage's ambition was in this way—to use Megill's phrase—aestheticist, and its synthetic power was not to be lost on Pound.

Later, in the Paris Letter of January 1922, Pound proposed that "in the search for international literary standards . . . the main interest is not in aesthetics." Rather, the pressing question which the postwar era must face "is a question of disapproving fundamentally of the claims of the modern

---

40. From Orage's regular column "Readers and Writers," in the *New Age* 18 (1915): 13; reprinted in *Orage as Critic*, ed. Wallace Martin (Boston: Routledge & Kegan Paul, 1974), 180. For Martin's estimation of Orage as critic, see his introduction to *Orage as Critic*, esp. 25.

41. Quoted in Martin, *Orage as Critic*, 195. The essay was originally published in the *New Age* in 1921 as "Perfecting English Prose."

42. For a study of Nietzsche's impact on Orage, see David S. Thatcher's *Nietzsche in England 1890–1914: The Growth of a Reputation* (Toronto: University of Toronto Press, 1970), esp. 219–268.

state. . . . Economics are up for discussion not in their technical, Fabian phases, but in the wider and more human phases where they come into contact with personal liberty, life, the arts themselves, and the conditions aiding or limiting their expression."[43] Here again was an attack on the inhumanity of utilitarian analysis, and more profoundly on its final irrelevance. By this time Pound had recognized that his first start on the *Cantos* was a false one, and it was in July of the same year that he sent Felix Schelling the letter distinguishing "a profounder didacticism" from the "patent medicine" of "the aesthete's critique" (*SL*, 180). Pound's notion of "a profounder didacticism" proposes in effect a synthesis of the aesthetic and the didactic—similar in aim to Orage's prose that "will be not only action itself but the cause of action." This notion of synthesis, of a form "profounder" than the mundane familiar, reinscribes the romantic ideology which requires the necessarily superficial antithesis between culture and material life. Pound's solution to the isolation of artistic production thus depends on the same conceptions which initially generated his problem. Arguably, at least in the forms in which it was disseminated by its nineteenth-century English prophets, the idea of "culture" requires from the outset constant crisis and transcendence. Certainly such attempted synthesis would become the hallmark of both the prose and the poetry that Pound produced once he was well into the *Cantos*.

The Symptomatic and Pound's "Aggregation of Particulars"

The French Revolution occurred because a chinless and hump-nosed monarch had seen fit to imprison Voltaire. The "Georgian" poets finished the Asquith administration. Neither of these statements is perfectly proportioned, and they do not express the direct line of causation. That is to say they are both lies, for a purpose, and they both contain a small fragment of truth. They are both lurid and melodramatic because they move from an apparently small cause to an apparently large result.
    —Ezra Pound,
        "The Revolt of Intelligence" (1919)

---

43. "Paris Letter," *Dial* 72 (January 1922): 73–78.

> I suggest that finer and future critics of art
> will be able to tell from the quality of a
> painting the degree of tolerance or intoler-
> ance of usury extant in the age and milieu
> that produced it.
> —Ezra Pound, *Guide to Kulchur*
> (1938)

As Marianne Korn has proposed, "Pound's development of a social concern can be seen in part as a result of his involvement with A. R. Orage's Guild Socialist weekly, the *New Age*. Writers in Orage's circle introduced Pound to Confucian social ethics, with its concern for right government, and broadened his ideas about poetry's social functions."[44] More recently, Wendy Stallard Flory has made an even stronger case for the importance of Orage's role in Pound's formation of a social conscience. Arguing that "Orage more than anyone else provided Pound with his real 'post-graduate education,'" Flory submits that "Pound's views of the didactic function of literature were shared by Orage," and quotes Orage's early conviction that "literature affects life for better or worse." Indeed, Flory sees the two men as having been much in agreement over the function of literature. Orage, she says,

> could have been speaking for Pound when he wrote, "Decadence, for me as a critic, is absence of mission, of a purpose, of a coordination of powers; and its sign manual in style is the diffuse sentence, the partial treatment, the inchoate vocabulary, the mixed principles." Orage's conviction of the moral responsibility of artists toward their society confirmed and intensified Pound's own sense of his jeremiac obligations. Already inclined to be eclectic in his interests, Pound was also encouraged by the example of Orage to make his broad range of interests even broader, particularly in the direction of exploring concrete proposals for social change.[45]

Although one might want to adjust her emphasis and say that it was Pound who shared Orage's view of the didactic function of literature, Flory's work can help substantiate the portentous impression Orage's eclectic socialism left on Pound. It remains as much as ever necessary work. In *A Serious*

---

44. Marianne Korn, *Ezra Pound: Purpose/Form/Meaning* (London: Pembridge Press, 1983), 54.
45. Wendy Stallard Flory, *The American Ezra Pound* (New Haven: Yale University Press, 1989), 48 and 51.

Character, for example, Humphrey Carpenter (one of Pound's centennial biographers) plays to old prejudices and dismisses the *New Age* as "unfashionable," "dull," "dreary and vaguely bad-tempered." That kind of dismissal remains blind to its dependence on ideas about "modernism" and "literature" such as we have discussed in Chapter 1. Carpenter is right to observe that Pound "thought [Orage] showed 'an unconscious antipathy to art.'" But his sense that the "pages of the *New Age* were [for Pound] an unlikely stamping ground" replays the major contest of Pound studies late in the twentieth century.[46] In this sense of the "unlikely," the strange or the apparently anomalous, is the difference between what Gadamer would call horizons of expectation. Pound's long association with the *New Age*, like his long interest in economic contestation, seems strange to us, or seems a departure from the usual business of poets, precisely because he failed to accomplish his broadest aims: he failed to win an audience for his "profounder didacticism," failed to carry poetry out of its splendid isolation and into the agora.

Pound's criticism began to show signs of commerce with Orage's Guild Socialism as early as January of 1912, hardly more than two months after Pound had met Orage. Significantly, Pound's overt topic was "technique." Taking up the question, "what have all men in common," Pound answered, "money and sex and tomorrow," and wryly observed that the first was most often called "fate," the second associated with poetry—at least ever since poetry "stopped being epic," and the third "we none of us agree on." Nevertheless, he continued,

> Every man who does his job really well has a latent respect for every other man who does *his* own job really well; this is our lasting bond; whether it be a matter of buying up all the little brass farthings in Cuba and selling them at a quarter per cent. advance, or of delivering steam engines to King Menelik across three rivers and one hundred and four ravines, . . . the man who really does the thing well, if he be pleased afterwards to talk about it, always gets his auditor's attention. . . . As for the arts and their technique—technique is the means of conveying an exact impression of exactly what one means in such a way as to exhilarate. (*SP*, 32–33)

---

46. Humphrey Carpenter, *A Serious Character: The Life of Ezra Pound* (Boston: Houghton Mifflin, 1988), 168–69.

Already, although not yet consistently, Pound was mixing his considerations of poetic technique with questions of money and trade. Whether he did so as a result of Orage's example, or whether he sought Orage's company because of his own inchoate interests, the two men began to meet regularly. It was the beginning of an association that would endure until Pound left London, and even then (1921) it was in the *New Age* that he would present his axiomatic "final testament" to English culture.[47]

After 1912, Pound's critical work commonly juxtaposed assertions about the properly "poetic" with convictions about the totality of human relations. Often the juxtapositions present uneasy and possibly unresolvable contradictions. Indeed, his convictions about cultural totality seem transparent: he sees "through" them rather than arguing for them. Pound's review of Jules Romains's *Odes et Prières* (August 1913) provides a useful example, especially because it is a product of that same period of time during which Pound was struggling with the formulations of "Imagisme." In this review we can just begin to see how his assumptions about cultural totality would exert a transformative pressure on his otherwise conventional attitudes about "pure poetry." Pound praised Romains as "one of the most interesting of Parisian poets," and found this particular book to be "a manifestation of unquestionable energy." Nevertheless, he considers Romains's poetry to be marred by "rhetoric":

> It is very fine and intoxicating rhetoric, no doubt, but as poetry it harks back to the pre-Victorian era, when Shelley set out to propagandize the world. It is of the time of Leopardi. If Romains had lived earlier he would have written "Night Thoughts on Death and Immortality" or on "The Grave"; now-a-days the craze is for social theory or crowd psychology. This work is symptomatic. It is post-Whitman with a vengeance.
>
> It is the same with Verhaeren's "City." It is good rhetoric, very good. If we had found the passage in a prose work we should have thought it rather fine. Perhaps it gains a little by being in verse, I am not sure; but it is not to be confused with true Helicon.[48]

---

47. McCarthy, in a very close study of the *New Age* during the years of Orage's editorship, points out that Pound's association was twice quietly punctuated by fallings out: first for a year after late 1913—as a result of his aggressive "Through Alien Eyes," and then again for a shorter period during 1916. See McCarthy, *Pound of Cure*, 125 and 215.

48. Pound's review of Jules Romain's *Odes et Prières*, in *Poetry* 2, no. 5 (August 1913): 187–89.

Pound's final charge against Romains is meant to be the most damning; *Odes et Prières* is not "true Helicon"—is not properly poetic because it includes the unrefined discourses of social theory and psychology. Romains's poetry is "rhetorical" because it exhibits designs upon its reader. This charge is joined to the previous perception of the "symptomatic": that is, in its inclusion of social theory and psychology, Pound regarded Romains's work as "post-Whitman with a vengeance" and "symptomatic" of its age. Presumably, had Romains not violated the springs of Helicon his poetry would not be symptomatic—it would not be of its age but for the ages. Ultimately, this critical approach suggests the relations between the notion of transcendental universality and the idea of poetic purity; but more immediately we should recognize the Ruskinian manner in which Pound was here using works of art to descry the moral failings of his day.

Again, the impress of Ruskin, or of the post-Enlightenment discourse of "culture" on Pound is not primarily a matter of thematics. With the possible exception of Lewis, no "modernist" was more self-consciously arch, more pursuant of the current of his time than Pound; and it is hence no surprise that he alluded to Ruskin but rarely. It is not in particular positions or causes that the discourse of "culture" left its impress so much as on the very ways that Pound conceived of or shaped up any of his positions. The continuity between Ruskin's "culture" and Pound's "kulchur" lies less in what Pound argued than in how he argued.

"The Serious Artist" provides a rich case in point. Incompletely serialized in the *New Freewoman* during its last two months (October and November, 1913), and written within weeks of "Robert Bridges' New Book," the essay was Pound's attempt "to rewrite Sidney's *Defence of Poesy* in the year of grace 1913." Pound plays with his awareness that he is repeating older arguments and expresses exasperation with the necessity of his having to do so. But his defense has little to do with Sidney and a great deal to do with nineteenth century ideas about "culture": it is conducted in strikingly Ruskinian terms.

Pound began in characteristic historicist fashion, identifying his age as "the age of Gosse" (and so by implication identifying himself as a voice in the wilderness), and then conflating the London of Gosse with the London of Bentham. With the help of a little play on names, this conflation in turn produces a parallel with the London of Stephen Gosson, the sixteenth-century satirist whose *Schoole of Abuse, Containing a Pleasant Invective Against Poets, Pipers, Plaiers, Jesters and Suchlike Catepillars of the Commonwealth* (1579) had motivated Sidney's *Apologie* (1581). This procedure of rapidly juxtaposing distant moments in time, which was quickly becoming a Poundian trademark, here served to identify as an ancient and perennial evil the same utilitarian enemy confronted by Carlyle, Ruskin, or Arnold. The "theorists" and the sellers of "patent medicines" whom Pound produces are indeed stock Carlylean villains. Similarly, when Pound sneers at the Webbs, he does so neither for the sake of personal slander nor even simply to denigrate the Fabian Society as a whole; his target is the broader utilitarian tradition from which Fabinism emerged: "We are asked if the arts are moral. We are asked to define the relation of the arts to economics. We are asked what position the arts are to hold in the ideal republic. And it is obviously the opinion of so many people less objectionable than the Sydney Webbs that the arts had better not exist at all."[49] Here again, as he had done in his review of Romains, Pound sought to establish the distinctive value of poetry on the basis of its removal from quotidian exchange. His language here, submitting several questions as but repetitions of one misconceived question, suggests the structure of a sermon. In "The Serious Artist" Pound would return to this structure more than once. His tone is of one embattled, straining to remain patient. In sum, he raises the question of poetry's relation to economics only to dismiss it. In the autumn of 1913 Pound could still understand such a question to be a mechanistic impertinence.

But already another of his righteous convictions was undermining that position, and its inclusive power was being generated by these same acts of exclusion. "Let us," Pound wrote, "pursue the matter in ethics. It is obvious that ethics are based on the nature of man, just as it is obvious that civics are based upon the nature of men when living together in groups. It is obvious that the good of the greatest number cannot be attained until we know in some sort of what that good must consist. In other words we must know what sort of an animal man is, before we can contrive his maximum happiness, or before we can decide what percentage of that happiness he can have without causing too great a percentage of unhappiness to those about him."[50] "The greatest number," "maximum happiness," and "per-

---

49. Pound's identification of the Webbs with the utilitarian tradition in general persisted for some time. In the second part of "Early Translators of Homer" (published in the *Egoist*, September 1918) he wrote that "it would be an ill day if men again let the classics go by the board; we should fall into something worse than, or as bad as, the counter-reformation: a welter of gum-shoes, and cocoa, and Y.M.C.A. and Webbs, and social theorizing committees, and the general hell of a groggy doctrinaire obfuscation; and the very disagreeabilizing of the classics, every pedagogy which puts the masterwork further from us, either by obstructing the schoolboy, or breeding affectation in dilettante readers, works toward such a detestable end" (*LE*, 270–71).

50. "The Serious Artist," *The Egoist*, 15 October–15 November, 1913; reprinted in *Literary Essays*, 41–57, quotation on 41.

centage of unhappiness" are, of course, tags identifying the utilitarian opposition. Pound's position develops for the most part by similar implication—as well as it might, since both sides of the argument would have been familiar to his audience. Pound's slash at the bishop of London (for encouraging slum dwellers to have children), like the axiom of Blake's implicit in his injunction not to "treat the ostrich and the polar bear in the same fashion" (compare to the conclusion of "The Marriage of Heaven and Hell": "One Law for the lion & Ox is Oppression") replicate the romantic resistance to the imposition of system on organism or "theory" on history or the substitution of analysis for vision. Indeed, Pound employs Arnold's unquantifiable criterion of "touchstone": "The touchstone of an art is its precision."

Pound's reference to the bishop of London, or his reference, say, to the architect of the Taj Mahal of Agra ultimately suggests more than mere analogies between poetry and other forms of cultural activity. Although willing to define "bad art" as art that falsifies its "reports to meet preconceived codes of ethics, the proprieties of a sovereign or the taste of the time," it was not in mere reportage that Pound located artistic value. That value lay in technique, so that Pound complained that "the people would rather have patent medicines than scientific treatment. They will occasionally be told that art as art is not a violation of God's most holy laws. They will not have a specialist's opinion as to what art is good. They will not consider 'the problem of style.' They want 'The value of art to life' and 'Fundamental issues.'" Under pressure here is the very notion of "utility": Pound's "Defence of Poesy" does not deny the use of poetry but works to reconceive it. In effect, like Ruskin or Morris before him, Pound was already treating aesthetic problems as moral and economic as well, already fighting to defeat the more comfortable inclination to "suppose that when something is wrong it is wrong with the arts ONLY" (*GK*, 60).

Pound's review "Robert Bridges' New Book" (*Poetry*, October 1915) illustrates how convictions about cultural integrity increasingly began to press his defense of "true Helicon." Pound took the occasion of this review to defend vers libre from its detractors by pointing to its use by Bridges, poet laureate and so the embodiment of orthodoxy. However, it is how Pound moved to that defense which is of interest here. He began by asserting that the various kinds of vers libre, like "practically all forms of verse, date from antiquity: China and Greece had free verse before some forgotten Italian got stuck in the beginning of a canzone and called the fragment a sonnet." Leaping then to the immediate past, Pound built toward a climax in good Ruskinian fashion—with a loosely biblical, catalogic "and": "And after all these things came the English exposition of 1851 and the Philadelphia Centennial, introducing cast-iron house decorations, and machine-made wood fret-work, and there followed a generation of men with minds like the cast-iron ornament, and they set their fretful desire upon machine-like regularity." Criticism like this may have been unusual in the pages of Harriet Monroe's *Poetry*, but Ruskin had established its precedent over a half-century earlier. Pound's move from technical discussion of verse form to sweeping jeremiad was sudden and unanticipated. That Pound should have scorned Victorian celebrations of capitalism, or sneered at "cast-iron ornament," is hardly more than cliché. Indeed, Pound does not even bother to explain what was wrong with these things — he does not need to: he is but trading on a half century of "cultural" outcry against the "philistinism" that underwrote the new middle-class concern with "art." What matters here is precisely the lack of argument. His catalogic "ands" asserted an inevitability between hypostasized verse forms, machine-made fret-work, and the deadening of desire that was righteously assumed rather than rigorously argued. But it is especially interesting to note here that, at a time when he still expected poetry to preserve the purity of Helicon's springs, Pound's criticism was already mixing aesthetic with social and moral discourses. This piece of journalism does not mark any turning point in Pound's thinking. On the contrary, it is the very fact that this was a book review that Pound wrote in haste, with no special self-scrutiny, that makes its evident assumptions of interest. Its transparency permits us to observe how Pound was already mixing aesthetic and economic discourse years before his 1919 conversion to Douglas's program of Social Credit. Without denying Pound's own originality, we should see that how he mixed these discourses was Ruskinian in manner and "Oragean" in focus.

Moreover, this kind of discursive mixture anticipates the experiments in genre so characteristic of what was arguably Pound's most productive — certainly his most prolific — period of work: the decade between 1930 and 1940, during which time he published *A Draft of the Cantos 17–27* (1930), *A Draft of XXX Cantos* (1930), *Eleven New Cantos* (1934), *The Fifth Decad of Cantos* (1937), and *Cantos LII–LXXI* (1940), as well as his "ABC's," *Guide to Kulchur*, and a large body of other didactic and critical work. What Pound developed, and pushed to the limits, was a poetics broadly contradictory to that which he had defended as a neophyte in London. Where the idea of "true Helicon" is exclusive, Pound's work of the twenties and thirties attempted with increasing ambition to develop a poetic marked by its ability to take up and guide all forms of discourse. This was Pound's "poem including history," and although he discussed "history" tirelessly, it was really his notion of "including" that most roundly confronted the expectations of the reading public—then and now. For poets since Homer have engaged history, and other poets were doing it in Pound's own time—and not just "modernists" like Yeats or Eliot. What was distinctive about Pound's work was his willingness and determination to include, as he wrote in *Guide to Kulchur*, "whole slabs of the record" in his poem: to inset long passages from even the driest of legal documents.

But these experiments were not first conducted in Pound's poetry; they are present in none of his trial poetic sequences of the late teens; not in "Near Perigord," "Moeurs Contemporaines," "Homage to Sextus Propertius," "Mauberley," or any of the canceled cantos of 1917 to 1919. Pound's first striking combinations of genre came in his prose work, beyond the check of his notions of "true Helicon," and so where his Ruskinian convictions about social organism met the least resistance. Consider, for instance, Pound's digressive and aggressive series "Pastiche the Regional," published serially in the *New Age* between June and November of 1919. "Pastiche" at once characterizes and departs from Pound's journalistic practice during his London years. It is one of ten longer essays Pound published for Orage, serially—in good Ruskinian fashion.[51] Each of these pieces combined aesthetic and socioeconomic analysis; each of them focused on problems of "culture" and used the particular news, issues, or events of the day as but springboards for considerations of purportedly more fundamental concerns. But in "Pastiche" Pound began altering the emphasis within the familiar features of Ruskinian argumentation-by-chance-example. In "Pastiche," Pound came to emphasize what he would call in *Guide to Kulchur* the "aggregation of particulars."

The first installment of "Pastiche" begins with Pound commenting on a dispatch in a local paper "taking note of Mr. Pickthall's sensible advice [that] the 'prejudices' of the Egyptians and the rest of the Moslem world are to be

---

51. The other serial essays were "I Gather the Limbs of Osiris" (in 12 parts, November 1911 to February 1912), an early example of the practice of restoring or reproducing life from fragments; "Patria Mia" (in 11 parts, September to November 1912); "America: Chances and Remedies" (in 6 parts, May to June 1913); "The Approach to Paris" (in 7 parts, September to October 1913); "Affirmations" (in 7 parts, January to February 1915); "Provincialism the Enemy" (in 4 parts, July to August 1917); "Studies in Contemporary Mentality" (in 20 parts, August 1917 to January 1918), a long critique of British journalism and its audience that Pound and Orage had originally hoped to publish in book form; "The Revolt of Intelligence" (in 10 parts, November 1919 to March 1920); and "Indiscretions: or, Une Revue de Deux Mondes" (in 12 parts, May to August 1920). "Pastiche the Regional" appeared in 18 parts, June to November 1919.

respected" in the current "Peace Conference." Pound regards that wisdom as an ironic illustration of the bigotry and prejudices of the French and British themselves, and of that provincialism which will be his subject through much of the rest of the series. A set of ellipses then breaks off Pound's attention to his dispatch, and sets off a condemnation of religion in general. The only justification Pound gives for that condemnation is his objection to the vicar of Kensington's enthusiastic ringing of church bells, to the "intense annoyance of the people who live nearer the church spire than he does." The lesson here, Pound offers,

> is purely allegorical. The act of bell-ringing is symbolical of all proselytising religions. It implies the pointless interfering with the quiet of other persons.
> . . . .

The second set of ellipses is an important clue to the nature of the argument that follows. Ellipses are generally an attempt to create continuity over textual disruption. In this case, however, nothing has been quoted; the ellipsis serves as an explicit disruption of continuity. The ellipses do not indicate a particular omission, but the eliding of continuity as a principle of exposition. Pound's motivation for such discontinuity emerges in the next sentence: "All religions are evil because all religions try to enforce a certain number of fairly sound or fairly accurate or 'beneficial' propositions by other propositions which are sheer bluff, unsoundness, will-to-power, or personal or type predeliction, regardless of the temperament or nature of others. Every religion is a 'kultur'; an attempt to enforce a type or cliché; an attempt to impose a thought-mold upon others." Pound's implication is that the ellipsis falls where the conventional argument would begin introducing the "other" kind of propositions: the kind that would make truth dependent on a system, or on a "kultur." Pound's association here of religion and kultur is an interesting clue to later developments: in both cases what he condemns is the attempt to systematize, rationalize, and impose.

This thematic tendency to attack the systematizing impulse was present in Pound's work even as early as "The Serious Artist," where he maintained that the subject of the arts "is man, mankind and the individual"—to provide "record" of the differences between individual human beings; a science like medicine by contrast addresses itself to the general laws of human being. But in "Pastiche," responding perhaps to Zola's studies of temperament, or the appeals to temperament of Conrad or Ford, Pound strove to develop a means of argumentation that can at one and the same time situate details within (a vision of) the totality of culture, and yet resist the inevitable differences of temperament.

The remainder of section 1 of "Pastiche I" executes similar, if unmarked, ellipses—leaping between the Virgin of Notre Dame des Douay, the Palais des Papes in Avignon, Machiavelli, and Pauthier's version of Confucius—until, beginning a second section, Pound apologizes for and explains again about "these arabesques." His explanations of method never, however, seem to him enough. In the second installment he interrupts himself again to affirm that "these fragmentary statements are not made haphazard." Even in the final installment of "Pastiche," Pound describes what he calls "the three troubled seasons of the writer"; the first is when the mind sticks, the second when it works but mechanically, and the third when "the mind suddenly bursts into 'too much' activity, functions profusely, but the sequences of ideas rush out in diverse swirls, intertwining rapidly, so that one loses the relations, or at least cannot state them in an orderly fashion either on paper or for oneself (typical condition of Coleridge as represented in tradition, reported effect of various drugs, etc.)." The opposition between the mechanical and relations profoundly beyond the organizing power of reason is of course a traditional feature of such writings about "culture," and Coleridge was among its first English advocates. Pound's metaphor of "sequences of ideas" that "rush out in diverse swirls" repeats his descriptions of the vortex, but in more fundamental terms it articulates his profound distrust of narrative order, and of strict analytical argument between examples. It is a manifestation of the "*anti*systematic" project that would lead Pound to insist, in *Guide to Kulchur* that we know the past, not "in chronological sequence," but "by ripples and spirals eddying out from us and from our own time."

This distrust of system followed from the examples of Carlyle and Ruskin, and the analogies between Pound's presentation of ideas in "Pastiche" with a work like *Fors* is unmistakable. But Pound grounded his attack against mechanistic history in the arguments of "culture" quite explicitly. In "Pastiche XIV" Pound attacked the triumph of conventional journalism, with its dependence on just this kind of mechanism, over "attempts to enrich the ideas or tones or ideas in circulation": "The newspaper criterion that 'an article must run straight through from start to finish' might be attributed to the tone of this period ['the Shavo-Bennetian of English secondary literature']; the criterion is of excellent newspaper technique; it is almost pure kinesis designed not to make the reader think, but to make him accept a certain conclusion; literature and philosophy constantly diverge from this groovedness, constantly throw upon the perceptions new data, new images, which prevent the acceptance of an over facile conclusion." Pound's notion of "enrichment" recapitulates Arnold's vision of "the function of criticism at the present time," just as his condemnation of "groovedness" responds in its way to Arnold's call for "disinterestedness." While respecting the great differences between their work, we should see in Pound's work the continuing vitality of that nineteenth-century vision of "culture" as an immaterial totality. The conclusion of Pound's attack on the criticism of "the Shavo-Bennetian" period bears out the fullness of his commitment to such principles. At issue, Pound claimed, was nothing less than "the salvation of the remnants of British culture": "In recognizing that the 'Daily Mail' has won the war, one should also consider that it would in due time create an order of things in which there would be no art, no literature, no manners, no civilization—nothing, in short, but Mr. Charles Whibley."

Charles Whibley (1859–1930) was among the most influential critics of his day, and made his reputation as the chief antagonist of the Ruskinian critical mode. His criticisms were very much the "popular" kind against which Bosanquet squared off: a reputation which makes it all the more interesting that the young T. S. Eliot should have so earnestly courted Whibley's favor. Indeed, Eliot's admiration was lifelong, and on Whibley's death Eliot published an appreciative memoir.[52] Richard Aldington surmised that Eliot found in Whibley the counterpart to his professor at Harvard, Irving Babbitt, and went on to describe Whibley as "a Fellow of Jesus College, Cambridge, a good scholar, but a hopeless crank about politics. He was the very embodiment of the English Tory don, completely out of touch with the realities of his time. 'Whig' and 'Whiggism' were his terms of contempt and insult to everybody he disliked, and anybody can see how Eliot picked them up."[53] Aldington's description is colored by the warmth of personal dislike, but the difference between Whibley's critical principles and Pound's is provocative, and instructive of both Pound's aims and of the differences between Pound and Eliot as critics.

By the second decade of the century, when Whibley was writing for such Tory periodicals as Lord Northcliffe's *Daily Mail*, or *The Spectator*, he had become friends with the great champions of French symbolism—Mallarmé,

---

52. "Charles Whibley: A Memoir" was distributed to members of the English Association in December 1931; it was then, as Donald Gallup reports, published in England as a pamphlet in January of 1932. Since 1932 it has been available in *Selected Essays*.
53. Richard Aldington, *Life for Life's Sake: A Book of Reminiscences* (New York: Viking Press, 1941), 220.

Verlaine—and had married the niece of J. M. Whistler (who had himself engaged Ruskin in a bitter lawsuit). But Whibley had first made his mark in the late eighties and early nineties, writing for W. E. Henley's *Scots Observer*, and then his *National Observer*. It was in this latter periodical that Whibley published his attack on Ruskinian principles: "Methodism in Art" (16 and 23 March 1889). "Methodism" meant two things for Whibley; it meant the elevation of theory or method over practice, and it meant the importation of "puritanical" fervor into the rightly detached discourse of criticism. In this Arnoldian vein Whibley complained that "under Mr. Ruskin's guidance every man has become his own art critic, though he has never ceased to look at pictures through Puritanical spectacles. Devoid of technical training, and misled by a few phrases which he repeats with parrot-like accuracy, the average man knows and cares nothing for the artistic aspect of a picture. He only attempts to find in it some response to the vague aspirations of his soul." Whibley's commentary is immediately directed against the criticism of painting, but its implications for Pound's work are unmistakable. Whibley champions many of the things that Eliot's edition of *Literary Essays* encourages us to find in Pound: he sees criticism as a matter for specialists and thinks that the critic should regard art in its own terms—line, color, form—and not in moral terms. The second installment of "Methodism" went further to condemn the practice of estimating "every artist entirely by his 'subjects,' never by his skill."

In this insistence on professionalism, it is Whibley who resembles Eliot's description of the critic limited by a concentration on craft: Whibley, not Pound. And yet Whibley was one of Pound's publicly announced antagonists. This discrepancy seems ironic only because we have too readily substituted Eliot's revision of Pound's career for the often unpleasant or unassimilable work known before the publication of the *Literary Essays*. The catalogic conjunctions of "Robert Bridges' New Book" are, for example, exactly the kind of substitution of "aspirations" for aspect that so exercised Whibley. And by 1919 that tendency in Pound's work was becoming increasingly marked.

"Pastiche VII" (21 August 1919) stands as a significant case in point. Here Pound did more than merely criticize "Shavo-Bennetian" technique; he put into action an alternative model of relations, one developed from the work of Carlyle or Ruskin:

> The city of Beziers was burned because Simon de Montfort attacked with a small force of knights and a great troup of "ribbands," tinkers,

and religious pilgrims or "croises." The tinkers broke through the walls and took possession of the rich houses and plunder; the knights drove out the tinkers in order to get the booty for themselves; the tinkers then burnt the place.

The violence of the Church ultimately profited the centralization of the French monarchy.

Richelieu destroyed Beaucaire. Montmorency was taken at the altar. Montsegur outlasted the treachery against the surrendered Albigeois, and was destroyed, I have been told, by order of Louis XIV.

If this statement is accurate, the gratitude for the gilded chaise-percé should be diminished, seeing that a Cantabrian sun-temple with a Roman superstructure is worth a great deal of gilt furniture.

Snippets of this kind build up our concept of wrong, of right, of history.

I put down these pellets in this manner, not merely as a confession of how I catch myself thinking, but because other people think no better, because the burnt-in detail is tied by no more visible cords to the next detail, and is found no more demonstrably into the underlying conviction-plus-passion.

. . . Any historical concept and any sociological deduction from history must assemble a great number of such violently contrasted facts, if it is to be valid. It must not be a simple paradox, or a simple opposition of two terms.

It is perhaps debatable whether Pound's "conviction-plus-passion" amounts to more than Whibley's "vague aspiration." But it is certain that the technique that Pound was developing here anticipated the technique of the *Cantos* by several years. This kind of history was resolutely antipositivist, and refused the narrative organization of cause-and-effect historiography. It is to be distinguished from the prose model of later works like *Guide to Kulchur*, or from the poetic model of the *Cantos* by one significant feature only.

Earlier in "Pastiche VII" Pound insisted that "it is the curse of our contemporary 'mentality' that its general concepts have so little anchor in particular and known objects." This preference for the concrete over the abstract (and "abstract" is always a term of opprobrium in the discourse of culture) then led Pound to the assertion that "any historical concept must assemble a great number of . . . violently contrasted facts, if it is to be valid. It must not be a simple paradox, or a simple opposition of two terms." These two statements describe "Pastiche" precisely, but they demonstrate no more than a preference for the concrete. In the next decade Pound would move from such a process of factual assemblage to the technique that most distinguishes his work from the allusive styles of other "modernists" such as H.D., Joyce, or Eliot: the process of concrete inclusion. The manifesto for that technique would not come for another fifteen years, but its first example emerged from the discarded fragments of the "Ur Cantos" of 1917 and became, after much work, the first canto of Pound's long sequence.

3

Epic Inclusiveness and the Innovations of *Eleven New Cantos*

> [The *Cantos* is] closely related in method and spirit to the kind of ideation found in Dante's Divine Comedy (which refers to Virgil, who refers to Homer). It is an ideation directed towards inclusiveness . . .
> —Louis Zukofsky, "The Cantos of Ezra Pound" (1931)

> A great poet is a poet who extends the uses of verse; who makes poetry out of what we took for granted to be only matter for prose.
> —T. S. Eliot, "John Dryden" (1930)

The Pressure of the Literary

Two related hermeneutics have shaped critical response to Pound's work. The first, the idea of the "literary," mediates readings of Pound's work by valorizing certain kinds of generic relations. Reading with the expectations, questions, and evaluative criteria of the idea of the "literary" emphasizes or constitutes generic configurations that Pound would have regarded as subordinate or tangential to the primary features of his work. The second, the idea of "culture," is one to which we are even more accustomed than Pound had been himself, and thus we no longer recognize its informative power. These problems suggest the value of developing a more precise means of examining our relations to historical work. We must remain aware of what our own critical activity brings to Pound's text; we must not forget what our own critical perspective programmatically excludes.

That the *Cantos* claims to be an epic has become an over-familiar proposition. As such, it wearies rather than excites attention. Weariness of this kind probably accounts for the inattention of Pound studies to how the professional reorganization of reading has altered, over the course of this century, expectations and associations about the idea of "epic." For the most part, critics now attempt to identify how the *Cantos* attempts epic form on the basis of features very different from those Pound believed himself to have included. Consequently, we mistake the force and nature of his proposition to write "a poem including history." A comment from Pound's 1928 review of William Carlos Williams's *Voyage to Pagany* can set the problem. Praising "the looseish structure" of that work, Pound ventured: "I would almost move from that isolated instance to the generalization that plot, major form, or outline should be left to authors who feel some inner need for the same; even let us say a very strong, unusual, unescapable need for these things; and to books where the said form, plot, etc., springs naturally from the matter treated" (*LE*, 397).[1] Although not altogether disclaiming interest in "plot" or "major form," Pound demonstrates that his own concerns were elsewhere as he was finally finishing the first thirty cantos. Unfortunately, whatever his own freedom from "inner need," formalist criteria have led many critics to invert his generalization. In more than a few accounts, subject matter springs critically from said form. An epic "needs" a struggle, as it does a hero.

In the words of one critic, "it has become a critical commonplace" that the Odyssean passage of Canto 1 functions as "a program piece for the entire poem." This "critical commonplace" reappears often, as in such generally uncontested proposals that Odysseus is "*the* recurring type in the *Cantos*," or that "the first canto sets the poem firmly in the Homeric tradition."[2] Indeed,

---

1. This review was originally published as "Dr. Williams' Position," in the *Dial*, November 1928. John Berryman noticed this same passage in "The Poetry of Ezra Pound," *Partisan Review* 16 (April 1949): 394, but Berryman emphasized that Pound only said that he would "*almost* venture" that plot should be left for those who feel a need for it.

2. The observation of the "critical commonplace" is James Longenbach's, from his *Stone Cottage: Pound, Yeats, and Modernism* (New York: Oxford University Press, 1988), 245; the reference to Odysseus as "*the* recurring type in the *Cantos*" is Walter Baumann's, see *The Rose in the Steel Dust* (Coral Gables: University of Miami Press, 1970); the second claim is William Cookson's, from his *Guide to the Cantos of Ezra Pound* (New York: Persea Books, 1985). For further examples, see also Michael Alexander, whose *Poetic Achievement of Ezra Pound* (Berkeley and Los Angeles: University of California Press, 1979) proposes that although it is only one among others, the *Odyssey* does provide a "narrative framework," if not quite a narrative model (124–25); Ronnie Apter's *Digging for Treasure: Translation after Pound* (New York: Peter Lang, 1984), which finds that the *Cantos* have a "hero" who is Odysseus's analog; Michael André Bernstein's *Tale of the Tribe: Ezra Pound and the Modern Verse Epic* (Princeton: Princeton University Press, 1980); George Dekker's *Sailing after Knowledge: The Cantos of Ezra Pound, a Critical Appraisal* (New York: Barnes & Noble, 1963); Forrest Read ("A Man of No Fortune" in *Motive and Method in the Cantos of Ezra Pound* [New York: Columbia University Press, 1954], 101–23) has proposed that "the Odysseus myth orders the experience Pound undergoes as he travels through the land of the dead and comes

for most of his critics, Pound's Odyssean beginning has proven provident, confirming the generic identification of the *Cantos* as epic. But the various versions of this understanding tend to presume that "epic" denotes story on a monolithic scale, and that in calling his poem an "epic" Pound invited us to discover within its diverse materials a consistent narrative. As Marianne Korn has observed, those expectations are at best ill-founded: "What the *Cantos* does not contain, in terms of an epic, is of course a narrative in the sense of an Aristotelian action with a beginning, middle and end, and a sequence of temporal and logical causality. . . . Put simply, we *expect* a fiction of such length to possess a plot. But this expectation is constantly defeated."[3] Korn's cautionary note is very much to the point, although her word "fiction" itself bespeaks a predominantly narrative orientation. But it raises as well the fundamental question of whence such expectations of narrative and plot arise. Neither the question nor its answer is self-evident. That critics have so repeatedly displayed such an expectation indicates that it is no individual or

---

out a different man"; Leon Surette, *A Light from Eleusis: A Study of Ezra Pound's Cantos* (Oxford: Oxford University Press, 1979), treats Odysseus, reinterpreted "in the light of Eleusinian models," as "central" to the poem's "story." Even revisionists who question linear associations tend to treat the Odyssean material of Canto 1 as material for the development of plot and character; Stephen Sicari, for instance, in his essay "Reading Pound's Politics: Ulysses as Fascist Hero," *Paideuma* 17 (spring 1988), argues that Pound's use of the "Ulysses" tradition owes as much to Dante as it does to Homer, yet treats "Ulysses" as a "paradigm for heroic action." Christine Froula offers a genuinely different understanding in *To Write Paradise: Style and Error in Pound's Cantos* (New Haven: Yale University Press, 1984), 7 and 171–73; Froula proposes that "the wandering that defines the genre is no longer closed by any such plotted 'redemption' as concludes the wanderings of Odysseus." She finds, rather, that "the significance of Pound's epic venture . . . is integrally bound up with the way his modern poem including history enacts the constitutive status of error in modern experience."

3. Marianne Korn, *Ezra Pound: Purpose/Form/Meaning* (London: Pembridge Press, 1983), 129. It is also important to remember that Pound did not consistently conceive of his project as "epic." In 1918 he complained to Margaret Anderson simply that "I desire to go on with my long poem" (*SL*, 128). In 1924 he protested to William Bird that "it aint epic. It's part of a long poem" (*SL*, 189). His problem, once again, was not so much with the inherent possibilities of epic as with its current received identifications. Thus when discussing Shakespeare's history plays, Pound claimed that they:

> form the true English EPOS,
>   as distinct from the bastard
> Epic, the imitation, the constructed counterfeit.
>   (*ABCR*, 59)

Interestingly enough, the topic provoked Pound to adopt here the presentation of the *Cantos*. His distinction is characteristically idealist—distinguishing between conventionalized material form and true spirit. "Epos," as the profound expression of a nation's spirit, recalls in this sense Pound's notion of "the tale of the tribe."

even collective "error": the expectations are raised by the *Cantos* itself—not only as a result of internal signals, but also by virtue of its inescapable participation in generic tradition.

"Generic tradition" in this sense does not indicate a linear development, but a more complex interaction between related discourses, all of which were changing and which exhibit their own internal dynamics. Understanding how generic tradition has informed critical discussion of the *Cantos* means more than considering historical changes in the composition of new epics—that is, how the *Cantos* relates to other poems which have been called "epic"—it also requires attention both to changes in the critical discussion of older epics, and to changes in the relations of epic poetry to other genres.[4] Needless to say, these changes are related. But whereas the first has received extensive critical commentary, that commentary has seldom extended to the others. Critics overlook the effect on Pound of the reconceptualizations of epic that took shape in the last third of the nineteenth century. These changes owed much to the formal dominance of the novel, and attention to them will facilitate a broader understanding of Pound's antinarrative determinations. To situate Pound's work within period discussions and translations of epic is to recover a fuller sense of the ground his poetic epic sought to reclaim.

That task is best begun by glancing back to the paradigmatic poetic and critical instances: the Homeric poems, and Aristotle's *Poetics*—which discussed epic primarily in its relations to other genres. Aristotle's concerns were with the physical features of different forms, and he valued tragedy and epic above other forms for the same reason he valued tragedy over epic. The criterion was comprehensiveness, the ability of one form to include elements and features from others: "All the elements of epic are found in tragedy, though not everything that belongs to tragedy is to be found in epic."[5] His

---

4. There have been quite useful historical studies of critical debates about the epic. See especially Donald Foerster's two books, *Homer in English Criticism: The Historical Approach in the Eighteenth Century* (New Haven: Yale University Press, 1947) and *Fortunes of Epic Poetry: A Study of English and American Criticism 1750–1950* (Washington, D.C.: Catholic University of America Press, 1962). H. T. Swedenberg's *Theory of the Epic in England 1650–1800* (Berkeley and Los Angeles: University of California Press, 1944) contains a digest of period commentary on the genre.

5. Aristotle, *Poetics*, trans. T. S. Dorsch (Harmondsworth, U.K.: Penguin, 1965), 1449b.19. Note also that in chapter 26 Aristotle reiterated this conclusion more particularly, noting that tragedy too can be read, just like epic, and that tragedy "can even use the epic measure; and as a not inconsiderable addition, it offers scenic effects and music, the source of a distinct feeling of pleasure. Then the effect is as vivid when a play is read as when it is acted. Moreover, this form of imitation achieves its ends in shorter compass, and what is more compact gives more pleasure than what is extended over a long period" (1462a.14–1462b.2).

reference to "elements"—the media, manner, and objects of imitation characteristic of particular forms—underscores the empirical basis of his discriminations. He sought to identify the features of heterogeneous forms, not to isolate homogeneous essence. And although he discussed types of "plot," he was careful to distinguish between what he saw as formal unity (the imitation of one complete action) and the attempt to tell everything that happened in the life of the hero: "If the presence or absence of something makes no apparent difference, it is no real part of the whole" (1451a, 35). Still, for Aristotle narrative was a subordinate concern. In his conception, epic was a form of poetry to be distinguished from others by the objects it imitated, and the means and manner of that imitation. He displayed no equivalent to our modern sense of "narrative" as a form. Certainly, he did not discuss the Homeric poems as "stories."

The *Odyssey*, in its recorded form, shows a less than perfect unity even by Aristotelian standards; but viewed from a perspective conditioned by three centuries of novel writing, during which time the prose story has supplanted and appropriated tragedy and epic alike, it can seem primitive in quite pejorative ways. It is not that it shows no interest in narrative—it contains in fact multiple narratives. But narrative relation is not its primary organizational feature. More simply, the Homeric epics are not in our sense of the term "stories." Pound himself noted, in "Dr. Williams' Position," shortly before his work on *Eleven New Cantos*, that "there is a corking plot to the *Iliad*, but it is not told to us in the poem" (*LE*, 394). That the *Odyssey* is relatively uninterested in narrative tension might be inferred from how it "gives away" the whole plot in its opening twenty-one lines. Those lines originally identified for their audience which parts of the body of familiar legend they were about to hear. Indeed, those elements which we now identify as digressive may have been the very features in which the earliest audiences most delighted: the genealogies and ancestral histories; the inset stories like those recounted in the courts of Menelaos or Alkinoös, or given of such curious figures as the fugitive prophet Theoklymenos; the speech-making and rhetorical exhibitions—quite apart from their nominal veracity; the poetic weaving of the long similes, or the recitations of prayer; the ekphrases; the descriptions of practical work or craft; all those elements, finally, which helped its earliest audiences to imagine a lost world, one revered as greater than their own, and in which every detail was by metonymic association worthy of grand poetic investment. Of course, the formulaic features of oral narrative are in themselves as much a particular kind of narrative as they are a configuration of principles antagonistic to modern conceptions of narrative. And it matters to reiterate that they are, as a means of presenting a tale, neither clumsy nor archaic, but the features of a different kind of poetry. In sum, the Homeric poems relate narrative without in any modern sense being narrative: they contain narrative as one important element among others.

With the advent of the literary epic, the balance of this mixture began to shift. Although it too contains a diversity of elements, Vergil's *Aeneid* conforms more nearly to modern narrative models. And for all its difference in character, the same may be said for Dante's *Commedia*, a poem also prolix in kind that nonetheless manages to relate a host of inset tales and conduct political, philosophical, and theological speculation within context of its narrative journey. Renaissance poets, however, especially in England, worked to subordinate narrative elements to others in the variety which epic form could encompass. Sidney, Spenser, and Milton all produced epics that were encyclopedic in kind, wherein narrative often performed a subordinate function. We share many terms with them, but within a very different set of relations and values.[6]

Renaissance poets made, as Barbara Lewalski has said of Milton, "constant, complex, and highly conscious use of the Renaissance genre system." All of them shared "the notion of epic as a heterocosm or compendium of subjects, forms, and styles." As Lewalski explains, "according to the major Renaissance genre theorist, Julius-Caesar Scaliger, epic is both a mixed form and 'the chiefest of all forms'; it is 'catholic in the range of subject-matter,' and it supplies 'the universal controlling rules for the composition of each other kind.'" Scaliger's definition turned on the Aristotelian criterion of comprehensiveness, and Milton's innovations within epic form were often tied to his manipulations of the received status of epic with regard to other genres.

Historically, because of its long dominance within the fluctuating hierarchy of genres, debates about the epic involved questions about the nature and extent of poesy, letters, or literature in general. To this aspect of the tradition Pound remained especially faithful. There was obviously much that changed between Milton and Pound, but concerning the relations between epic and other genres we can make two conclusions: the epic declined in importance,

---

6. For valuable historicizations of seventeenth-century critical language, see Alastair Fowler, *Kinds of Literature* (Cambridge: Harvard University Press, 1982); Barbara Lewalski, *"Paradise Lost" and the Rhetoric of Literary Forms* (Princeton: Princeton University Press, 1985); and Douglas Lane Patey, "The Eighteenth Century Invents the Canon," *Modern Language Studies* 18, no. 1 (1988), 17–37.

and whereas it had for centuries been identified on the basis of generic inclusiveness, it came increasingly to be understood in terms of its narrative scope. In 1742 Henry Fielding could conceive of *Joseph Andrews* as a "comic epic poem in prose," but such generic heterogeneity came to strike romantic writers as inappropriate. The "epic" novels of Scott preserved a more elevated tone. Southey's work more resembled Scott's poetic romances, its claim to epic stature resting on its narrative scope and sweep. Wordsworth, with his incomplete chronicle of "the growth of a poet's mind," and Keats, with his two attempts to tell of the fall of Hyperion, both in their different ways imitated Milton and aspired to write of first things; but unlike Milton both envisioned their task in narrative terms.

This "basic" difference belies a still more fundamental reorganization of generic relations—although to historicize this reorganization is to refuse its enabling precept. That is, Renaissance critics typically took an inclusive view of the extent of "literature." For period critics such as Patrizi, Scaliger, and others, "literature extended to a whole *paideia* or curriculum of learning. Minturno held that philosophers such as Empedocles or Lucretius wrote poesy."[7] But there was an oppositional view—an opposition that by the end of the eighteenth century had successfully circumscribed the "literary" in what has largely remained our own sense of the word. As we have seen with Eliot's editorial work on *Literary Essays of Ezra Pound*, such disputes over frontiers bring the heartland into similar contest. Fowler speculates that the constriction of Renaissance "poesy" to nineteenth-century notions of "literature" indicates, perhaps, "a reaction to the temporarily over-extended concept that underlay Augustan literature, with its extreme georgic or didactic emphasis"(9). This is an admittedly normative reading, but the inclusiveness of the Augustan concept presents an important if ironic precedent for Pound's experiments with epic form. Pound was, in this sense, half-right to have complained in "René Crevel" that "it was only in the groveling age of usura and usuriocracy that letters were lowered to mean merely 'belles lettres' and that the subject matter was reduced to personal titillations."

Nevertheless, it was not simple antipathy to overrefinement that marks the singularity of Pound's epic. Carlyle before him had endeavored to extend "the meaning of epic from the literary to the practical."[8] But "epic" embod-

---

7. Fowler, *Kinds of Literature*, 9. This observation is especially interesting in view of Pound's return to the idea of a "whole paideia"—what he called, after Frobenius, "paideuma."
8. John Clubbe, "Carlyle as Epic Historian," in *Victorian Literature and Society: Essays Presented to*

ied different concerns for Pound, who regarded it as the ultimate expression of a culture—and herein lies the key. Whereas "culture" might be said to have been a conscious ideal for Carlyle, it formed Pound's conceptual horizon. The point can be made in reference to the complaint in "René Crevel." Although Pound recognized the historicity of "literature," his historical sense had developed well within the discourse of culture and he took the "reduction" of "letters . . . to mean merely 'belles lettres'" to be a symptom of his "age"—a sign of the times. He recognized the weakness of the modern conception of "literature" largely because he had so internalized another one of the ideals that "culture" promoted. That is, Pound's conception of inclusiveness differed from earlier understandings in that he aspired to make that inclusiveness *total*. His vision of totality was imaginable only within the discourse of culture.

Narrative in Epic and Epic Narrative

"Better mendacities / Than the classics in paraphrase!" These bitterly ironic lines from "Hugh Selwyn Mauberley" (1920) reflect the drubbing that Pound took over "Homage to Sextus Propertius," and they set out what he saw as a neat antithesis: lifeless and only literally accurate translation versus vital paraphrase. The first remains mendacious because it renders form without its spirit; the second preserves spirit in formal approximations. The constructions of "Mauberley" represent the former as characteristic of "the age," but Pound's antithesis is misleading. It not only identifies "the age" with an academic minority, but misrepresents the dramatic controversies then engaging classicists and translators. In fact, Pound's "Propertius" appeared at a time when paraphrases of the classics were proliferating as never before. It may well have been the growing public appetite for paraphrase that goaded Professor William Garner Hale, of the University of Chicago, into attacking Pound publicly. Certainly there was little professional detachment in Hale's public charge that "if Mr. Pound were a professor of Latin, there would be nothing left for him but suicide."[9]

Hale believed he was merely correcting error; but subsequent commen-

---

Richard D. *Altick*, ed. James R. Kincaid and Albert J. Kuhn (Columbus: Ohio State University Press, 1984), 139.

9. William Garner Hale, "Pegasus Impounded," *Poetry* 14, no. 1 (April 1919): 52–54.

tators have established that his issue with Pound more fundamentally involved different conceptions of paraphrase and its proper license. It is a similar confounding of terms that has frustrated critical debate over both parts of Pound's claim to have written "an epic," a "poem including history." But there is a special value in examining period disputes over the nature and relative merits of translation and paraphrase. Pound's response to these played out his contrary impulses, on the one hand to pursue high art, and on the other to "popularize" and reform his world. The extensive body of Homeric translation and paraphrase in English offers a valuable perspective on the formation of the earliest sequences of the *Cantos*, because it exhibits the gradual displacement of inclusiveness by more recent notions of artistic purity. The valorization of generic heterogeneity yielded in time to concern for narrative order; the perception that poetry was the necessary medium for the transmission of epic was subordinated to a sense that the proper language of epic was unadorned and simple—in other words, the language of prose. Pound's resistance to narrative order is well documented, but that resistance did more than affect his handling of epic conventions: it was a motivating factor in his very choice of epic as form, because Pound was already thinking of epic in other than predominantly narrative terms.

Of the *Odyssey* alone, since that is the example most relevant to argument about the *Cantos*, there were published between 1615 and 1945 over thirty complete verse and prose translations, and over twenty complete prose paraphrases—that is, retellings that worked from other translations rather than more "directly" from the Greek. This distinction, between translation and paraphrase, is not, however, so clear as might first seem the case. As translators often acknowledge, their own work aims to redress perceived imbalances or imperfections in previous translations: they work inevitably with other translations in mind, or even before them. Moreover, paraphrases of the classics emerged as a distinct genre only in the nineteenth century. Charles Lamb published the first in English in 1808, an adaptation of George Chapman's translation of 1615, which Lamb called "The Adventures of Ulysses." Although there was German precedent for Lamb's work—Karl Friedrich Becker published his *Ulysses von Ithaka* in 1802—the paraphrase was yet a distinctly romantic innovation.[10] It owed in large part to a growing

---

10. Lamb's "Ulysses" was by and large available in popular editions until 1939, by which time it had seen nineteen different editions. Becker's *Erzählungen aus der alten Welt für die Jugend* (*Ulysses von Ithaka. Achill. Kleinere griechische Erzählungen*) was translated into English as *Ulysses of Ithaca* by George P. Upton (Chicago: A. C. McClurg, 1912).

middle-class readership, and its most distinctive feature was its emphasis on the Homeric poem as a *story*.

This new emphasis was itself a significant "translation" of a different kind, a translation from one form to another—from poetic epic to prose narrative. There had been prose cribs before Lamb's adaptation, as there would continue to be for most of the remainder of the century. But these were often printed on facing pages to the Greek, and were not meant to stand as independent texts. The advertisement of Oxford professor Henry Cary's translation (1823) can serve to establish the difference. Cary claimed only to have "translated into English prose, as literally as the different idioms of the Greek and English languages will allow—with explanatory notes."[11] For scholars like Cary, the rendering into prose required apology and explanation; for Lamb, the rendering into prose was precisely what he expected would make his work attractive. Cary and Lamb were appealing to different audiences; but by the end of the century Cary's audience had largely disappeared, while Lamb's was still growing.

That growth proves to be tied up with a significant change in the valorization of epic and the perception of its relations to other forms. These changes were stirred as well by more academic sources—chiefly by the celebrated debate (1860–61) between Matthew Arnold and Francis W. Newman. Arnold insisted that translation should attempt to "affect our countrymen as the original may be conceived to have affected its natural hearers." Newman—whose translation of the *Iliad* in 1856 had incited Arnold's criticism—countered that the translator ought rather "to retain every peculiarity of the original, so far as he is able, with the greater care the more foreign it may be."[12] In her study *Translation after Pound*, Ronnie Apter remarks that Pound's translations, "imbued with a sense of the wondrous otherness of the past," show an orientation to Newman's principles.[13] Other scholars, for example J. P. Sullivan on "Homage to Sextus Propertius," suggest that Pound was quite capable of resorting to Arnoldian tactics where they suited his purpose. But Apter's conclusions reveal yet another place where Pound's inclinations isolated him from most readers, even though they developed dialogically with popular traditions, for it proved to be

---

11. Henry Cary, *The Odyssey* (London: G. & W. B. Whittaker, 1823).

12. Arnold outlines both positions in his essay "On Translating Homer," reprinted in *The Complete Prose Works*, vol. 1, ed. R. H. Super (Ann Arbor: University of Michigan Press, 1960); see esp. 98.

13. Ronnie Apter, *Digging for Treasure: Translation After Pound* (New York: Peter Lang, 1984), 21.

Arnold whose principles most often guided the hand of subsequent translators.

More broadly, the public's apparent appetite for paraphrase indicates the extent to which Arnold's criterion of impact had supplanted that of Newman's literal fidelity to source. Nineteenth- and twentieth-century readers alike have craved the past in recognizable form, and that form most characteristically involves the plottings and subordinations of post-Enlightenment fiction.[14] Pound recognized "what the age demanded." His correspondence with W.H.D. Rouse even implies that he saw in this antipoetic trend a means of clearing ground for his own "profounder" attempt to reconstitute the poetic epic. But the understanding of epic most pervasive in the early twentieth century was wholly antagonistic to Pound's undertaking.

Consider those renderings of the *Odyssey* first published between 1879, the year of Butcher and Lang's long-popular prose translation, and 1900, the year of Samuel Butler's. During this especially productive period there were published four verse translations, four prose translations, and eight prose paraphrases.[15] By contrast, during the twenty years before 1879, seven of

---

14. The celebrated work of Mikhail Bakhtin on the difference between epic and novel stands here as intelligent and ironic testimony. Bakhtin was theorizing the difference between novel and epic (and indeed any other genre) at approximately the same time Pound was at work on his epic. The first edition of *Problems of Dostoevsky's Art* appeared in 1929 and, as Michael Holquist has observed, by the time that book appeared in a second edition (1963), Bakhtin's ideas were fully developed. In short, Bakhtin argued that the novel was to be distinguished from all other forms on the basis of its inclusiveness—its ability to place in "dialogic" relation conflicting class attempts at "absolute" language. The very nature of Bakhtin's argument testifies to how thoroughly the conventions of the novel had entered critical discourse by the heyday of European modernism. The account I have just given of changing conceptions of the "epic" does not challenge Bakhtin's work because it establishes that the epic is actually more inclusive than the novel, but because it exemplifies how all genres are by nature combinatory. Bakhtin's perception that the novel was not a monolithic form remains important; but to make that point it is neither necessary nor accurate to submit that other forms are by contrast incapable of historical or political accommodations. See "Epic and Novel," reprinted in *The Dialogic Imagination: Four Essays by M. M. Bakhtin*, ed. Michael Holquist, trans. Caryl Emerson and Michael Holquist (Austin: University of Texas Press, 1981), 3–40.

15. The verse translations were done by George Augustus Schomberg (London, 1879), Arthur Sanders Way (London, 1880), William Morris (London, 1887), and John Graham Cordery (London, 1897); the prose translations were done by S. H. Butcher and Andrew Lang (Oxford, 1879)—which by 1912 had been reprinted fifteen times, Roscoe Mongan (Dublin, 1880), George Herbert Palmer (Boston, 1891), and Samuel Butler (London, 1900); the prose paraphrases were done by C. M. Bell (London, 1881), Charles Henry Hanson (London, 1884), Frances Younghusband (New York, 1885), Alfred John Church (London, 1891), Edward Brooks (Philadelphia, 1892), Agnes Spofford Cook (Bloomington, 1897), Michael Clarke (New York, 1900), and Francis Sydney Marvin (London, 1900). Over the next twenty years, prose paraphrases outnumbered verse

nine published renderings were verse translations, the lone exceptions being John Allen Giles's painstakingly completed prose crib (London, 1858–78), and W. Lucas Collins's prose paraphrase (Edinburgh, 1870). The explanation for such a marked contrast cannot be simple; the economic fortunes of the publishing industry, the growth of lending libraries, and the increasing demand for school primers must all be considered, as should the repercussions of the Arnold-Newman debate. But giving shape to these factors was the consolidation of the novel as the dominant literary form of its day, and the resulting inclusion of the features of prose narrative in other forms.

Samuel Butler's translation of 1900 here stands as a resonant example. Hitherto, although prominent poets had often turned their hand to translating Homer (Pope, Cowper, Bryant, Morris), Butler was the first novelist to do so. While he was a man of wide interests—engaging in the debates over Darwinianism, or producing his polemical claim to have identified "the authoress of the *Odyssey*"—his precedent here is not merely a matter of coincidental, personal initiative. Indeed, his claims about the "authoress" of the *Odyssey* are not eccentric; their orientation is novelistic, effecting a domestication of the epic and of the sublime.[16] Butler's translations of Homer, probably unintentionally, accomplish something very like this end. His translations treat the poems as stories and read rather like a late-Victorian novel.

Butler advertised his translation as a "rendering into English prose for the use of those who cannot read the original," but it was much more than this. It might have been said of the verse translations of Pope or of Morris that they were "for the use of those who cannot read the original." Neither was Butler's use of prose without precedent. The innovation of Butler's translation lay in its presentation of poetic materials in almost strictly narrative terms, and for this project the work of Butcher and Lang served as both positive and negative example. Testifying to the impact of Arnold's position, Butcher and Lang had justified their translation into prose by submitting that

> the epics are stories about the adventures of men living in most respects like the men of our own race who dwelt in Iceland, Norway,

---

translations ten to two; between 1920 and 1940 there were published in English eight more paraphrases, four more prose translations, and two translations in verse.

16. The force of that domestication was, of course, also at work on tragedy. See Edward Payson Vining's *Mystery of Hamlet: An Attempt to Solve an Old Problem* (Philadelphia, 1881), which theorized that Hamlet was a woman in order to explain away what seemed otherwise incongruous dramatic elements.

Denmark, and Sweden. The epics are, in a way, and as far as manners and institutions are concerned, historical documents. Whoever regards them in this way, must wish to read them exactly as they have reached us, without modern ornament, with nothing added or omitted. He must recognize, with Mr. Matthew Arnold, that what he now wants, namely, the simple truth about the matter of the poem, can only be given in prose, for in a verse translation no original work is any longer recognizable. It is for this reason that we have attempted to tell once more, in simple prose, the story of Odysseus. We have tried to transfer, not all the truth about the poem, but the historical truth, into English.

This argument is laden with telling assumptions, and its notion of epic as historical document offers context for Pound's notion of "a poem including history." Butcher and Lang's repeated emphasis on "story" is crucial to their undertaking, as their distinction between "historical truth" and "the truth of the poem" is definitive. Their conclusion that the truth is best served by "simple prose" is, finally, the logical consequence of their prior perception that the Homeric material constitutes a "story." The rendering into prose is thereafter but a part of their translation, and it is in this respect that their work most constitutes an important example for Butler's more flamboyant rendering.

Like Butcher and Lang, from whom he quotes to differentiate his own work, Butler believed "that a translation should depart hardly at all from the modes of speech current in the translator's own times." But he held, with more conviction than any translator previously or since, that a prose rendering alone could once again make Homeric poetry "live." "We know," he wrote in the preface to his *Iliad*, "the charm of Elizabethan translations, but he who would attempt one that shall vie with these must eschew all Elizabethanisms that are not good Victorianisms also." Referring to that claim in the preface to his *Odyssey*, Butler added that "the initial liberty of translating poetry into prose involves the continual taking of more or less liberty throughout the translation; for much that is right in poetry is wrong in prose, and the exigencies of readable prose are the first thing to be considered in a prose translation." Where Butler's work differed from earlier prose translations was the degree to which he expected his prose narrative to take on a life of its own—the degree to which he was willing to sacrifice accuracy to Homer to the demands of modern narrative. In so doing, he approached the realm of paraphrase: certainly classical scholars have treated his translations with only slightly more respect than they show his arguments in *The Authoress of the Odyssey*. But then Butler did after all regard *The Authoress* as a companion text to his translations, quoting from it in his preface, just as his polemic had borrowed from his translations.

Butler's endeavor to foreground the narrative elements of Homer's poem is evident in both frame and form. His table of contents provides "arguments" for each book, synopses of "story" that effect considerable continuity between books. To take but one example, of book 5 we are told that "Hermes is sent by Zeus to Ogygia to tell Calypso to let Odysseus go. Odysseus builds a raft and sets sail. The Raft is broken by a storm, but Odysseus battles the waves and reaches Scheria." The synopsis of book 6 continues the narration: "Exhausted, Odysseus hides himself and sleeps." Earlier translations had provided arguments or summaries; sometimes these indicated narrative progress, but they did so without in themselves constituting a narration. Compare Philip Stanhope Worsley's synopsis of 1861: Worsley's translation into Spenserian stanzas was also a conscious response to Arnold, but his tabular arguments made few concessions to the requirements of narrative. Of book 5 he notes simply that it tells of "The Building of the Ship—Odysseus Leaves Calypso and is Wrecked—Arrives at Scheria." The difference in Butler's table exemplifies the narrative overdeterminacy of his translation, how his representation of a poetic epic as a prose narrative effected a multiplicity of accompanying formal changes.

Although, as Hugh Kenner has said, Butler's arguments about "the authoress" of the *Odyssey* "put him beyond serious consideration,"[17] his novelistic approach to the epic proved a successful consolidation of earlier trends, just as it offered a model for subsequent work. Kenner has situated Butler's work in the context of late-century views about Homer's historical accuracy, as well as the "new psychology of creation" characteristic of "the age of the novel." Valuable as these explanations are, we need at once to expand them and to narrow them. Innovating within a tradition, Butler's redactions of Homer develop further the interaction between the rapidly growing body of paraphrase and the realm of "serious" translation: the same conceptual shifts evident in the popularity of Homeric paraphrase informed scholarly argument about the nature of epic. This interaction, one of several that becomes evident in the study of Pound's combinatory procedures, provides a valuable opportunity to examine the relations between popular

---

17. Hugh Kenner, *The Pound Era* (Berkeley and Los Angeles: University of California Press, 1971), 44–48.

and polite writing. Butler's decisive emphasis on the *Odyssey* as a story appropriated the most salient feature of popular paraphrase. This is not to deny the continuing, if diminished appearance of scholarly verse translations. But between 1900 and 1945 there were published only three complete translations of the *Odyssey* into English verse, all in London: John William Mackail's in 1903, Henry Bernard Cotterill's in 1911, and Francis Caufield's in 1921. That same period saw four translations in prose and nearly twenty prose paraphrases.

Numbers in and of themselves prove very little; if it were true that these paraphrases left no mark on the activity of translation proper, we might simply conclude that the quantity of paraphrase simply testifies to its ephemerality. Granted, in the second half of the twentieth century the appearance of important verse translations by scholar-poets like Cook, Fitzgerald, or Lattimore suggests a process beyond our focus here. But in our century's first half the most influential new translations were in prose, and in a kind of prose that follows Butler's model. Of these, the most significant instances remain the prose translations of T. E. Lawrence (published by Oxford University Press in 1932), and of W.H.D. Rouse (in 1937).

In his prefatory note, Lawrence finds that the *Odyssey* lacks "the attributes" of "great art," but nonetheless maintains that "by its ease and interest [it] remains the oldest book worth reading for its story and the first novel of Europe." There is an analogy here with Butcher and Lang's distinction between "the truth of the poem" and its "historical truth." Lawrence considers the poetic features of Homer's work secondary attributes. For Lawrence, the *Odyssey* is a story and, like Butler, he detects in the *Odyssey* a domestication of the "huge and terrible." "Every big situation," he wrote, "is burked and the writing is soft." Lawrence's identification of "this novel" with its story is so thorough that he even criticizes Homer for "his thin and accidental characterization." "Only the central family stands out," he finds, but Penelope is "sly" and "cattish," Odysseus is a "coldblooded egotist," and Telemachus is "the priggish son who yet met his master-prig in Menelaus." "It is," Lawrence concludes in the final words of his preface, "sorrowful to believe that these were really Homer's heroes and exemplars." This concern with characterization testifies to Lawrence's readiness to reconceive the Homeric poems in novelistic prose. It helps not only to clarify the nature of his criterion of "art," but also the formal argument which Rouse would shortly, though implicitly, lodge against him.

That Lawrence's version anticipated many of the chief features of Rouse's is evident from the prominent place Rouse gave to a kind of disclaimer usually seen only in the most scholarly contests for the authority invested in first treatment. In his brief acknowledgments, before even his preface, Rouse protested that "to guard against possible mistakes I add that the translation was made before T. E. Lawrence's *Odyssey* was published." That Rouse had cause for anxiety is evident from the embarrassingly familiar claim of his preface: "This is the best story ever written, and it has been a favourite for three thousand years." But as Rouse develops it, this claim emerges as a polemic. Despite the apparent misunderstanding in the phrase "ever *written*," Rouse was primarily interested in the *Odyssey* as a story passed word-of-mouth. His express intention was to address a popular rather than a scholarly audience, and he hoped to strip away the encrustations of three hundred and fifty years of translations. So it was that he presented Keats's "On First Looking into Chapman's Homer" as an epigraph: he hoped to deliver his English readers an experience of Homer less mediated than any hitherto possible—to open up for them a whole new world. Needless to say, what he offered his readers was not an unmediated experience of Homer, but a differently mediated one. Rouse too referred to the conventions of modern fiction—but not to the same "literary" tradition within which Butler had worked. Instead, Rouse promised excitement to the lovers of "thrillers and detective novels"—pulp fiction—and of fairy tales. His references were to popular traditions, no longer folk traditions, and his translation vowed to avoid all "attempts at a poetic language which Homer himself is quite free from."

Undoubtedly, every translation or even paraphrase strives to avoid phony poeticisms, but there is a difference here. As Butler had done, Rouse first published a "theoretical" study. But unlike Butler's *Authoress*, Rouse's *Adventures of Ulysses* (1932) in many ways epitomized the new attitudes toward a historically reliable Homer. Having traveled to the lands of Homeric adventure, Rouse claimed to discover enduring elements of the Homeric oral tradition. In the preface to his *Odyssey* he recalled a moment when he "heard far-off echo [of the *Odyssey*] in a caque on the Aegean Sea, when the skipper told me how St. Elias carried an oar on his shoulder until some one called it a winnowing fan." *The Story of Odysseus*, as Rouse called his translation, aimed to reproduce that oral preliterary tradition. In fact it owed less to ancient oral formulas than it did to a mixture of Arnoldian concern for effect and modern ideas about story—a peculiar combination that found encouragement from an equally peculiar source. Rouse corresponded with Pound for nearly two years (1934–35) and attracted from him a keen interest. Pound praised the essentially ahistorical manner in which Rouse endeavored to recover a sense of oral presentation, and enthusiastically reiterated the importance of maintaining "the drive of narration."[18] In general, Pound urged Rouse toward two goals: to make "as straight a tale for adults" as had Homer, and to recover the "raw cuts of concrete reality combined with tremendous energy, the contact with natural force."

Pound's recommendation to include "raw cuts of reality" was consonant with the most central procedures of the *Cantos*—what Pound calls the inclusion of "whole slabs of the record." But Pound himself not only avoided the relation of "straight tales," he programmatically attacked narrative order in both his poetic and his critical work. Yet his advice to Rouse was consistent with his discussion of Homeric translation elsewhere. The most important example is the series of essays he wrote between 1918 and 1919 and, in an evocation of Arnold's polemic, titled "Translators of the Greek: Early Translators of Homer." Here Pound praised Chapman's excellence "in the plainer passages of narrative"; he condemned "Leaf-Lang prose" (Leaf was Lang's collaborator on the *Iliad*) as "the nadir of Homeric translation," regretted that no translator had yet caught "the authentic cadence" of Homeric speech, and in a concern that anticipated Lawrence's, praised the ability of Hugues Salel (1545) to render exactly the "mental attitude" of Homeric characters. For all his interest in Homer's "magnificent onomatopoeia," with what he later called in his letter to Rouse "the raw cuts of concrete reality," Pound was nevertheless evaluating the history of Homeric translation in novelistic terms. In short, he engaged the tradition of Homeric translation with expectations different from those which attended his own effort to create a modern epic.[19]

The import here is not merely that Pound contradicted himself, or even that he contradicted himself on an issue that was for his own work so crucial. For we can understand this inconsistency in terms of another, no less central to his work. On the one hand, it was for Pound a precept that his work should "present," firsthand, the textual embodiments of human history. On the other hand, Pound was endlessly interested in historical transmission and dissemination, a process that inevitably mediates, alters, and corrupts. The analogy is simple. He expected his own work to exemplify the comprehensiveness of Homeric epic, and his own reading of Renaissance poets and critics undoubtedly amplified his sense that comprehensiveness, the ability of

18. See *SL*, 263, 268, 271.
19. Originally published as "Early Translations of Homer" (3 parts) and "Hellenist Series" (3 parts) in *The Egoist*, August 1918–March/April 1919; condensed and redacted in *Instigations* (1920) and reprinted in *Literary Essays*, 249–75.

epic to include all other forms, was the quality that made it so vital to the ancients. Other critics contemporaneous with Pound celebrated the inclusive property of epic: Mackail's Oxford lectures on poetry (published 1914) had affirmed the essentially Arnoldian view that "poetry is greater, not as it purports to deal with a greater subject, but as it gathers and absorbs into itself more of life."[20] But even this understanding of epic still identified epic "scope" with spiritual qualities, rather than with the quantitative and formal qualities recognized by Aristotle, and by most critics prior to neoclassical revisions. At the same time, Pound recognized quite clearly the dominant features and functions of epic translation in the twentieth century. He concluded, as had his Victorian predecessors, that only in prose could the Homeric epics recover for a modern audience their power and effect.

In Pound's advice to Rouse we thus can see him treating translation as a genre unto itself: one distinct from his own epic ambitions but authentic in its own right. He was not simply preserving the distinction between the popular and the polite; his attention to Rouse indicates an interest in popular work, as do his many primers and his hopes for the *Cantos* itself. The distinction can at last help us appreciate more fully the boldness of Pound's experiments, his attempt to create without modern antecedent a work that might recover the characteristic inclusiveness of the ancient epos.

As Philip Furia has proposed, "When Pound called the epic a 'poem including history,' he was going back to the original function of epic as tribal archive."[21] The word "archive" should not be confused with the postmortem display of a museum; such an archive proposes a living tradition that draws on the panoply of human concerns. Pound's discussions of epic reveal a similar orientation. That the epic should be a "poem including history" not only advances claims about its truth value; it suggests as well that history is to be found as one element among many others. This is the same emphasis found in Pound's description of the *Cantos* as "a cosmographic volcano": a writing (*graph*) that includes the universe (*cosmos*) will include history—as one element among many others. Indeed, this same emphasis informs the

---

20. John William Mackail, *Lectures on Poetry* (London: Oxford University Press, 1914), 37. Mackail's verse translation of the Odyssey appeared in 1903. In *Guide to Kulchur* Pound "suspected" that "McKail [sic] is a paterine product, and one can read McKail's *Latin Literature*" (207). Certainly there are signs that Pound read him. Pound's insistence, quoted above, that Romain's *Odes et Prières* "is not to be confused with true Helicon" (1913) suggests Mackail's *The Springs of Helicon: A Study in the Progress of English from Chaucer to Milton* (New York: Longmans, Green & Co., 1909).

21. Philip Furia, *Pound's Cantos Declassified* (University Park: Pennsylvania State University Press, 1984), 3.

often quoted claim of *Guide to Kulchur* that "there is no mystery about the *Cantos*, they are the tale of the tribe." It is true that Pound here speaks of "tale" or narrative; but, more important, he also speaks of "the tale," speaks of his work as somehow embodying all the narratives that could be told by Western culture. To be "the tale" the *Cantos* could not possibly constitute any single narrative. It is the claim of narrative to complete a whole action, but what Pound wanted was to "reconstitute" a wholeness of which all other narratives are but fragments. This is the impulse behind Pound's idealist notion of subject-rhymes, wherein individual "rhymes" suggest without denoting precise and limited parallels. It is a romantic position that recalls Shelley's distinction between story, that mere "catalogue of detached facts" which refers only to a unique historical moment, and poem, "the creation of actions according to the unchangeable forms of human nature."[22]

Given the fevor with which both Shelley and Pound sought to "reestablish" the centrality of poetry, the similarity between their positions is not surprising. Nevertheless, how each sought to recover that centrality differed vastly. Shelley developed a poetic language that renounced the limitations of the concrete; Pound sought by contrast to incorporate language in all of its forms, and history in all its materiality. As Bernstein has proposed, "Pound was attempting to write a tribal encyclopedia, one adequate to the needs of his own day, and thus, of necessity, incorporating far more, and often quite different kinds of, material than sufficed for the Homeric age."[23] It is therefore in its insistence on the principle of inclusiveness that we can identify the nature of Pound's project. That the *Cantos* fails as either "history" or "poetry" in their conventionally romantic senses is here a secondary issue, not least because Pound sought to undermine the value of either tradition in its distinct and exclusive form. The fundamental question about the *Cantos*, a quarter century after Pound left off, is how its inclusionary and combinatory procedures really work.

The vision of a "universal" art consistently informs Pound's work and typically figures in even his critical writings more as assumption than as argument. But really, Pound did not need to argue this point, because for early twentieth-century critics and readers the historically contingent premise that art should be "universal" had itself come to seem "natural" and "universal." Here again our subject constitutes for Pound less a conscious idea than a transparent part of the very language with which he conceived of

22. Percy Bysshe Shelley, "A Defence of Poetry" (1821 [pub. 1840]).
23. Michael André Bernstein, *The Tale of the Tribe: Ezra Pound and the Modern Verse Epic* (Princeton: Princeton University Press, 1980), 127.

his work. Consider as an almost random instance Pound's "Paris Letter" of September 1922, where he averred that "Flaubert's art was the art of 'generalization,' that is he presumably sought conditions, facts, relations which would be unaltered by *milieu*; I take it that Mr. Eliot has this in mind in the current issue of the Tyro when he complains that no American has yet done for America what James Joyce has done for Ireland; that is, he, Eliot must mean that no American author has yet so written of things in America that they would be equally profound and equally true for the rest of the Caucasian world."[24] The quest for facts "unaltered by *milieu*" neatly describes much of Pound's work in both the *Cantos* and in much of his didactic work; and in this quest we can see how Pound's rejection of narrative closure derives from the same convictions as his totalizing conception of culture. To consider "culture" in terms of its integrity is to envision it as an organism in which different parts nevertheless comprise a whole life. Romantic thinkers after Coleridge applied the same principle to artistic composition. "The doctrine of organic form," insofar as it develops from the recognition that an organism is "no singleness but rather a manifold," presupposes "that perfect wholeness, which must be a singleness, tends to be outside the fact—to become as it were a hypothetical construct."[25] Pound's conception of wholeness, his conception of totality, was both figural and configurative.

Thus it is no mere coincidence that the *Cantos* begins with a fragment of Odyssean narrative, but that fragment in and of itself does not indicate the basis for Pound's conception of his work as epic. The *Odyssey* appears only in this and other still smaller fragments; moreover, the fragment that opens Pound's poem seemed to him an element of more distant antiquity than the rest of the poem—a part of some earlier work which Homer had included in his work, just as the *Odyssey* itself was later included in Divus's notebook, and Divus was included in the *Cantos*. Canto 1 begins in medias res and breaks off in mid-sentence. The address to Andreas Divus near the end of Canto 1 indicates that Pound's interest lay less in the *Odyssey* itself than in the transmission of texts. As Korn observes, "Pound's decision to translate a section of the *Odyssey* into an Anglo-Saxon verse form and use it as a statement about tradition and cultural beginnings in Canto 1 was a deliberate attempt to leave present certain signs of the strangeness and pastness of the past" (*Ezra Pound*, 44). Pound's command, "Lie quiet Divus," is really a

---

24. "Paris Letter, August, 1922," *Dial* 73, no. 3 (September 1922): 332–37.
25. See Thomas McFarland, *Romanticism and the Forms of Ruin* (Princeton: Princeton University Press, 1981), 4.

command to stir and speak. To "lie quiet" would be, as Pound put it in *Guide to Kulchur*, deliberately echoing Eliot, to lie anesthetized on the table—which is by implication how history resides in the body of traditional histories of which the *Cantos* is a pointed critique.

Pound's decision to salvage the Odysseus—or Divus—material from the abandoned sequences of 1917–19 followed his discovery of an organizing principle. But that principle was not finally thematic. It had to do rather with a way of generating meaning.[26] In one respect this was a characteristic procedure of literary epic: just as Milton proposed to supersede Homer by describing prior and greater things, Pound proposed to include the mighty Homer as but one among many other texts. Certainly the presence of this material from the *Odyssey* was, like everything else in the *Cantos*, overdetermined. We have, for example, Pound's explanation of the metaphorical progress of the *Cantos* to his father:

> A.A. Live man goes down into world of Dead
> C.B. The "repeat in history"
> B.C. The "magic moment" or moment of metamorphosis, bust thru from quotidian into "divine or permanent world." Gods, etc.
>
> (*SL*, 210)

Nevertheless, Pound was unable to sustain, or lost his interest in sustaining, or felt threatened by the closure implied by too strict an observance of, any thematic hierarchy. He did, however, not only retain the principle of concrete inclusion developed so dramatically in Canto 1, but pursued it with increasing enthusiasm. Between *A Draft of Cantos 17–27* (1928) and the publication of *Eleven New Cantos* (1934), Pound reached well beyond the "literary" sensibility evident in the explanation to his father and seized upon documentary and epistolary materials of the most overtly prosaic quality.

The Prose of the *Pagany* Cantos of 1931

It is with the documentary materials of the much discussed "Malatesta" sequence (Cantos 8–11), or of such Cantos as 24 ("Thus the book of the

---

26. In fact, as Humphrey Carpenter notes, by the time of his 1956 recording of Canto 1, it was evident that "he no longer approved of the poem's resonant opening." *A Serious Character: The Life of Ezra Pound* (Boston: Houghton Mifflin, 1988), 824.

mandates") or 25 ("The Book of the Council Major") that the fullest implications of Pound's principle of inclusiveness become apparent.[27] For with these materials Pound questioned the very value of poetry for the modern world. Browning may have set a precedent for delving into documentary materials in *The Ring and the Book*, the meticulous diction and prosaic rhythms of which test the limits of metrical convention. But as the celebrated ring metaphor of Browning's opening lines attests, he was yet interested in transforming his materials into poetry, just as he was interested in the murder trial of Count Guido Franceschini as a particular story. Pound's treatment of similarly unliterary documents, especially in and after *Eleven New Cantos*, generates no such closure, nor does it in the same way "transform" its materials.

The inclusion of the prosaic in *A Draft of XXX Cantos* anticipates the inclusion of prose itself in *Eleven New Cantos*. Canto 25, for example, "The Book of the Council Major," presents a series of mandates whose prosaic quality remains largely unchanged by Pound's carefully shaped poetic lines:

> It being convenient that there be an end to
> the painting of Titian, fourth frame from the door on
> the right of the hall of the greater council, begun
> by maestro Tyciano da Cadore since its being thus
> unfinished holds up the decoration of said hall on
> the side that everyone sees.
>
> (Canto 25/119)

This prosaicness was a deliberately imported quality; Pound elected not only to include mandates but to do so in generally long and capacious lines. By contrast, at other points such as the cantos of *Section: Rock-Drill* and *Thrones: 96–109 de Los Cantares* (1959), Pound handled similar materials either in short, chiseled lines, or in verse that alternated irregularly between shorter

---

27. Some critics find in the Malatesta sequence the first instance of prose in the *Cantos*. Lawrence S. Rainey's splendidly researched *Ezra Pound and the Monument of Culture: Text, History and the Malatesta Cantos* (Chicago: University of Chicago Press, 1991), 64–75, examines the composition of these cantos with unprecedented precision and detail. Carpenter, however, makes the point simply: "Here," he writes, "for the first time the *Cantos* drop into prose." *Serious Character*, 420. "Drop into" is a good way of describing the way prose there appears—in individual phrases, usually indented, although Canto 9 includes entire letters and prints them with justified margins. But the prose of the Malatesta cantos figures as a subordinate generic feature. More important in this case is a new "prosaic" texture to much of the poetry. The work of the *Pagany* cantos may be distinguished by the dominance of its prose features.

and longer lines. Like his resolve that his poem must include history in concrete form, the introduction of the prosaic, and even of prose itself in the final cantos of *XXX Cantos* was considered and polemical.

Nevertheless, Pound labored on *XXX Cantos* for fifteen years, through false starts and abandoned resolves. Its prosaic elements are striking, but hardly dominant. It is important that *XXX Cantos* concludes with the highly lyrical and overtly archaic "Compleynt I hearde upon a day." But if that conclusion functions to reaffirm the place of *XXX Cantos* within the poetic tradition, it also underscores the further departures of *Eleven New Cantos*. Few of Pound's readers could have been prepared for what they met in Cantos 31–33, the opening sequence of *Eleven New Cantos*, and originally published in the July/September 1931 issue of *Pagany*.[28] Reviews were largely unfavorable, and their complaints about *Eleven New Cantos* as a whole apply most forcefully to its opening sequence. Reviewers complained that these cantos were "cluttered" and "crowded . . . with insignificant detail," that the poems lost Pound's characteristic "lyrical balance and dignity" in a "staccato of violent quotations." The conclusion of Philip Blair Rice, who reviewed *Eleven New Cantos* in the *Nation*, was typical. Rice found that "only a small portion of the new Cantos can be called poetry." And while he was not adverse to the idea of poetry addressing social concerns, he regarded Pound's attempt at such address as a failure: "It remains a matter for regret, however, that [Pound] seems to have been stumped by the problem of combining poetry and economics, when younger poets, most of them his own disciples, are already proving themselves equal to the task."[29] In short, critics discerned Pound's failure to be a "poetic" one, finding that his materials too often remained—as critics continue to say—untransformed.

The criticism of Pound's reviewers suggests a disappointment of expectations. These reviews were anything but hostile to the idea that poetry might address social and ethical issues; after all, even Tennyson had done that. But unlike Tennyson or Browning, Pound no longer satisfied the reviewers' sense of the properly "poetic." Clearly, Pound was capable of producing such writing; the poems of *Ripostes* (1912) or of *Lustra* (1916) were often flamboyantly "poetic," and even *Mauberley* (1920), Pound's ironic farewell to aestheticism, turned on resonant and intense lyrics:

28. Carpenter, *Serious Character*, 489, points out that Canto 34 was part of the group, but was published independently in *Poetry*.
29. Philip Blair Rice, "Education of Ezra Pound," *Nation*, 21 November 1934, 599–600.

> For three years, out of key with his time,
> He strove to resuscitate the dead art
> Of poetry; to maintain "the sublime"
> In the old sense. Wrong from the start—[30]

Eleven New Cantos contains writings of this kind, but in unfamiliar generic mixtures. No longer the dominant element of Pound's poem, such lyrical elements change in function. The judgments of Pound's reviewers were sound, in that the qualities for which they looked were but inconstantly present in *Eleven New Cantos*, and this disappointment serves as an index of Pound's innovations in poetic tradition.

Pound's determination to recover what he took to be the ancient centrality of poetry had led him to create a broadly heterogeneous poem that included the various discourses in which cultural and political power was most immediately manifest. At the same time, remaining convinced of the value of poetry, Pound's ambitions made the pursuit of his topical concerns in conventionally didactic forms impossible. Seeking "a profounder didacticism," Pound's experiments in genre endeavored to transform alike utilitarian notions of the didactic and cultural notions of the literary.

In *Eleven New Cantos*, Pound pursued such transformations both between and within individual cantos. In it he carefully interspersed the resonantly lyric with the disturbingly prosaic. Opening with the *Pagany* sequence, which he could have expected would prove unsatisfactory as "lyrics," Pound sustained that quotidian texture for five cantos before offering lyrics whose candences and archaic diction verge on the histrionic: lyrics such as Canto 36 ("A lady asks me") or Canto 39 ("Desolate is the roof"). In this alternation between cantos of predominantly prosaic and predominantly lyrical generic mixtures Pound discovered something of a formula to which he returned throughout the prolific thirties. In *Cantos LII–LXXI* (1940), for instance, the prose of Canto 44 is followed by the archaic lyricism of 45, the so-called Usura Canto. But Pound was perfectly able to mix prose and impassioned lyric within cantos as well. Canto 36 includes Pound's translation of Cavalcanti's "Donna me Prega" in a manner similar to his inclusion of Divus's *neukia* in Canto 1: the lyric is followed by quotations from Scotus Erigena, references to the Albigensian crusade, and fragments from a letter of Pope Clement IV, all of which reframes and alters its reception.

---

30. "Hugh Selwyn Mauberley (Contacts and Life)," Part I, 1–4, in *Personae: The Shorter Poems of Ezra Pound*, ed. Lea Baechler and A. Walton Litz (New York: New Directions, 1990), 183–202.

The generic mixture of the last of *Eleven New Cantos* might serve as the representative instance of this process, beginning with the short, trochaic lines of Pound's later lyric manner, and moving into the bookkeeping of "the Count de Vergennes. Paris, August. 1785":

> Consumption tobacco, esteemed in francs
> 15 to 30 million pounds, let us say it may be 24
> delivered in ports of France @ 8 sous
>   9 million 600 thousand
> at the rate 6 sous to manufacture
>   7 million and something
> revenue to the King 30 million
> to the consumer   72
> expense of the tax in collection is therefore
>   say 25 million
> presumptuous to assume
>   (Canto 41/205–6)

Writing of this sort can only be considered "lyrical" if we permit a vastly extended and metaphorical notion of lyricality. This is what Robert Langbaum means when he proposes that "even the cantos that quote prose letters are intended to give a lyric effect through presentation of the prose in fragments intended to set up poetic vibrations."[31] Such an explanation preserves the idea of "lyricality" by transforming it from a kind of writing into a particular kind of effect, or modality. In so doing, it recapitulates those romantic conceptions of wholeness which, as we have seen, played a powerful role in Pound's development.

But, finally, metaphors of "poetic vibration" and lyric "effect" interfere with the historical understanding of Pound's generic experiments. By the thirties Pound was investing received ideas about lyricality in both his poetic practice and critical promulgations—and was doing so with increasing exasperation. In the year before he published *Eleven New Cantos*, for example, he accepted the invitation of Social Credit advocate Gorham Munson to attack public ignorance of economics in the pages of *New Democracy*. That attack soon turned to ideas about the properly lyric:

---

31. Robert Langbaum, "Pound and Eliot," *The Word from Below: Essays on Modern Literature and Culture* (Madison: University of Wisconsin Press, 1987), 210.

> An epic is a poem *including* history. Any man who thinks he can understand history present or past *without* understanding economics is a mere piffling pigeon. Criticism of poesy in the age of idiocy, Abercrombie, georgian anthologies, neo-georgian anthologies welcomed by poor whats his name in *The Symposium* as the NEW, and by the London mugger press as the that which is to be fatted up for the maintenance of the habitual garbage of the Garvin school Observer, whats its name, the other guy and the rest ov 'em. . . .
>
> Malice in England and ignorance in America conducing to parallel dunderheadedness. . . .
>
> Criticism of poesy, to return to the start of this sentence, has been, by habit, restricted to the lyric and the epileptic. [ellipses Pound's][32]

Here again, Pound's emphasis on the inclusiveness of epic develops hand-in-hand with his rejection of traditional, and here specifically "Georgian," circumscriptions of the lyric. But Pound's identification of "lyric" with "epileptic" implies more than idiocy (probably in Ruskin's and in Shaw's senses of purely private concerns obliterating public awareness); it also invokes the romantic identification of poetry with heightened vision—epiphany—prophetic fits. However ineffectually, Pound focuses his attack not so much on the idea of lyricality as on contemporary versions of it. His aim was not to destroy the "lyric" but to transform it; his epic "included" lyricism and history in a manner that transformed both.

Nevertheless, it is important to remember the contradictions within Pound's own originating premises. The internalization and mystification of the "poetic" developed as a symbolist response to the perceived dangers of a moralizing and utilitarian age. Pound's conception of "a profounder didacticism," or of "a poem including history," sought to reinvigorate poetry by restoring its contact with those "quotidian" discourses in which society conducted the negotiations of power. Moreover, Pound often presented the prose elements of his poem in units more sustained and extended than "fragments." The *Pagany* cantos of 1931 are here exemplary, almost as if Pound had set out to prove his claim that "no method is justified until it has been carried too far."[33]

In Canto 33 in particular Pound includes prose in a way and to an extent unprecedented in post-Enlightenment poetry. Although in Cantos 31 and

32. "'Writers!' (as Joe Gould says) 'Ignite!'" *New Democracy* 1, no. 4 (25 October 1933): 6.

33. Pound, "Paris Letter," *Dial,* April 1922. See also John Childs, *Modernist Form* (Selingsgrove: Susquehanna University Press, 1986), 16.

32 he includes long excerpts from the correspondence of Thomas Jefferson, he transposes the letters into poetic lines. Those lines tend to be long and loosely constructed; they are typically "flat" by the strandards of romantic lyric convention—and are certainly "flat" by comparison with the poetry Pound had been writing up through the early twenties. But they are nonetheless distinguishable as "poetry"; they are at least not prose. They are so distinguishable chiefly by virtue of their appearance on the page: Pound repeatedly employs ellipses to break off from Jefferson's narratives or explanations, so that ellipses become a common line-ending. The varying length of Pound's lines becomes a way of creating emphasis, and of altering the relations between Jefferson's ideas. In what follows, the ellipses and line spacing are Pound's:

> "English papers . . . their lies . . .
>
> in a few years . . . no slaves northward of Maryland . . .
>
> "Their tobacco, 9 millions, delivered in port of France;
> 6 millions to manufacture
> on which the king takes thirty million
> that cost 25 odd to collect
> so that in all it costs 72 millions livres to the
> consumer . . . . . .
>
> (Canto 31/154)

It is important in passages such as this that Pound's treatment disrupts the expository sense of Jefferson's letters, seizing on details rather than argument, but treating those details as though they were germs from which, and between which, we might imagine Jefferson's "world" as a totality.

Canto 33 includes the same kinds of materials as the previous two *Pagany* cantos, drawing extensively on the letters of Jefferson and Adams. But it carries the process of inclusion still another step further:

> If the troops cd. be fed upon long letters, I believe the gent. at the head of that dept. (in this country) wd. be the best commissary on earth. But till I see him determined to act, not write; to sacrifice his domestic ease to the duties of his appointment, and apply the resources of this country, wheresoever they are to be had, I must entertain a different opinion of him.
> T. J. to P. Henry, March '79.

This is not merely prosaic, it is prose. The rest of the canto continues in kind, individual sentences sometimes interrupted with ellipses, but more typically presented in paragraph-length prose excerpts. In this respect, Canto 33 is unique within the *Cantos*. Hereafter Pound would frequently include prose excerpts in prose form, but never again would any canto be so nearly and so completely unpoetic. Canto 33 begins, it is true, with nine lines of poetry, material such as found in the preceeding two cantos. But how the poetry then breaks off finds only one parallel elsewhere in the *Cantos*: the sudden punctuation of seven lines of poetry in Canto 75 by a page and a half of musical notation.

The singularity of the generic mixture of Canto 33 suggests the value of considering the relations among its diverse elements. The opening lines offer Pound's version of John Adams's meditation on the nature of despotism. This way of describing the lines is descriptive, and yet not exact; for although Pound preserves the words of Adams's letter, he disrupts their significance by how he places them on the page. The meditation ceases to be Adams's. To call it Pound's version of Adams—while strictly correct—is to underestimate the effect of Pound's presentation. Ultimately the meditation becomes Pound's own:

> . . . . . Is that despotism
> or absolute power . . . unlimited sovereignty,
> is the same in a majority of a popular assembly,
> an aristocratical council, an oligarchical junto,
> and a single emperor, equally arbitrary, bloody,
> and in every respect diabolical. Wherever it has resided
> has never failed to destroy all records, memorials,
> all histories which it did not like, and to corrupt
> those it was cunning enough to preserve . . . . .
>   (Canto 33/160)

Pound excerpted this material from the opening of a letter which Adams had written to Jefferson. The date was as Pound gives it, except that Pound transposed Adams's formal "13 November, 1815" into more colloquial, contemporary American practice: a transposition characteristic throughout the *Cantos* of his handling of historical materials, frequently even when his object was to establish their alterity. The opening of Adams's letter appeared in the *Collected Works* as follows:

> The fundamental article of my political creed is, that despotism, or unlimited sovereignty, or absolute power, is the same in a majority of a popular assembly, an aristocratical council, an oligarchical junto, and a single emperor. Equally arbitrary, cruel, bloody, and in every respect diabolical. Accordingly, arbitrary power, wherever it has resided, has never failed to destroy all the records, memorials, and histories of former times, which it did not like, and to corrupt and interpolate such as it was cunning enough to preserve or to tolerate. We cannot therefore say with much confidence what knowledge or what *virtues* may have prevailed in some quarters of the world.

Pound omitted only one sentence in full from Adams's letter, which was significantly enough Adams's speculation about the unreliability of the historical record. Although Pound believed that the dark forces of international finance had always sought to "bury" the record of their evil, the *Cantos* is predicated on the principle that such burying was typically accomplished by a diffusion of attention, by separating the inquiries of the human mind into its separate sciences and disciplines—and so obscuring the totality of relations. As he put it in *Guide*, "There is one enemy, ever-busy obscuring our terms; ever muddling and muddying terminologies, ever trotting out minor issues to obscure the main and basic, ever prattling of short range causation for the sake of, or with the result of, obscuring the vital truth" (*GK*, 31). Adams's doubts about the recoverability of the record would, then, have struck Pound with the same dread with which Carlyle, say, regarded Enlightenment deism or atheism.

Twice Pound elides subjects of Adams's sentences. These elisions reflect Pound's ideas about the epic. By omitting the nominative phrase of Adams's first sentence, Pound begins this canto in medias res. Such an opening serves Pound in several ways. It fosters what one critic has described as a chief characteristic of the *Cantos*, "the illusion of plenitude."[34] In this case, such a beginning suggests a characteristic technique of Ruskin's *Fors Clavigera*, the use of the random example to illustrate "the main and basic" principles of history. Pound's opening does not entirely elide the identity of the speaker; he might have expected his readers to identify Adams on the basis of the heading "Quincy Nov. 13, 1815." But the omission of Adams's salutation exemplifies how Pound's presentation works to minimize the generic fea-

---

34. See Marjorie Perloff, *The Poetics of Indeterminacy: Rimbaud to Cage* (Princeton: Princeton University Press, 1981), 155–99.

tures of the letter, and to offer it instead as part of a public and even universal record.

Pound's other ellipses are more problematic, and his practice of indicating omissions unconventional. For example, his ellipsis in line 2 stands for the loss of but one word, an "or"; but he drops a three-word phrase between lines 2 and 3 with no indication. Similarly, the sentence beginning midway through Pound's sixth line lacks its initial nominative phrase. Pound apparently felt that "despotism" was a suitable synonym for "arbitrary power," and assumed that his readers would take the pronoun of line 6 to refer to the subject of the previous sentence; but his construction suggests an unwillingness to name the enemy: "Wherever it has resided / has never failed to destroy all records, memorials." In Adams's prose a comma falls after "resided," since what is the beginning of Pound's sentence was but a periodic modification of the subject in Adams's. Pound's seventh line thus seems to lack a word when it actually does not. The end of the subsequent line, by contrast, elides Adams's phrase "and to interpolate such as" with, again, no indication. Such apparent inconsistency results from Pound's confidence that he was including Adams's meditation "whole"—however idealistic that sense of "wholeness" or "totality" may have been. The ellipsis with which the poetry breaks off underscores the extent to which Pound foregrounds the process of transmission. Where Adams's account went on to doubt the ability of the historical record to endure, Pound's ends with a note of promise, with the infinitive "to preserve." Indeed, Pound's retention of Adams's heading here assumes a new significance. The last of Adams's sentences that Pound included begins with what here becomes a qualification; "wherever" despotism has prevailed, it has sought to destroy the historical record, but "Quincey," and by extension America, is a place free from such invidious power.

The emphasis on the transmission of texts continues through the prose fragments of the rest of the canto—even where Pound paraphrased rather than quoted. The paragraph referring to *Das Kapital* offers a striking example:

> limits of his individuality (cancels) and develops his power as a specie. (Das Kapital) denounced in 1842 still continue (today 1864) report of '42 was merely chucked into the archives and remained there while these boys were ruined and became fathers of this generation . . . for workshops remained a dead letter down to 1871 when was taken from control of municipal . . . and placed in hands of the factory

> inspectors, to whose body they added eight (8) assistants to deal with over one hundred thousand workshops and over 300 tile yards. (Canto 33/162)

As Furia has observed, Pound is quoting Marx, who was quoting from an 1864 report on British factory conditions, which in turn had quoted from an 1842 report by a Parliamentary commission on child labor conditions. There is no question here of deception: such language as "report of '42 was merely chucked into the archives" is obviously Pound's own. Pound's text presumes to present the force of its sources, not their form. And although it is true that the other prose excerpts that make up Canto 33 remain closer to their originals than does the material from *Kapital*, it is nevertheless not "documents" that we meet here but a digest.

Pound would never abandon this technique, but within five years, by the time he was at work on *The Fifth Decad of Cantos* (1937) and on *Guide to Kulchur* (1938), his emphasis had changed. This change was in keeping with the innovations of *Eleven New Cantos*, and in a sense it was the result of retrospective understanding of the value of the generic mixture of Canto 1. That is, after the mid-thirties Pound came to insist on that toward which in 1931 he had only gestured: the principle of concrete inclusion. His notion of including history became at last doggedly empirical, while his justifications of method remained no less extremely idealistic. The *Guide* was Pound's major effort to expound the historiographical method pursued in the *Cantos*, a method which marks the periphery of his blindness as surely as it informs his vision in its most compelling moments. In his insistence that "the 'new' historic sense in our time demands . . . whole slabs of the record in the latin of such men as Claudius Salmasius," Pound was making several demands, distinct but related in their impulse to present history in an unmediated form. All of these demands reflected Pound's unconscious and enabling historicism—his conviction that his method must be appropriate to "the age." He wanted a historical method that included "concrete" pieces of historical evidence, rather like the way that, in collage, found objects are affixed to one surface (this parallel is inexact and we shall see that the claims of Pound's text to truth inevitably generated different semiotic problems). He wanted a method that could include that evidence "whole"; and because the force of his claims for universal truth rested on a primary demonstration of multifariousness of evidence, he wanted a means of presenting his evidence in its alterity—its original "latin"—that nevertheless would prove intelligible and assimilable to his own didactic purpose.

It is worth pausing over the relation between this formulation, this call for "whole slabs of the record," and the several manifestoes from Pound's polemical London years. Pound's notions of "image" or "vortex" or "ideogram" all emphasized intensity and lyricality. But even in these Pound was beginning to consider how it is that poetry might gather into itself other forms of discourse. Even as such talk about imposing pattern and energy posits distinctions between the poetic and the nonpoetic, it reveals an interest in bringing them together. In another of Pound's contributions to *New Democracy*, an inflammatory "warning against high financial skullduggery" titled "Hands Off Alberta" (15 November 1935), Pound reflected on the nature of revolution. As though answering the jejune questions of angry young men, Pound demonstrated he could be angrier than anyone: "Do I," he queried, "expect economic revolution with SOCIAL revolution?" The very question, he insinuated, depended on a misconception of the autonomy of the different areas of cultural activity: "BOTH these revolutions are GOING ON, and a lot of small town intelligentsia are still sitting round WAITING, and suggesting that I shd. aim toward a group of dead and fixed ideas FROM WHICH and OUT OF WHICH earlier revolutions proceeded." Pound was quoting his own definition of "vortex" of twenty years past—that "from which, through which, and into which, ideas are constantly rushing"—as though it should have been a familiar part of the public record. That he was appropriating his vorticist manifesto for new ends is less important than his own perception of an integrity between his poetics and politics. The term common to both expositions is "ideas," and it implies an equation. Poetry, of all forms of discourse, contains the greatest density of ideas, and it is ideas "from which and out of which" revolutions proceed. Such an equation underscores the complex irony of Pound's quotation from the letters of John Adams in the third of the *Pagany* cantos that "Litterae nihil sanantes" (Canto 33/161). Whether one regards Pound's use of Adams's phrase as ironic or as disapproving in large part depends, of course, on how one reads the *Cantos*, but its importance to him is suggested by the space between its two quotations. Pound first used it in 1931, when the radical inclusiveness of his "epic" was becoming for him a principal concern; he quoted it again in 1962, in Canto 116, the last of his completed cantos.

Pound discovered the phrase in a letter that Adams sent to Jefferson in June of 1812. In a previous letter, devoted almost entirely to affairs of state, Adams had closed with something of a non sequitur, asking if there was "any book that pretends to give any Account of . . . the confused traditions of Indian antiquities." Ignoring in this case Adams's political reflections, Jefferson responded with what is much like a long annotated bibliography, the effect of which on Adams proved somewhat daunting. Adams was quick to express his puzzlement over what "had turned my Curiosity to inquiries after the metaphysical Science of the Indians," and to admire Jefferson's "perspicuity and Elegance." "But your letter," Adams continued, "has given me great Satisfaction" because

> while it has furnished me with Information *where* all the knowledge is to be obtained, that Books afford: it has convinced me that I shall never know much more of the Subject than I do now. . . . The various Ingenuity which has been displayed in Inventions of hypotheses to account for the original Population of America; and the immensity of learning profusely expended to support them, have appeared to me, for a longer time than I can precisely recollect, what the Physicians call the Litterae nihil Sanantes. Whether Serpents' Teeth were sown here and sprung up men; whether men and women dropped from the Clouds upon this Atlantic island; whether the Almighty created them here, or whether they immigrated from Europe, are questions of no moment to the prospect or future happiness of Man. Neither Agriculture, Commerce, Manufactures, Fisheries, Science, Literature, Taste, Religion, Morals or any other good will be promoted, or any Evil averted by any discoveries that can be made in answer to those questions.

Adams's impatience with the abstruse speculations outlined by Jefferson derived from an impatience with historicist attempts to systematize history. Later in the letter he parodied arguments about God as "the mechanician of the universe," the great "watchmaker" who had in his head an "Idea of the System of the Watch" before he made it. "I am," Adams wrote,

> weary of contemplating notions from the lowest and most beastly degradations of human Life, to the highest Refinement of Civilization. I am weary of Philosophers, Theologians, Politicians and Historians. They are immense Masses of Absurdities, Vices, and Lies. Montesquieu had sense enough to say in Jest, that all our knowledge might be comprehended in twelve Pages in Duodecimo: and I believe him, in earnest. I could express my Faith in shorter terms. He who loves the Workman and his Work, and does what he can to preserve and improve it, shall be accepted of him.

Adams's reflections had for Pound a multivalent resonance. He welcomed the skepticism about systematic treatments of history, as well as the confidence that the lessons of history could be compressed into a small digest. Probably, Adams's love of "the Workman and his Work" also resonated with his own Ruskinian ideals. But Pound's treatment of Adams's reflections narrowed, surprisingly enough, their range—or perhaps this narrowing is not surprising at all.

Adams's phrase opens a short paragraph about fifty lines into Canto 33 (the ellipses are Pound's):

> Litterae nihil sanantes whether serpents' teeth sprang up men . . .
> cannot appease my melancholy commiseration for our armies
> in this furious snow storm (Quincey, November 15th.)

The second two lines of this passage are from a letter written four months after the letter reflecting on "Indian metaphysics," and their juxtaposition here alters the reference of Adams's phrase. Where Adams voices skepticism about the value of abstruse or historicist system-making, Pound presents a less philosophical derision of writing or "letters" in general. Pound's construction "rhymes" with the fragment of Jefferson's letter included earlier in the canto (lines 10–17). That fragment offers its own sarcasm: "If the troops cd. be fed upon long letters, I believe the gent. at the head of that dept. (in this country) wd. be the best commissary on earth." Thus, Pound's reconstruction of Adams's letter provides an amplification of Jefferson's annoyance with writing that stops short of real action.

Pound's long insistence on "ideas which are intended to 'go into action,' or to guide action and serve us as rules (and/or measures) of conduct" (*GK*, 34) cannot be overemphasized, especially with regard to the constructions of *Eleven New Cantos*. In a letter of early 1934, for instance, Pound complained that even though Farrar had agreed to print *Eleven New Cantos*, they had decided to "hold it back" until autumn. It ought, Pound objected, "to have been in print last November or at any rate before Roose took over the Fed. Res. deposits" (*SL*, 253). Pound's confidence in the efficacy of his own work may have been, as the doctors at St. Elizabeths later believed, the result of delusion, but it was certainly not bluff. If it was the product of "delusion," it was more immediately the delusion of faith, or of unexamined assumptions, than it was of madness (a term whose precision in Pound's case may yet prove more metaphorical than clinical).[35]

Pound's conviction that the earlier publication of *Eleven New Cantos* might have altered the economic policy of a nation had the sanction of "great" literary tradition: it was Flaubert's lament that "if they had read my 'Education Sentimentale' these things [the Franco-Prussian War] would not have happened." That those words impressed Pound is evident from the variety of ways in which he applied them during the war years. In 1916 he grumbled that "if more people had read *The Portrait* [sic] and certain stories in Mr. Joyce's *Dubliners* there might have been less recent trouble in Ireland." In 1917 he used Flaubert's lament as an epigraph for his serial essay "Provincialism the Enemy," and attributed America's entry into the war to the exhibition of Lewis's paintings in New York. In 1918 he quoted Flaubert once more to insinuate how much the English-speaking "multitudes" had lost by neglecting Henry James. Pound's insistence on such connections grew fiercer with time. Over forty years later, in Canto 107, for instance, he sought to link the execution of Charles I to the public assimilation of Shakespeare's history plays (which he called in *ABC of Reading* "the true English EPOS"), and of the juridical writings of Edward Coke. Ill-founded though this conviction of an immediate tie between "literature" and history might have been, it was one Pound refused to relinquish. He sought to produce writing that would "be not only action itself, but the cause of action."

"Litterae Nihil Sanantes"

Neither Mr. Sandburg nor I, nor even Mr.
Ben Hecht, is likely to invade the halls of
congress or lead anyone over the barricades.
— Ezra Pound, "Mr. Pound on Prizes"
(1927)

---

35. Several critics have ventured this important idea. Wendy Stallard Flory's book *The American Ezra Pound* (New Haven: Yale University Press, 1989) is so far the most reasoned and judicious, and may well prove to be so for some time to come; E. Fuller Torrey's contentious *The Roots of Treason: Ezra Pound and the Secret of St. Elizabeths* (New York: McGraw-Hill, 1984) also denies that Pound was ever insane, but does so only to vilify him, and creates so many further misunderstandings in the process that it discredits itself.

> Barometers, wind-gauges, cannot be used as engines.
> —Ezra Pound, *ABC of Reading* (1934)

Neither Adams's aphorism, nor Pound's use of it—either in Canto 33 or later in 117—refer immediately to "literature" in its restrictive sense. And yet because Pound necessarily includes the quotation in a highly ambitious poetic context, it cannot function merely to dismiss writing as a substitute for action. If the explicit thematics of Canto 33 concern the better use of resources, its constructions propose that "letters" or writings are themselves among those uselessly ingenious histories. Pound's elision of Adams's weariness over the endless systems proposed by universal and systematic historians is significant, since the *Cantos* itself proposes to offer such a universal history—epic, or tale of the tribe. But Pound expected that his renunciation of narrative as an organizing principle would avoid the inevitable failures of earlier systems, the "fatal lacunae" of "anesthetized" academic histories. Pound's very inclusion of prose, and the manner of that inclusion, was therefore in itself a rejoinder to Adams's skepticism.

The manner of that inclusion raises, however, another question about Pound's use of the aphorism. *The Companion to the Cantos* translates the phrase as "literature curing nothing," but Adams's subsequent reflection about the uselessness of such "writings" to "Agriculture, Commerce, Manufactures, Fisheries, Science, Litterature, Taste, Religion, Morals, or any other good" indicates the different sense the word had for him. Adams's target was abstruse system-making, not "literature" in our modern sense. Alert to the historicity of the term, Pound was convinced that the academy had played a major role in fostering what he saw as its diminished modern sense. Thus in "The Jefferson-Adams Letters as a Shrine and a Monument," published in the *North American Review*, in the winter 1937–38 issue, he grumbled that "it is probable that I could pick one crow a week with the American university system 'for the rest of my natural', but two immediate crows are quite obvious, one with the modus of teaching history omitting the most significant documents, and second the mode of teaching literature and/or 'American literature', omitting the most significant documents, and assuming that the life of a nation's letters is restricted mostly to second-rate fiction" (*SP*, 147). Pound's purpose was not to dismiss the value of fiction, but to inveigh against its isolation from the forms of cultural exchange.

"Europe went blind" into the Great War, Pound insisted later in the same essay, "because all general knowledge had been split up into fragments. Because literature no longer bothered about the language 'of law and of the state' because the state and plutocracy cared less than a damn about letters" (*SP*, 153). The circularity of argument here is precisely the point, since he was asserting the ineluctable ties among all kinds of work.

But elsewhere, especially in essays written more contemporaneously with his work on *Eleven New Cantos*, Pound more directly identified the isolation of literature as a cause and not merely effect of its impoverishment. In "The Individual in His Milieu: A Study of Relations and Gesell," Pound complained that "the diseased periphery of letters is now howling that literature and poetry in especial, should keep within bounds. I find this limitation entitled 'respect itself', which phrase is perverted to mean that literature should eschew the major field by omitting and leaving untackled a great deal of the subject matter that interested such diverse writers as Propertius, Dante and Lope de Vega" (*SP*, 272). Pound's critique is radical: it is the very defining of "literature" that necessarily removes writing to the "periphery" of cultural activity, and engenders its modern disease and triviality. By *Eleven New Cantos*, "literature" had become for Pound a pejorative term. It implied a thin-blooded aloofness from real events and a false circumscription of the poetic sphere. His alternative, a broadly Carlylean or Ruskinian perception of cultural integrity, is exemplified in his title, "The Individual in His Milieu: A Study of Relations and Gesell." Even though Pound's immediate concern was Gesell's rethinking of money and value, he still found it necessary to posit first, and once again, the relatedness of economic and artistic endeavor.

Pound did not regard his essays into economics as departures from his principal activity. In the issue of *Pagany* immediately preceeding that in which he published the opening sequence of *Eleven New Cantos*, he considered "the possibility of criteria"—and did so in totalizing terms that Carlyle or Ruskin would well have understood. "Literature does not exist in a vacuum," Pound intoned repeatedly, but is "part of the general and social existence. . . . The condition of man in social organism and the working of the latter, are parts of legitimate subject matter. All major literature has taken count of the relation of the one to the rest." This "social organism" was for Pound the ennabling principle for all forms of production and exchange. Without the integrity between them, the different arts would wither into insignificance. As for "aht and licherchoor," Pound drawled—in another article published within a month of the *Pagany* sequence—"the whole drift of plutocratic kultur is toward devitalization of letters and scholarship."[36]

If, then, the translation of "litterae" in the *Companion to the Cantos* as "literature" is misleading, it observes all the same an association that is for modern readers probably inevitable, and which is moreover encouraged by Pound's fragmentary inclusion of Adams's letter. But if we accept that association, then we must recognize that even in its most superficial appearance, the texture of Canto 33—or for that matter of most of *Eleven New Cantos*, and most of the cantos that Pound wrote between 1930 and 1946—is an affront to most of what the term "literature" traditionally denotes. Canto 33 not only presents its readers with the problem of examining the role of prose within a larger poem, but exacerbates that difficulty by taking up such subject matter as the discounting of bills, the language of the Factory Act of John Hobhouse, or extracts from the minutes of a Senate speech concerned with regulating commerce between the states. Pound's inclusion of this material goes out of its way to emphasize its difference from romantic notions of the lyric, both in subject matter and in form. The nine lines of poetry with which Canto 33 opens serve more than anything else to call attention to an activity hitherto alien to the composition of lyric writing: the preservation and inclusion of history, and the attempt to mediate political and economic power.

Pound was explicit on this point, even with regard to the *Pagany* sequence, which heralded the innovations of *Eleven New Cantos*. In "The Jefferson-Adams Letters as a Shrine and a Monument," Pound affirmed that literature had "gone to pot," had grown steadily "duller and duller by limitation of subject. Balzac, Trollope and Henry James extended the subject. EXTENDED the subject, they as Dante before them and as every real writer before them or since, extended the domain of their treatment" (*SP*, 153). Contemporary readers may here find Pound's references puzzling, at least with regard to Balzac and James. The difficulty arises because Pound's canon took shape around issues of cultural engagement. His Flaubert was less the great stylistic innovator, the master of "free-indirect discourse" than a writer whose stylistic precision ennabled penetrating social critique (*Sentimental Education*) and satire (*Bouvard et Pécuchet*): the Flaubert who believed that his *Education Sentimentale* might have prevented the Franco-Prussian War. Balzac Pound regarded as a near epic commentator on the human comedy. In fact, Pound similarly respected James, Eliot, Lewis, and Joyce primarily as

---

36. "Fungus, Twilight, or Dry Rot," *New Review*, August/September/October 1931.

tenchant cultural critics. The difference between Pound's view of these writers and the prevailing academic views of our time parallels precisely the difference that we have noted between early and late-twentieth-century receptions of Ruskin. Pound's inclusion of the Jefferson-Adams letters into the *Cantos* was a programmatic "extension of subject."

"The Jefferson-Adams Letters as a Shrine and a Monument" exemplifies how Pound's Ruskinian assumptions about culture inform the generic experiments of *Eleven New Cantos*. He began the essay by submitting that American history could be divided into four periods: the period of "civilisation" (1760 to 1830); the period of decline (to 1860); the period of despair (to 1930); and the contemporaneous period, which he believed held out the possibility at least of revival. The language with which Pound described and explained this fall in effect reinscribes the "cultural" tradition, even as it can help us account for Pound's rejection of the idea of culture as it had developed by the thirties.

Pound attributed the initial fall of American culture to "a scission between the life of the mind and the life of the nation," in other words to the divorce of culture from the realm of material civilization—the shattering of experience as a lived totality. Similarly, the period of "despair" witnessed a further shrinking of the inner life from the commonality of material conditions, so that culture became increasingly elite: a "division" arose "between the temper, thickness, richness of the mental life of Henry Adams, and Henry James, and that of say U. S. Grant, McKinley, Harding, Coolidge and Hoover." Such a prognosis set the terms for Pound's prescription for the future: "The possibilities of revival, starting perhaps with a valorisation of our cultural heritage, not merely as something lost in dim retrospect, a tombstone, tastily carved." Pound objected to the commodification of "culture," the expectation that it meant only the preservation of tasteful "monuments"—"tombstones"—to the past: "two gross broken statues" and "a few thousand battered books." Like Carlyle before him, Pound identified "culture" with the energy of total being, of "a still workable dynamo." From here his attack turned to the exclusion of such materials as the Jefferson-Adams correspondence from the teaching of history, and the restriction of "literature" "mostly to second-rate fiction."

Pound's rejection of "literary" privilege was, like his admiration for the Adams correspondence, generated by romantic convictions about cultural totality. But his many discussions of "culture" can confuse the issue, unless we see that his target was not that vision of a "whole" life held out by the

Victorian sages, but the reified and commodified form that "culture"—as both concept and community—had in his time assumed. This discrimination, which had led him two decades earlier to attack "kultur" as opposed to "culture," in the thirties prompted him gradually to abandon the term. In "The Jefferson-Adams Letters," the seminal values of culture thus remain intact even as Pound refuses its familiar terminology: "If we are a nation, we must have a national mind. Frobenius escaped both the fiddling term 'culture' and rigid 'kultur' by recourse to Greek, he used 'Paideuma' with a meaning that is necessary to almost all serious discussion of such subjects as that now under discussion. His 'Paideuma' means the mental formation, the inherited habits of thought, the conditionings, aptitudes of a given race or time." Although Frobenius was an anthropologist, his term "paideuma" differs from the ostensibly neutral anthropological uses of the term "culture."

As Pound recognized, Frobenius essentially wanted a term that could recover the initial force of the term "culture." Its emphasis was not, as it is in the anthropological sense of "culture," on the gestalt of communal praxis; rather, "paideuma" emphasized possibility and imagination, the relation of mind to matter. As Pound explained his orientation further, its reproduction of nineteenth-century oppositions becomes increasingly informative. He decried "ideology," and did so in a way that presents Mussolini as a modern Napoleon: "In Italy there is current the adjective 'anti-storico' to describe unlikely proposals; ideologies hung in a vacuum or contrary to the natural order of events as conditioned by race, time, and geography" (*SP*, 148). Asserting that the "lesson" of this article "is against raw ideology, which Napoleon, Adams, Jefferson were all up against, and whereto, as Adams remarked, Napoleon had in those days given a name" (*SP*, 158), Pound instanced as "antistorico" Henry Adams's theory of history. The problem was that Adams "wanted a science, almost a mathematical science of history—overlooking, or does he specifically say he didn't overlook, the impossibility of laboratory methods" (*SP*, 149). Once more associating science with the lifeless and mechanical, Pound argued the final inadequacy of scientific method before the questions of history. "The laws of material science," he said, "presuppose uniformity throughout the cosmos, but they do not offer an hierarchy of anything like the earlier coherence. Call it an hierarchy of evaluation."[37]

---

37. Ian F. A. Bell, in his impressive *Critic as Scientist: The Modernist Poetics of Ezra Pound* (New York: Methuen, 1981), has made a study of Pound's debts to period science. Bell documents how frequently Pound's most "aesthetic" formulations depended on scientific analogy, and how

Again, the oppositions on which Pound depends are so familiar that we hardly notice them. But the conclusion of "The Jefferson-Adams Letters" depends on assumptions of totality and on a distinction between "totality" and "uniformity" that illuminates the innovations of *Eleven New Cantos*. Referring to the novelistic tradition, Pound claimed that "in fact the whole of Flaubert, the whole of the fight for the novel as 'histoire morale contemporaine' was a fight against maxims, against abstractions, a fight back toward a human and/or total conception." Behind this claim is the association of uniformity with abstraction.[38] The ideal of totality, by contrast, derived from related romantic ideals of organism. In such a view, the whole depends on the differences of its parts, but to abstract any of those parts is to destroy its life. For Pound, the struggle of the modern was to restore the fullness of life by refusing uniform and universal law, the division into disciplines that abstracted political economy from the arts. "A total culture such as that of Adams and Jefferson does not," Pound averred, "dodge such investigation [as the search into the nature and source of transference or money]. A history of literature which refuses to look at such matters remains merely a shell and a sham" (*SP*, 157). It was, finally, toward the recovery of the "life not split into bits," the recovery of vitality, of totality, that Pound determined to write "a poem including history."

The rapidity with which Pound was completing cantos throughout the thirties attests to a new certitude of purpose; but after the breaks with lyrical tradition in *Eleven New Cantos* the further innovations of the thirties were largely implicit in his earlier practice. The incorporation of ideograms in *Cantos LII–LXXI* (1940), for instance, only makes explicit what Pound's arrangement of words on the page had been doing implicitly: substituting visual-perceptual organization for syntactic, and subverting a strictly narrative order with constructions that worked toward a simultaneity of signifi-

---

Pound's was often a "mixed vocabulary," in the case of "The Wisdom of Poetry," for instance, a "sifting of terms from technology, religious mysticism and Platonic idealism." I am not arguing, against Bell, that Pound consistently vilified science. But it is important to emphasize that Pound's attempts to establish the "aesthetic" in scientific terms have important historical precedent— Ruskin's "Science of Aspects" (see *Modern Painters* III, vol. 5 of the Library Edition of the *Works of John Ruskin*, ed. E. T. Cook and Alexander Wedderburn [London: George Allen; New York: Longmans, Green and Co., 1907]) to name the most crucial. Such endeavor was not friendly to science, but an attempt to legitimize what might otherwise seem a less rigorous activity; for where so much prestige attends to scientific success, to be less rigorous threatens to be less valued.

38. For an account of Pound's aversion to abstraction that situates it within contemporaneous philosophical developments, see Sanford Schwartz's *Matrix of Modernism: Pound, Eliot, and Early Twentieth-Century Thought* (Princeton: Princeton University Press, 1985), esp. chaps. 1 and 3.

cations. Of course, the extensive inclusion of ideograms unreadable to his Western audience changed the generic mixture of his poem. But here too Pound had already employed this technique in his prose; *Guide* had incorporated numerous ideograms two years earlier. Like the experiments of *Eleven New Cantos*, the generic mixture of *Guide to Kulchur* developed directly from Pound's convictions about cultural totality. Like those earlier experiments too, the innovations Pound there undertook would have dramatic implications for his subsequent work on the *Cantos*.

4
Popularizing Primers and the Discourse of Culture

> The ultimate goal of scholarship is popularization.
> —Ezra Pound, "Provincialism the Enemy" (1917)

> I am merely a popularizer who has perhaps dug up a few historic instances the better to clarify the expression of what the good economists know.
> —Ezra Pound, "More on Economics" (1933)

The Popularizers of Romance

Pound's didactic primers have won few admirers. Often obscure in reference, difficult in manner, and latterly objectionable, these books and pamphlets are failures. They are, however, failures of a particular kind. They participated in a busy tradition whose mastery Pound believed, early and late, material to his poetic work. But today that tradition is so seldom even recognized that his popularizing work has come to seem anomalous. In describing the nineteenth-century tradition of popularized scholarship, I shall at times rely on lists of books rather than on sustained analyses of individual instances because the profusion of pertinent examples is here more important than any one in particular. My purpose is not to imply that such books rank with Pound's, but rather to expose the oppositions (popular vs. polite, "Victorian" vs. "Modernist," didactic vs. aesthetic) that interfere with our understanding of his work.

As George Dekker has observed, Pound's first sustained critical work, *The Spirit of Romance* (1910), "arrived on one of the last surges of the flood of

Victorian popularizations."[1] This "surge" of popular interest in romance contributed to the production of scholarship of a distinctly "popularized" kind. Hugh Kenner and Peter Makin have noted the debt of this activity to seventy-five years of Continental and romantic scholarly tradition,[2] but Dekker emphasizes Pound's belatedness in an English and popularized tradition. As he observes, the first romance study immediately relevant to Pound's was a book by Ford Madox Ford's father: Francis Hueffer's *Troubadours: A History of Life and Literature in the Middle Ages* (1878). The lateness of Pound's arrival, Dekker proposes, "may be gauged by the fact that the last general book on the troubadours in English was published by H. J. Chaytor in 1912"—only two years after *The Spirit of Romance*. Even at that, Chaytor was in 1912 an established figure, having published *The Troubadours of Dante* ten years earlier.[3] It is at last a rather poignant spectacle. Pound set out as a young man to carry a standard for which few of his contemporaries could still muster any enthusiasm. It was not that his concerns, or the earnestness he brought to them, were in themselves strange to the other anti-Victorians whom he sometimes mistook for allies; what struck them as strange was the presence of such things in a young poet affecting "modern" ambitions.

Commenting on the romantic seizure of "Provence" as a "cause," Makin notes that "romantic currents have always been behind the more public side of interest in Provençal culture—the literary interest (Mistral, the Pre-Raphaelite period), the local interest (the crushed heretics of Languedoc, language revival, and separatism), and the historical-romance interest.[4] Cer-

---

1. George Dekker, *Sailing after Knowledge: The Cantos of Ezra Pound, a Critical Appraisal* (New York: Barnes & Noble, 1963), 111–12.

2. See Hugh Kenner, *The Pound Era* (Berkeley and Los Angeles: University of California Press, 1971), 109–12, and Peter Makin, *Provence and Pound* (Berkeley and Los Angeles: University of California Press, 1978), 2–5.

3. Henry John Chaytor was a prolific author who remained active until his death in 1954. In the years between the two books on the troubadours, for instance, he published inter alia *A Companion to French Verse* (1903), *The Greatness and Decline of Rome* (1907), *A First Spanish Book* (1908), *The Teaching of History* (1908), *The Transmigration of Souls* (1909), *Christianity and Islam* (1909), *Paul and Jesus* (1909), and *The Story of Israel and Judah* (1911). The number and variety of these studies indicates much about the nature of the studies themselves. Chaytor's *Troubadours* (1912), in its concern with the troubadours' ostensible identification of love and poetry (chapter 2), exemplifies the focus of many popular studies, such as John Rutherford's *Troubadours: Their Loves and Lyrics* (1873), or Justin Smith's *Troubadours at Home: Their Lives and Personalities, Their Songs and Their World* (1899). The idea was distinctively late-century: that these poets aestheticized their lives, and lived their art. Hueffer's book is worth additional mention in that its second and third chapters are devoted to distinguishing between "popular" and "artistic" epics, Hueffer seeing both as a species of narrative poem.

4. Makin, *Provence and Pound*, 2–3.

tainly one other place where this question reached popular attention was the arena of Homeric translation and paraphrase. Like the paraphrases and most of the translations of the seventies and after, books like Hueffer's, or like Ida Farnell's *Lives of the Troubadours* (1896) narrativized older materials, expanding on the *vidas* (lives) and *razos* (explanations) that often accompanied the poems in the old "troubadour" manuscripts. It was in this form, rather more than in the translations of Rossetti, or Pound, that Provence attracted its widest attention.

Writers like Hueffer owed their audience in one part to the medievalism cultivated by Carlyle, Ruskin, the Pre-Raphaelites, or Morris, and in another to the late-century backlash against it. For the late seventies were precisely when Burckhardt's *Kultur der Renaissance in Italien* (1860) began to find its peculiar English reception. Whereas Victorian medievalism had elegized the organic unity of a simpler world and regarded the Renaissance as a fall from which the world has yet to recover, writers like Walter Pater or John Addington Symonds established the now familiar sense of the Renaissance as a rebirth.[5] Pater celebrated its cultivation of "aesthetic" experience, Symonds its cultivation of "humanism." When Pater began *The Renaissance* (1873) with "Aucassin et Nicolette," later revised (1877) as "Two Early French Stories," he associated the study of romance with serious "aesthetic" concerns. Symonds drew another kind of analogy between romance and his activity as its scholar; in "The Romantic Epic" in his three-volume *Renaissance in Italy* (1875–86), he emphasized the "Plebeian origins" of the romantic epic as a means of explaining its generic heterogeneity. Symonds too was writing for a popular audience, even while working to create a verbal texture that reproduced (the phrase is inevitable) the spirit of romance. Thus when more recent commentators conclude that Symonds's work is long on the picturesque but short on scholarly rigor, they describe the book accurately,

---

5. What makes Hueffer of interest here is that he made a career of romance scholarships, and constituted "romance" in a way that embraced both medieval and Renaissance elements—and so mediated much of the period contention. In 1875 he published *A Literary Friendship of the Fourteenth Century*—a study of Boccaccio and Petrarch; his *Troubadours: A History of Provençal Life and Literature in the Middle Ages* appeared in 1878. In subsequent years, Hueffer would publish many other such studies. But early works like these already lent him enough authority that, in 1880, he could publish his *Lectures on Troubadours at the Royal Institution*. Advances in scholarship and the self-definition of the field as a profession would shortly make such appointments less likely, and it is noteworthy that whereas Hueffer could lecture at the Royal Institution, Pound (albeit a young and unestablished figure) was lucky to get a stint as lecturer for the London Polytechnic.

but mistake its purpose, because they miss the tradition in which and for which it was written.[6]

In this extended sense, the notion of romance joined Pound not only to such popularizers as Hueffer, but also to Ruskin and such of his revisionists as Pater or Symonds.[7] Call it "popularized scholarship," but it shaped Pound's ideas about the significance of romance for the modern world, as it did the ideas of the preceding generation; moreover, it provided the young Pound with a model for how one established oneself as an authority on poetry and on the tradition. As Marianne Korn notes, Pound "consulted" Mackail's *Latin Literature* (1895) "throughout the composition of his own book, as a generic model for a period study in literary history aimed at the general reader."[8] *The Spirit of Romance* was a highly self-conscious book, conceived and executed within a genre that an earlier audience would have recognized, but which has since wholly faded from popular memory. Like much of Pound's work that now seems idiosyncratic or brashly original, his romance studies derived from his most conservative tendencies. Dekker observes that "the faith in popularization of which [*The Spirit of Romance*] is a manifestation did not survive Pound's days as an apprentice poet; and, indeed, the faith in popularization in general seems to have died out in scholarly circles (in English speaking countries anyway)."[9] Pound, however, kept that faith. His first published essay, "Raphaelite Latin," defended the "dilettante" against "the scholar" who "is bowed down to this Germanic ideal."[10] In 1909, he told his father that he hoped *The Spirit of Romance* would "cauterize" German scholars;[11] although that hope was not fulfilled, he afterward attempted two

---

6. See the account of Symonds in *The Oxford Companion to English Literature*, 5th ed., ed. Margaret Drabble (Oxford: Oxford University Press, 1985), 956–57.

7. Wyndham Lewis too discerned in the notion of "romance" a major issue for his time. He also believed that in Pound's case it represented a definitive and pernicious influence. Lewis called the first chapter of his 1927 attack on Pound "Some of the Meanings of Romance." See Lewis, *Time and Western Man* (London, 1927); new edition ed. Paul Edwards (Santa Rosa, Calif.: Black Sparrow, 1993).

8. Marianne Korn, *Ezra Pound: Purpose/Form/Meaning* (London: Pembridge Press, 1983), 40. John William Mackail, the author of *Latin Literature*, was of course the translator of Homer mentioned above: indeed, his translation of the *Odyssey* was one of the only four complete verse translations published in English in the first half of the twentieth century. Mackail is not, in other words, a good example of the "popularizer" in its pejorative sense, although he retained a sense of the value of general knowledge.

9. Dekker, *Sailing after Knowledge*, 112.

10. "Raphaelite Latin," *Book News Monthly* 25, no. 1 (September 1906): 31–34.

11. Humphrey Carpenter, *A Serious Character: The Life of Ezra Pound* (Boston: Houghton Mifflin, 1988), 125.

further studies of romance—the "Gironde" and "Cavalcanti" projects. By 1917 he had grown defiant. In the third installment of "Provincialism the Enemy," as he declared that "the ultimate goal of scholarship is popularization," he anticipated drawing "groans from the scholar, the aesthete, the connoisseur!" But rather than offer apologies, Pound dismissed the lot as themselves characters of a most provincial type. "Fitzgerald's 'Omar,'" he explained,

> is worth all the Persian scholarship of a century. Yet, in my undergraduate days I was accustomed to hear England damned as an unscholarly country, and to be told that practically no authoritative books on any subject had come out of England for many decades. This may, for all I know, be, from some angles, true, but a harping on this point of view shows an ill-sense of proportion. I am not saying that nine hundred small philologists and researchers should all of them have been trying to be second and third Fitzgeralds. I do say that all literary research should look toward and long for some such consummation, and that only with such a hope can it be healthy and properly oriented. And in every department of scholarship or of life I demand a similar orientation. (SE, 198)[12]

The longing for consummation that Pound demanded "from every department of scholarship or of life" reflects his dreams of totality, and those dreams shaped the peculiar significance he attached to popularization. Far from being marginal to his main project, the work of popularization occupied a sustained and central position in Pound's activity as a writer, informing the generic experiments of the *Cantos* as well as of his programmatic prose. Popularization became for him a weapon against provincialism: a means of fostering a world fit to produce great art, and so greatness of soul.

Although Pound's efforts did little to rejuvenate scholarly faith in general knowledge, after a century of scholarly condescension, bookstores still provide titles of the "difficult made easy" sort in most disciplines, and the business of popularization remains a staple of the book trade. This is not to say that we should suddenly start admiring these writings for their "literary" value, or that we should learn to overlook the simple fact that most of these books, nowadays at least, are published for no nobler purpose than the

---

12. Ezra Pound, "Provincialism the Enemy III." Originally published in the *New Age*, 26 July 1917.

making of money. Indeed, that vulgarity of purpose largely accounts for the decline of the genre in relation to those genres respected by "serious" or "literary" writers. Nevertheless, it matters to see that the genre has changed and that popularization has not always meant exploitation. Pound himself came of age reading earnest and high-minded popularizers. In the mid-nineteenth century, popularization attracted some of the best minds of the time—not only poets like Fitzgerald, but also intellectuals like Martineau, Ruskin, Huxley, or Shaw. But after the Great War such activity was increasingly left to journalists and "hack" writers, literary jobbers hired out by publishers to provide a marketable commodity. It is no irony here that *Guide to Kulchur* was one of the few books for which Pound had a contract before he started writing.[13]

The insistence of Pound's popularizing impulse does not, simply, contradict the elitism documented by Longenbach in his study of the Stone Cottage years. It suggests rather the need to rethink the opposition between popular and elite "culture." Pound's elitism can be understood as an attempt to transform himself more perfectly into the popular conception of "the poet": once acquired, that persona would lend him the kind of authority which he believed necessary to pursue his ambitions. More fundamentally, the tension between Pound's mandarin and populist impulses was generated by the history already carried within the idea of "culture." There is much in Pound's talk of artists as "the antennae of the race"[14] to suggest the kind of synthesis that a John Stuart Mill might attempt, an attempt to demonstrate the "utility" of culture. The implications of Pound's postwar determination to develop "a profounder didacticism" resisted the traditional opposition between didactic and aesthetic writing. By the time that he was writing the *Guide*, Pound frequently described the *Cantos* as though it were itself a kind of primer. A letter of 1937 suggests a conscious contrast between the "elite" culture of Eliot's *Waste Land*—which its explanatory notes—and the *Cantos*: Pound wrote that "part of the job is *finally* to get all the necessary notes into the text itself."[15] Pound often liked to discuss "the writer's task," but the word "job" as he uses it here has more quotidian and worklike connotations. That Pound's epic does not provide most readers with "all the necessary

---

13. See Pound's letter to Frank Morley in *SL*, 288 and 294, and also Carpenter's *Serious Character*, 542.

14. See "Henry James" (originally published as "A Shake Down," *Little Review* 4 [August 1918]: 62–64), reprinted in *LE*; and "Murder by Capital," *Criterion* 12, no. 49 (July 1933): 585–92, reprinted in *SP*.

15. See Pound's letter to John Lackay Brown, April 1937, in *SL*, 293.

notes" is not beside the point; it is rather testimony that the generic experiments by which Pound hoped to produce his "profounder didacticism" had failed.

A Proliferation of Alphabets

Bad economics are complicated . . . good
economics are simple.
    —Ezra Pound, "Ezra's Easy Economics"
    (1934)

By the thirties Pound was regularly combining the generic features of his popularizing and poetic writings, proof that his explanatory activity was no departure from his true vocation. During the thirties Pound produced both kinds of work at a furious pace. Especially considering that his work as an anthologist was itself a form of polemic, hardly a year passed without bringing from him some attempt to expound fundamentals. In the years bounded by *A Draft of XXX Cantos* and *Cantos LII–LXXI* there appeared: "How to Read" (1931), *Profile* (1932), *ABC of Economics* (1933), *Active Anthology* (1933), *ABC of Reading* (1934), "Child's Guide to Economics" (1934), *Social Credit: An Impact* (1935), *Jefferson and/or Mussolini: Volitionist Economics* (1935), "Moneta Fascista" (1936), *Ta Hio* (1936), "L'economia ortologica" (1937), *Guide to Kulchur* (1938), *What is Money For* (1939), and the *Introductory Textbook* (1939). Of these titles, only *Active Anthology* does not overtly address itself at least in part to political-economic questions. In its concern with economic principles, this body of work participated in a genre heavily trafficked then, and still busy today, albeit more often in the form of textbooks than in primers for the general public. In Pound's time it comprised a body of frequently (but by no means usually) passionate writing that sought to check the growing divergence of economic discourse from common parlance.

    The popular exposition of economic principles is nearly as old as modern economic science. Arguably, the political economists of the eighteenth century needed no such redaction; but with the abstractly theoretical work of David Ricardo, economics began to emerge as a distant, and distinctly inaccessible, discourse. Indeed, the first popular primer marketed as such appeared only a year after Ricardo's influential *Essay of the Importance of a Low*

Price of Corn on the Profits of Stock (1815). Jane Haldimand Marcet (1769–1858) was just then beginning a long career as a popularizer. Most of her dozen or more books were written as "Conversations," the form which since the Renaissance had generally been deemed most appropriate for the education of "the gentler sex."[16] Marcet's *Conversations on Political Economy, in which the Elements of that Science are Familiarly Explained* (1816) was hugely successful. Her success attracted numerous imitators, including the formidable Harriet Martineau. Serialized from 1832 to 1835, Martineau's *Illustrations of Political Economy* (25 volumes) discarded the conversation mode for exemplary fables and simple fictional narratives, and regularly sold up to ten thousand copies of its monthly installments. Sheer length, however, rendered her *Illustrations* ineffective as a primer, so that when John Ramsey McCullough surveyed the field in 1845, he pronounced Marcet's *Conversations* to be "the best introduction to the science that has yet appeared."[17]

But although Marcet was instrumental in establishing the economic primer as a genre, few subsequent writers showed much interest in the conversation as form or vehicle. Richard Whately's *Easy Lessons on Money Matters for the Use of Young People* (1833), for instance, published by the Church of England's Society for Promoting Christian Knowledge (and which remained in print for twenty-two years), adopted a more directly pedantic approach. Writers seeking an adult audience, but still interested in promoting "Christian Knowledge," tended to follow Martineau's example rather than Marcet's, exploiting the traditional association of fables with moral instruction. Most eminent among these are the economic primers of John Ruskin—*A Joy Forever* (1857, 1880), *Unto This Last* (1860, 1862), and *Munera Pulveris* (1863, 1872). That Ruskin's discussions of political economy can be read today without relation to other books of the kind says much

---

16. For discussion of the historical association of the "Conversation," as a literary genre, with writing for women, see Isabel Rivers, ed., *Books and Their Readers in Eighteenth Century Britain* (New York: St. Martin's, 1982), especially the essays by Terry Belanger, Pat Rogers, and John Valdimir Price. Marcet's other "Conversations" show a consistent interest in the "scientific" engaging: chemistry; mineralogy; natural philosophy; the Evidences of Christianity; Vegetable Philosophy; Grammar; Chronology; Scenes in Nature; Animals, Vegetables and Minerals; Harmony; and Land and Water. Most primers tended to explain "scientific" knowledge, although this was not consistently true. In 1862, for instance, the fortuitously named A. B. Child wrote an *ABC of Life*; but by the 1880s the genre was more usually associated with the unfamiliar, the scientific, or the scientist.

17. *The Literature of Political Economy* (London: Longman, Brown, Green & Longmans, 1845),
18. McCullough himself, incidentally, published an economic primer in 1870. As for Harriet Martineau, twenty-five volumes did not exhaust her interest in writing about economics; in 1834 she published the five-volume *Illustrations of Taxation* (1834).

about his talent, but it also demonstrates the generic variety of nineteenth-century economic primers. That variety was not to endure. The generic features of popularizing discourse were available for innovation only so long as the principles of political economy themselves appeared stable.

That stability shattered in the last quarter of the century. In promulgating the principle of "marginalism," theorists such as W. S. Jevons, Carl Menger, and Leon Walras rendered classical political economy obsolete. Their professional success changed popular economic discourse forever. Thereafter, economic primers appeared to compensate for the new uncertainties of their subject by becoming themselves predictably "generic." Marginalist theory also helped create an arena for contests that were, from a professional view, utterly illegitimate. The popular exposition of economics became newly available to the factitiousness of political conviction, and an unprecedented outpouring of economic handbooks and primers followed. Even Alfred Marshall's synthesis of political economy with the economics of marginalism (*Principles of Economics: An Introductory Volume*, 1890), which prepared the ground for neoclassical economics, did not thereafter slow the production of these books. Among the "alternative" economic models that appeared in the early twentieth century, promising to restore certainty, promising that economics is after all fundamentally simple, must be numbered those of such Poundian heroes as C. H. Douglas and Silvio Gesell.

At this point, a short catalog suffices to suggest the relation of such primers to Pound's. Looking first to instances prior to Orage's *Alphabet of Economics* (1917), which may have first fixed Pound's attention on writing of this kind, we might cite such books as Simon Newcomb's *ABC of Finance; or, the Money and Labor Questions Familiarly Explained to Common People in Short and Easy Lessons* (1877); Graham McAdam's *Alphabet in Finance: A Simple Statement of Permanent Principles and Their Application to Questions of the Day* (1880); Phillip Henry Wicksteed's *Alphabet of Economic Science: Elements of the Theory of Value or Worth* (1888), which was atypical in its insistence on a first "forty pages of almost unbroken mathematics"; Andrew Carnegie's *ABC of Money* (1891), George Coffin's *ABC of Banks and Banking* (1903); J. A. Hobson's *Science of Wealth* (published in 1911 as part of Williams and Norgate's "Home Universal Library"); or *The ABC of the Federal Reserve System* (1918) by E. W. Kemmerer—who alone between 1910 and 1940 authored seven primers, and some dozen other economic studies.[18]

---

18. Wicksteed and Kemmerer are interesting examples of those authors doing "economics-made-simple," for both were also respected economists. Indeed, others of Wicksteed's books, such

This sampling of the titles only begins to represent the activity of late-century primers and hardly mentions the profusion of still cheaper pamphlets. Some of these were done solely for profit, others were published by various benevolent organizations—most notably by the Fabian Society, which saw education as the spearhead for the forces of socialist change. Under the leadership of Beatrice and Sydney Webb, the Fabians founded the London School of Economics (1895), and after the *Fabian Essays* of 1894, programmatically issued topical tracts, distinctive in their utilitarian reliance on statistical evidence.

But although the Fabians laid the foundation for the British welfare state, their activity had little impact on the discourse of popularization. Indeed, by comparison with nineteenth-century models, the economic primers of the early twentieth century were vulgar—and that vulgarity increased with mounting social tensions. In the first quarter of the twentieth century the genre came to be very attractive to conservative thinkers, insofar as it offered a means of opposing the popular appeal of first socialist and then Marxist critiques of capitalism; of course, socialist or Marxist critiques themselves sometimes took the form of popular primers, as with Harvey Moyer's *ABC of Socialism* (1900), Nikolai Bukharin's *ABC of Communism* (English edition 1921), or Alexander Berkman's *ABC of Communist Anarchism* (1937). We can discern something of the strength of this appeal in the ease with which, by 1912, Rudyard Kipling could adapt it for his dystopian story "Easy as ABC"[19]—or in the even more unlikely fact that W. B. Yeats originally intended to title his "little philosophical book" *Per Amica Silentia Lunae* (1917), "An Alphabet." In 1924 the Catholic distributivist Hilaire Belloc published *An Economic Guide for Young People*; four years later the Fabian Shaw offered his opinions about distribution in *The Intelligent Woman's Guide to Socialism and Capitalism* (1928). Not surprisingly, the economic turmoil of

---

as *The Commonsense of Political Economy* (1910), although similar to the primers in title, are in fact writing of a very different kind. Kemmerer's *ABC of the Federal Reserve System* was published by Princeton University Press; he was a professor at Cornell from 1906 to 1912, and at Princeton from 1912 to 1943; he became chairman of the American Financial Commission, and in 1926 was president of the American Economic Association. The publication of handbooks in such series was a regular and sometimes regularizing feature of the genre. Kemmerer, in particular, frequently published books as numbers in a series of handbooks for the general reader, but neither he nor Hobson were singular in this regard: Newcomb's *ABC of Finance* appeared in Harper's "Half Hour Series"; and McAdam's *Alphabet in Finance* (reprinted five times by 1884) was one of Putnam's "Popular Manuals."

19. The story is reprinted in *A Diversity of Creatures*, vol. 26 of *The Writings in Prose and Verse of Rudyard Kipling* (New York: Charles Scribner's Sons, 1917).

the thirties occasioned the publication of a renewed welter of such economic primers, books like George Clare's *ABC of the Foreign Exchanges* (1931), J. S. Wardlaw-Milne's *ABC of £.s.d.: The Plain Man's Guide to the Money Problem* (1931), Harvey Sieg's *ABC of Wall Street* (1935), G.D.H. Cole's *Intelligent Man's Guide Through World Chaos* (1932)—or his *What Everybody Wants to Know about Money* (1933), or Louis Lebenthal's *ABC of Municipal Bonds* (1937). These primers were ready to reassure a confused public that despite Western economic collapse, the fundamentals of investment and exchange were yet comprehensible matters. In this welter were numerous books by "social creditors" known to Orage—and to Pound. Elisabeth Sage Holter offered her own version of *The ABC of Social Credit* (1934). About the same time, Albert Newsome published "a glossary for the plain man," which he titled, formulaically enough, *An Alphabet of the New Economics*. Philip Mairet, a frequent contributor to the *New Age* and later one of Orage's biographers, also prepared a "handbook . . . outlining Social Credit": *The Douglas Manual* (1934). As Europe convulsed again in war, even the symbolist poet F. S. Flint published a pamphlet on economics—"Economic Equilibrium."

Holter's *ABC of Social Credit* is representative. Appearing in both an English and an American edition, and contemporaneous with Pound's economic handbooks, it offered "an introduction to the plan set forth in Social Credit by C. H. Douglas." But although Holter's book praised Douglas's ideas, it departed from his arguments. Economics handbooks by definition must suppose that economic privation is unnecessary, but in Holter's case this supposition was joined to Douglas's theorem that privation resulted on the national level from bad accounting rather than any paucity of resources. Holter thus emphasized (as Pound also often did) Douglas's claim that the modern world was in fact an age of plenty, and went on to argue that "in an age of plenty the only proper function of an economic system is to produce the goods and services required with the least possible expenditure of effort." Consequently, "it is the aim of Social Credit to restrict the economic system to this proper function." "After all," she continued, "there is nothing esoteric about Economics. As its etymology implies, it is only the law of the household writ large."[20]

Here again it is not Holter's ideas that were important; they were general

20. *The ABC of Social Credit* (New York: Coward, McCann, 1934), 77–78. The assumption of natural abundance is common through most Ruskinian economic studies, and though Pound had always rejected the idea of material scarcity, he did so more vehemently and frequently during the mid-thirties—the period of Holter's and most other Social Credit primers; see Pound's "Loeb Report (A Refresher)," *New English Weekly*, 2 February 1936, or his "Man vs. Merchandise: Fascism in Action," *British-Italian Bulletin*, 13 June 1936.

even beyond the focus of Social Credit, and they were ancient. But in reminding her readers of the etymology of "economics" she was not so much proposing the household as the model for political economy as she was striving to domesticate a scientific and specialized discourse. In this respect too Holter's work was anything but original: writers of economic primers had been adopting such strategy for much the same purpose for over fifty years. In 1886, for instance, R. R. Bowker published an *Economics for the People: Being Plain Talks on Economics, Especially for Use in Business, in Schools, and in Women's Reading Classes*. For all its detail, Bowker's title did not exactly single out a specific audience—it wasn't meant to: it functioned rather to advertise the broad utility of Bowker's explanations. Bowker began his book autobiographically, recounting boyhood adventures in the buying and selling of postage stamps, the account of which led him to etymologize "economy." But neither in Holter's case or in Bowker's was this etymology a gesture toward history. Instead, most of these manuals worked to persuade their readers that historical knowledge was unnecessary for the understanding of economic principles, and worked to disseminate them by overt heuristic models. These models often related accounts of small enterprise similar to Bowker's, but they could also take a more exotic or metaphysical turn. Wicksteed thus imagined the situation of Robinson Crusoe, and both Alan Dane (*Economics for Boys and Girls*, 1935) and Gorham Munson (*Aladdin's Lamp*, 1945) developed explanations around the motif of Aladdin's genie-haunted lamp, in rather different attempts to reduce problems of monetary exchange to first principles.

Pound too sometimes developed his explanations around exotic metaphors, as in his unfortunate "Dam Nigger and the Banana Tree" (1936); but generally his pedantics diverged from such models, both because of his determination that the case for economic reform or for Social Credit in particular could be improved by a knowledge of history and because his concern with cultural integrity led him to substitute an "ideogrammic" presentation for the more familiar constructions of expository writing. But even here many of Pound's departures had precedent, for the body of popular economic handbooks manifested the turbulence of more specialized economic contention.

By 1932 books of this kind were appearing with such frequency that Eliot too took notice, giving to them the whole of his "Commentary" in the January *Criterion*.

> For the last few months we have been peppered with a succession of little books on financial and economic problems; little books aimed

at that large part of the "reading public" which normally is not only ignorant of such matters, but prefers to remain so. I myself am normally ignorant as anybody, with the normal disinclination to take up any subject which I did not study in my youth. But the repeated impact of these small books upon the eye cannot fail to make an impression on the conscience. Of old it seemed that the economists preferred to discuss their mysteries among themselves, and in two-volume works priced from fifteen to thirty shillings; and that was a happy age for the man who desired to know nothing of their subject. But now economists issue into the market-place to harangue and convert the people; they almost buttonhole you, by publishing these modest volumes which seem to say "it is now *your* duty to learn what's what in these deep matters; I am just the book to make it all clear even to your intelligence, written down exactly to your level."

Bantering aside, Eliot regarded the appearance of these economic primers as a new development and was vaguely suspicious of the intrusion of "market-place" interests into what had hitherto been a scientific field. There was no single instance that Eliot found important, but "the repeated impact" of many. The four primers Eliot chose to discuss were all "unorthodox": Angell and Wright's *Can Governments Cure Unemployment?* Baker's *Money and Prices*, Demant's *This Unemployment*, and Hobson's *Poverty in Plenty*. Eliot found all of them unsatisfactory. Nevertheless, he took an extended interest in Hobson's work, not just because Hobson was also a "serious" economist, but because Hobson found the privation of the thirties to stem from "profound" rather than material origins.[21] "My thesis," Hobson wrote, "is that our main economic troubles are of a distinctly moral origin."

John Atkinson Hobson (1858–1940) figures prominently among the mediators of Ruskin's early twentieth-century reception. He was explicit about his debt to Ruskin, and determined to resist "the growing tendency to endeavor to convert Economics into a purely quantitative science."[22] What Hobson called for—and he himself understood this to be "the basic thought" that he drew from Ruskin—was "the necessity of going behind the current monetary estimates of wealth, cost and utility, to reach the body

---

21. Tim Redman has also discussed Hobson's work from the perspective of Douglas and Pound in *Ezra Pound and Italian Fascism* (Cambridge: Cambridge University Press, 1991), 59–60. Redman accounts for the profusion of popular economic primers by observing the extent to which "the Depression did much to discredit the economics profession" (58).

22. Hobson, *Free Thought in the Social Sciences* (New York: Macmillan, 1926), 112.

of human benefits and satisfaction which give them real meaning."[23] He published his monograph *John Ruskin: Social Reformer* two years before Ruskin's death; by the time Eliot was reviewing *Poverty in Plenty* he had published nearly forty books, struggling throughout to associate Ruskinian organicism with his own mathematical and rationalist bent. But however trenchantly Ruskin motivated his thinking, Hobson never strove for the ideal of *Fors Clavigera*: he did not attempt to move from chance observations to the vision of cultural totality. For all that it challenged classical economics, Hobson's work continued to seek out (in vain, for the most part) the professional audience. Pound's primers did not. Instead, Pound sought to disgrace professional economics by appealing directly to the greater public. His procedures were Ruskinian, but because Pound proved in certain ways more Ruskinian than Ruskin, because he seized upon the most "aesthetic" qualities of Ruskin's writing, the tendency to develop his position from "chance" illustrations took on a different function.

Pound's *Social Credit: An Impact* (May 1935) exemplifies this difference. Dedicated to "the Green Shirts of England," it first presents a "motto" ("'The Earth belongs to the living'—T. Jefferson"), and then definitions of Douglas's notions of "increment of association" and "cultural heritage": all of which functions as an epigraph to guide the reader's response to what follows. This initial strategy distinguishes Pound's primer from such books as Hobson's and the others reviewed by Eliot. To compare *An Impact* with other tracts for Social Credit, like Holter's, is to see that whereas the latter strove to present the unfamiliar in familiar terms, to explain Douglas's ideas in a manner calculated to anticipate the prejudices of the average reader, Pound's text works from the start to assail preconceptions and to change—more than what the reader thinks about economics—the very *way* that the reader thinks about economics and his or her relation to it.

The Impact of Fact, or History as Table Talk

Poetry is not greatly concerned with what a
man thinks; but with what is so imbedded in
his nature that it never occurs to him to

---

23. Hobson, *Confessions of an Economic Heretic* (London: G. Allen & Unwin, 1938), 42.

question it; not a matter of which idea he
holds but of the depth at which he holds it.
        —Ezra Pound, *Profile* (1932)

That Pound's "profounder didacticism" aimed to change the *way* his readers thought was not absolutely out of keeping with the premises of the popularizing handbook; it shared with them what Eliot recognized as an assumption that its reader hitherto had been uninterested in economic discussion. Uninterest, of course, often follows from incomprehension or intimidation and, unlike Holter, Pound did nothing to mitigate such feelings. But Pound presumed that popular ignorance of economics existed not because of its perceived difficulty but, more fundamentally, because of the popular perception of economics as an isolated field of interest only to specialists.

This was the attitude that Pound's economic primers set out to change. Consider the salvos that open *Social Credit: An Impact*:

> An epic is a poem including history.
>
> No one can understand history without understanding economics. Gibbon's History of Rome is a meaningless jumble till a man has read Douglas.
>
> My generation (that born in the 1880's) was dragged up in black ignorance of economics, an ignorance in part of the product of malice, in part of sheer sloth and incompetence.

Few of Pound's readers could have understood why a work ostensibly devoted to Social Credit would begin with a definition of epic, except perhaps to grumble that poets find their craft in everything. Nevertheless, this opening derives from Pound's understanding of an epic as a poem able to engage the totality of human relations. So it was that, further on, Pound insisted that "certain facts must stand in the common tongue. These root facts must go to the PEOPLE, they must go into the one everlasting repository, the MIND of the people. They must go into the folk-lore, into men's proverbs." The realm of folklore and proverb is the realm in which Pound hoped to situate the greater part of his work—an observation that suggests that Gertrude Stein was more right than she knew when she described Pound as "the village explainer." Folklore he assumed, was woven from the very fabric of everyday life, and implied a *whole* way of life.

Pound's understanding of folklore resonated with longer-held notions about "epic," but ironically his growing interest in oral forms would remove him yet further from the broader audience he imagined. His incorporation of anthropological observations into his poem not only tended to distance him from the experience of most readers, but introduced the additional mediation of anthropological detachment. Sometimes the pursuit of folklore led him to disregard his own judgment; sometimes it prompted him to reinterpret earlier enthusiasms. Thus he devoted section 48 of *Guide to Kulchur* to Doughty's *Arabia Deserta*, even through Pound himself found Doughty "a bore," and declared in section 49 that the modernity of Confucius lay "in his interest in folk-lore." Indeed, Pound continued, "all this Frazer-Frobenius research is Confucian" (*GK*, 272). These claims refer to Pound's more celebrated definition of culture as "what is left after man has forgotten all he set out to learn" (*GK*, 195), "culture possessed and forgotten" (*GK*, 98).

Folklore is then for Pound an entangled bank wherein one might discern the totality of cultural relations, and *Guide to Kulchur* frequently returns to it to dispute the value of systematic knowledge. Largely on the richness of its evidence, Pound moved on to "dissociate" knowledge from both "true" understanding and from "culture." "Knowledge" he dismissed as the product of mechanism and rote, of dead catalogues, abstraction, and system; "understanding," by contrast, he held to develop from lived experience and "process." The opposition is familiar, and having so defined it against the vital and the whole, it is hardly surprising that Pound insisted too that "knowledge is not culture. The domain of culture begins when one HAS 'forgotten-what-book'" (*GK*, 134).[24] This attitude was not new to Pound's work; in a 1920 essay on Arthur Symons, for instance, Pound asserted that "one remembers a poem in broken lines and by phrases," and professed that he was "deliberately beginning this essay from memory."[25] But whereas in earlier statements it can seem a mere flaunting of his own sensibility, by the thirties it had come to represent for him an immediate and vital way of knowing. This valorization of the oral informs Pound's concern that Confucius passed his wisdom on "directly" through interlocutors, and that these

---

24. Isolated from living process, and identified with the factitious, "knowledge" much resembles what François Lyotard calls "information" in his *Postmodern Condition: A Report on Knowledge*, trans. Geoff Bennington (Minneapolis: University of Minnesota Press, 1984). In Lyotard's distinction between knowledge and information the latter term denotes that which can be stored and processed by the machinery of the postmodern age. The opposition serves his "report" much as Pound's served his "guide": the opposition reinscribes romantic rhetoric, depending on binary oppositions that include the primary one between culture and civilization (see the first sentence of Lyotard's report), and positing a kind of unity for the age, albeit in a purportedly qualified fashion.

25. "Arthur Symons," *Athenaeum*, 21 May 1920.

men were not interested in knowledge but were "responsible," and thought "for the whole social order" (*GK*, 29). Here again, Pound was working to identify a totality of experience and doing so in a way that followed the century-old examples of, say, Coleridge's *Table-Talk*, or of Carlyle's displacing of the profound truths of experience from intellect and reason to intuition and temperament. The opposition reenacts the difference between Teufelsdröckh and his editor (*Sartor Resartus*), or between Monk Samson and modern utilitarian government (*Past and Present*).

Pound's suspicions, however, extend to the sovereignty of writing itself. In both his prose primers and in the *Cantos* he sought to work back through his source texts and recover the immediacy of speech and conversation.[26] Pound's histories sought, in effect, to reverse the academic process of recorded history, which strives to sort out "facts" from hearsay. Pound sought to detranscribe facts back into conversation. One might say that Pound was reviving the oral model of Herodotus, opposing it to the academic model of documents and statistics. Pound's work contains elements of formal histories, but it uses them in ways that emphasize the process of verbal transmission, which though susceptible to distortion, was more proof against destruction than the written record. Unlike written histories, the oral record of "culture" embodied the accumulated wisdom of the ages, and so—Pound believed—was impervious to ideological manipulation. As Pound argued in the second section of *Guide*, "The New Learning":

> It may or may not matter that the first knowledge [of history] is direct, it remains effortlessly as residuum, as part of my total disposition, it affects every perception of form-colour phenomena subsequent to its acquisition.
>
> Coming even closer to things committed verbally to our memory. There are passages of the poets which approximate the form-colour acquisition.
>
> And herein is clue to Confucius' reiterated commendation of such of his students as studied the Odes.
>
> He demanded or commended a type of perception, a kind of trans-

---

26. Allen Tate had described something of this aspect of the *Cantos* in his review of *A Draft of XXX Cantos*: see "Ezra Pound's Golden Ass," in the *Nation*, 10 June 1931, 632–34. Tate wrote that "the *Cantos* are talk, talk, talk; not by anyone in particular to anyone else in particular; they are just rambling talk. At least each canto is a cunningly devised imitation of polite conversation, in which no one presses any subject very far."

mission of knowledge obtainable only from such concrete manifestation. (*GK*, 28)

In this metonymical "axis," as Pound would have it (*GK*, 195), the term "concrete" emphasizes immediate, firsthand perception more than it does monumental presence. It means writing "coming ever closer to things committed verbally to our memory." Pound's idea of a "total disposition" reiterates his model of "kulchur" not only with regard to the totality of relations, but also by underscoring its essentially irrational, or more than "merely" rational, nature ("disposition").

The popular image of Pound's elitism (Bob Dylan, for example, singing of Pound and Eliot "fighting in the captain's tower," aloof and isolated from the common lot) makes this view seem ironic. Yet Pound was peculiarly anti-intellectual, peculiarly because his was an anti-intellectualism rooted in arcane symbolist prejudice against reason. Pound's totalizing ambitions, and his impatience with "mere" ideas, account for much of the apparent quirkiness of his didactic work. For example, in any traditional handbook, the chapter called "Culture"—in a book called *Guide to Kulchur*—would be self-evidently crucial. But Pound's chapter, "The Culture of an Age is what you can pick up and/or get in touch with, by talk with the most intelligent men of the period?" provides little more than a page of conversational fragments about such topics as the wife of "the Geheimrat." Precisely this combination of apparent levity and opaque erudition in *Guide to Kulchur* has led to its neglect both popular and scholarly. To be sure, the chapter would be of little help to Pound's general reader. But it functions adequately enough according to Pound's own implicit premises; its levity militates against "highbrow" circumscriptions, and the randomness of Pound's examples reflects his confidence that from any fragment the true critic (the Carlylian or Ruskinian seer) *can* reproduce the culture of an age. "Real knowledge goes into natural man in tit bits," Pound affirmed (*GK*, 99), and his treatment of the Adams-Jefferson correspondence in the *Pagany* cantos as scraps of conversation exemplifies how this same conviction was already leaving its impress on the *Cantos*.

Pound's antagonism to "mere ideas" relates as well to his decision to focus on the "impact" of Social Credit rather than provide an analysis of its fundamental ideas. In Pound's view the "impact" of ideas may distort them, but it is precisely as ideas go into action that they gain force. One of Pound's most commonly used phrases in both the *Cantos* and in his prose is "out of," as in "Out of Zeno, out of the dogged as does it system results may have emerged." Pound's interest is in what comes "out of" something rather than in what that thing may be, or mean, in and of itself. The paratactic configurations of Pound's primers and of the *Cantos* in this way offer themselves more as seismometers than proper digests. Examples abound: in the preface to the *Guide*, he writes that no other single man's effort "registered" as did Sigismundo Malatesta's; as appendix to the *Guide* he lists "As Sextant" four books without which a "sane man" cannot "measure the force" of other books. Indeed, when he invokes such seismographic metaphors as "Blast" or describes the *Cantos* as a "cosmographic volcano" he engages in just this kind of thinking.

In the *Guide*, this displacement of "truth" from the realm of writing and reason to that of lived experience becomes central. Pound's etymology of the ideogram "to study" offers a convenient example. "The dominant element in the sign for learning in the love of learning chapter is," he explained, "a mortar," meaning that "knowledge must be ground into a fine powder" (*GK*, 24). Later, Pound treats Zeno, Epicurus, and Pythagorus in a like manner, proposing that they each taught "a modus vivendi, did advocate modes of life, and did not merely argue about certain abstractions" (*GK*, 25). His point is that the label "philosopher" misrepresents these teachers, since they considered the totality of human relations, whereas "philosophy as the word is currently used means a highbrow study, something cut off from both life and from wisdom." This prejudice against "philosophy" is closely akin to those against political economy or academic history. It is thus no accident that Pound should move from such a distinction to an observation about the nature of epic: "the shored relics of a very human and high state of culture as immortalized in the *Iliad* and the *Odyssey*" (*GK*, 24). The epic remained for him the one form inclusive enough to be able to register the impact of ideas from and upon all aspects of human endeavor, and from and upon the relations between them.

In both *Social Credit: An Impact* and the *Guide*, the nature of epic enters into Pound's presentation of his most fundamental concerns, and in *ABC of Reading* he turns to epic to illustrate why anyone should study literature (*ABCR*, 15). Pound's didactic prose tracts typically turn on the opposition between cultural totality and utilitarian mechanism; in *Social Credit* the utilitarians appear as "amoral technocrats [who] have gathered statistics of production"; in the *Guide* they emerge as the obscurantists who are "ever muddling and muddying terminologies, ever trotting out minor issues to obscure the main and basic, ever prattling of short range causation for the sake of, or with the result of, obscuring the vital truth" (*GK*, 31). Within the paradigm of "culture" that Pound was developing, "vitality" is always a synecdochical trope for ideal totality, as in *Social Credit*, for instance, where Pound refers to "the vitality, the *whole* health of a nation" (emphasis added). A culture is vital when possessed of a sense of itself as a totality, "the perception of a whole age, of a whole congeries and sequence of causes" (*GK*, 136).

The point here is to provide neither a thematics for Pound's didactic prose nor a sketch about his ideas about culture so much as it is to observe: first, why "culture" was for him an important issue; second, how his assumptions about cultural totality informed his generic innovations. Pound himself was self-conscious about his departures from more usual expository practice and eager that they should not be (as they have so often been) confused with "mere" incoherence. Pound eschewed "cause and effect" exposition because he believed the sense of cultural totality to be inconceivable by strictly linear representation, and because his aim was to change how his readers perceived economics as much as what they thought about it. This objective derives, again, from fundamentally romantic precepts. But like Pound's ideas about economics, his ideas about "culture" were mediated by more contemporaneous figures. Numerous commentators have remarked the importance for Pound of Leo Frobenius (1873–1938), a German anthropologist especially concerned with the origins of culture. Because Frobenius is canonized both in the *Cantos* and in such didactic primers as the *Guide* or "The Jefferson-Adams Letters as a Shrine and a Monument," it is important to recognize how his work amplified—not only Pound's thematic motifs—but also his compositional and combinatory principles.

Frobenius and the Constructions of *Guide to Kulchur*

I reiterate our debt to Frobenius for his sense
of the reality in what is held in the general
mind.
    —Ezra Pound, *Guide to Kulchur* (1938)

Many of the singular generic features of Pound's didactic primers can be understood in reference to Frobenius's arguments about culture—although the principal values Pound discerned in Frobenius's work generally but confirmed his own implicit tendencies. Even the crucial emphasis on folklore was previously a part of Pound's practice, his reversion to something like the historiography of Herodotus.

Like the German idealists of the late Enlightenment, like Carlyle or Ruskin, or like Pound, Frobenius proposed that "there are two main ways of apprehending reality, which may be called the mechanistic and the intuitive."[27] Precisely because the distinction has become overfamiliar and apparently natural, it demands our further reflection. In his *Paideuma*, Frobenius explained the distinction in a way consonant with the Ruskin of *Fors Clavigera* or the Hobson of *The Social Problem*:

> In the mechanistic view the world consists of a system of facts which can be analysed into cause and effect, elements and combinations, and from which it is possible to deduce relationships of universal validity. It is a type of biological or psychological approach based on albumen tests, laws of association, motives and impulses, ganglion cells and nerve tissues, all duly classified and reduced to dry formulae. The intuitive observer, by contrast, seeks to enter with his whole being into the lawless profusion of spiritual activity, at the same time distinguishing the significant from the trivial, the expressive from the merely accidental. He surrenders to the inner logic of growth, evolution and maturity, a realm which system and experiment are powerless to unlock. Instead of petrified laws and formulae, he discovers symbolic events and types of living, breathing reality. (19)

The familiar binary opposition structures the argument and produces those conclusions which carry in them an inevitable response: the "mechanistic" world of "facts" is "dry" and dead; the "spiritual" world lives and breathes and transcends its opposite. More interesting is Frobenius's explanation that although "lawless," the cultural explanation can yet distinguish "the significant from the trivial, the expressive from the merely accidental." Instead of "laws," it produces "symbolic events." Although, in *Guide to Kulchur* and elsewhere, Pound liked to talk about uncovering the "causes" that drive cultural prosperity or decay, he relied on the juxtaposition of "luminous" details to outline the patterns of causation. In the language of "Pastiche: The Regional" (1919), where Pound first published his technique of historical

---

27. *Paideuma—Umrisse einer Kultur—und Seelenlehre* (1921), in *Leo Frobenius 1873–1973: An Anthology*, ed. Eike Haberland, trans. Patricia Crampton (Wiesbaden: Franz Steiner Verlag, 1973), 19.

"assemblage," "snippets of this kind build up our concept of wrong, of right, of history."[28]

Frobenius's valorization of the "symbolic event" reinscribes the principal patterns of the discourse of "culture." Consequently, Frobenius was for Pound another mediator rather than a "source." But Pound seized on the importance Frobenius attached to folklore and oral transmission with enthusiasm enough to alter the emphases of his work. Orality had already figured in Pound's work, but after reading Frobenius he invested it with unprecedented importance. Frobenius's assertions about the nature of poetic composition seem particularly to have registered: "True fables, myth and fairy tales present themselves to us in perfected form as an inheritance from remote ages" (*Paideuma*, 24). Their perfected form results, Frobenius thought, from their having developed as an expression of the entire culture. The stories of the civilized West lack such perfection because the nature of "literary" production isolates both author and reader: "Strictly speaking we no longer possess stories—we can only read them or, still worse, hear them recited at literary evenings. We have lost the world of living magic" (25). Moreover, whereas the literary story only tells "what happened once upon a time" and "once and for all," oral folktales "can happen today, tomorrow or yesterday" (26). "Clearly," Frobenius concludes, "the despised African is closer to a daemonic or intuitive apprehension of the core of his civilization than are we intellectualized Westerners, from whom the paideuma is hidden by an accumulation of soulless, objective facts" (27).

Each of these propositions suggested something salient about Pound's work after *Eleven New Cantos*. Frobenius's appreciation of the timelessness of folktales encouraged Pound to recover "symbolic events" from the constrictions of "literary" narrative history ("once upon a time" or "once and for all"). "The perfected form," which Frobenius believed the legacy of folk culture, helps explain many of the most obtrusive generic inclusions of the *Guide*. In chapter 34, for instance, Pound includes his own verse translation of Rudolf Prietze's text of a folktale of the Haussa tribe of the Sudan: "The Lioness Warns Her Cubs"; chapter 35 is comprised solely of Pound's verse translation of a folk song of the Siberian Teleuten, "Praise Song of the Buck-Hare"; chapter 36 ("Time Lag") includes Pound's translation of Pére Lacharmés' Latin transcription of a Confucian Ode—another example of Pound reading "through" a literary text to recover its oral origins. "Even from the Latin one cd. get [this much]" he implies, as he then cuts to the ode.

---

28. "Pastiche: The Regional," *New Age* 7 (21 August 1919): 284.

And, in chapter 37 ("The Culture of an Age is what you can pick up and/or get in touch with, by talk with the most intelligent men of the period?"), Pound presents scraps of a conversation between himself and none other than Frobenius. The "meaning" of these inclusions is not to be derived from any intrinsic thematic readings, but from the very fact of their inclusion.

These inclusions nevertheless remain problematic as constituent parts of a "guide" or primer. In "The Jefferson-Adams Letters as a Shrine and a Monument," Pound complained that "people often think me crazy when I make a jump instead of a step, just as if all jumps were unsound and never carried one anywhere." Interestingly enough, his complaint repeats Browning's famous protest to Ruskin: "I cannot begin writing poetry till my imaginary reader has conceded licenses to me which you demur at altogether. . . . You ought, I think, to keep pace with the thought tripping from ledge to ledge of my 'glaciers,' as you call them; not stand poking your alpen-stock into the holes and demonstrating that no foot could have stood there; suppose it sprang over there?"[29] But the parallel between Pound and Browning suggests, more than the similarities between them, the nature of Pound's generic reconceptualization, especially because in the same letter Browning allowed that the license he demanded for his poetry ought not to be allowed in prose. Pound's "ideogrammic" constructions thus exemplify what Siskin has described as the "lyricization" of postromantic genres, or Patey and Eagleton the accelerating dominance of the category of the "aesthetic."[30] Pound's inclusion of a lyrical organization of content in a popular primer reconceives one of the fundamental features of explanatory writing. The difficulties of Pound's didactic texts arise not so much from any difficulty of thought, willful obscurity, or perverseness of character, as they do from (to appropriate Hugh Kenner's language) self-interfering generic combinations.

In chapter 5 of the *Guide* ("ZWECK or the AIM") Pound proposed that "the value of Leo Frobenius to civilization is not for the rightness or wrongness of this opinion or that opinion but for the kind of thinking he does" (*GK*, 57). Quoting Frobenius's reflection that "where we found these rock drawings, there was always water within six feet of the surface," Pound

---

29. From Browning's letter to Ruskin of 10 December 1855; quoted in W. G. Collingwood, *The Life and Work of John Ruskin* (Cambridge: Riverside Press, 1893), 1:232–33.

30. See the introduction to Clifford Siskin's *Historicity of Romantic Discourse* (New York: Oxford University Press, 1988); Douglas Lane Patey's "Eighteenth Century Invents the Canon," *Modern Language Studies* 18, no. 1 (1988), 17–37; and Terry Eagleton's *Ideology of the Aesthetic* (Oxford: Basil Blackwell, 1990), esp. 1–12 and 366–415.

submitted that "that kind of research goes not only into the past and forgotten life, but points to tomorrow's water supply. This is not *mere* utilitarianism, it is a double charge, a sense of two sets of values and their relation"(*GK*, 57). The identification of "mere" utilitarianism implies, of course, the possibility of more desirable forms as well—of what Pound elsewhere calls "a profounder didacticism." Here too Pound and Frobenius share a series of binary oppositions, which lead both to similar valuations of the epic. "If," Frobenius explains in *Paideuma*, "we consider epic tales like that of Samba Gana, Gorobo Dike, Sambakullung or Gossi [all Sahel folk epics], we find them imbued with spiritual greatness: the heroism and energy of the main characters is not diminished by any philosophy imposed from without, but is governed and directed by their own inner qualities" (37). The opposition most pertinent here repeats romantic myth, opposing spiritual vision to "mere" ideology. But the emphasis on the essential directedness from within raises another important and related aspect of Pound's own arguments.

In "The Jefferson-Adams Letters as a Shrine and a Monument," an essay begun shortly after his completion of the *Guide*, Pound elaborated his idea of culture. When positing four periods of American history—civilization, decline, despair, and possibility of revival—Pound attributes America's decline to "a scission between the life of the mind and the life of the nation" (*SP*, 147). Pound saw "the possibilities of revival" as "starting perhaps with a valorization of our cultural heritage, not merely as something lost in dim retrospect, a tombstone tastily carved." In other words, "culture" was not to be objectified or commodified, but to be recognized "as a still workable dynamo." Here again is the Frobenian notion of culture as the still living, vital energy within. By now these words—culture, life, vitality, energy—should be recognized as a cluster of equivalences: defining the thing or idea in self-similar terms. Subsequently, Pound moves to attack the inevitable enemy: "In Italy there is current the adjective 'anti-storico' to describe unlikely proposals; ideologies hung in a vacuum or contrary to the natural order of events as conditioned by race, time, and geography." The rest of Pound's argument follows from here. As opposed to ideological and mechanical narratives, Pound discerned in the Jefferson-Adams correspondence a "total" account of American life:

> The MAIN implication is that they stand for a life not split into bits. Neither of these two men would have thought of literature as something having nothing to do with life, the nation, the organisa-

tion of government. Of course no first-rate author ever did think of his books in this manner. If he was a lyrist, he was crushed under a system; or he was speaking of every man's life in its depth; if he was Trollope or Flaubert he was thinking of history without the defects of generic books by historians which miss the pith and point of the story. . . . In fact the whole of Flaubert, the whole of the fight for the novel as "histoire morale contemporaine" was a fight against maxims, against abstractions, a fight back toward a human and/or total conception. (*SP*, 152 and 155)

Several critical features here exemplify how Pound's notion of popularization had changed since his early work *The Spirit of Romance*. Such work as "The Jefferson-Adams Letters" no longer mediates in any primary sense between the realms of popular and polite discourse (a distinction that is also, as Patey observes, "aesthetic"). Instead, Pound's tiltings against the mills of ideology had led him to an almost anthropological sense of culture. His concern was now with the articulation and explanation of lived praxis. But as the title of his essay might suggest, this more totalizing sense of "culture" was joined to, rather than substituted for, the more elitist or mandarin sense of the term. Whereas a "shrine" might well be an integral part of daily life, a "monument" can be so only in the sense that it stands to remind us of something greater than ourselves.

In Pound's poetic and prose texts alike, this was an uneasy mixture, but in *Guide to Kulchur* it produced a peculiar problematic. Pound was able to use the title "Guide to Kulchur" only in the Faber and Faber edition; his American publishers insisted on the simpler and less outrageous title of "Culture." And yet even the Faber edition was something more serious than Pound had hoped for. His first idea was to call the book "The New Learning," figuring that "Paideuma" was "too long a word for the public" (*SL*, 288),[31] but following a possibly ironic suggestion from Frank Morley, he was soon ready with " 'Kulch,' or Ez' Guide to Kulchur." But even as it stands the tone here matters a great deal. Pound's own comment, in "the title chapter," which he withheld for 183 pages, was purposively self-reflexive: "Ridiculous title, stunt piece. Challenge? Guide, ought to mean help other fellow to get there. Ought one turn up one's nose?" Pound's spelling "Kulchur" did not just allude derisively to German *kultur*; it suggested generic, if parodic, ties to the baedeker. "Kulchur," that far-off, exotic and

---

31. See also Carpenter's *Serious Character*, 535–42.

little known land, was a joke most any reader might appreciate. But Pound's expositions repeatedly confuse the issue. As we have seen, he identified "culture" with the totality of a people's life, using the word sometimes in an anthropological sense, while elsewhere retaining the notion of culture as the rarefied and privileged—the transcendental perfection toward which as a young man he had always aspired. The fourth paragraph from the chapter "Guide to Kulchur" reveals both senses of the word operating side by side:

> Ideogram of this "culture"/division between the Best, the 95% and upward, and the second division of writing, painting, sculpture, cooking or any other damn process.
> "And pause a while from letters to be wise."
> (rhyming with "turn thine eyes"). Saml. quite right if this means that the culture (damned word if there ever was one) ought NOT to be a blighted haystack of knowledge so heavy it crushes or smothers.

In such passages as this Pound was working to synthesize two rather different understandings of the idea of culture. He insisted on the one hand that "culture" was neither "knowledge" nor the dead weight of so many museum pieces; neither was it just a matter of artistic accomplishment ("letters"), but a matter of vision ("eyes"). His concern that culture be recognized as a mode of experience and thought (imagination) tempered Pater with Arnold. But Pound's continuing respect for that Arnoldian "best" rests uneasily with such of his other inclusions as "Praise Song of the Buck-Hare."

This attempted synthesis is analogous to the project of forging "a profounder didacticism," and in the *Guide* it produces many of the same difficulties and contradictions so prevalent in the *Cantos*. Rather than proving useful as an entry into the *Cantos*, the *Guide* remains an ancillary textual problem. Although the poem aspires to achieve "epic" status, and the *Guide* the status of primer, both works are similarly totalizing in scope, and after *Eleven New Cantos* consistent in their combinatory procedures.

Similar procedures will, however, inevitably produce different results in different generic mixtures, and attending to the relations between Pound's work in different genres ought not to eliminate the perception of difference. Two key factors distinguish *Guide to Kulchur* from the *Cantos*: the functions of Pound's verse, and the peculiar dynamics in *Guide* between chapter headings and the content of the chapters themselves. The *Cantos* develops no such irony: individual cantos are headed only numerically, and only *Cantos LII–LXXI* (1940) includes any explanatory apparatus. In the *Guide*, each chapter title suggests as it were a different aspect of "kulchur," almost like the headings of a baedeker organize different kinds of local attractions, and raise and then exploit typical generic expectations. As we have seen, the variegated materials in Pound's "guide" do "meet" these expectations, but only in implicit and metaphorical ways. Terribly, it would only be in the two "Italian cantos," 72 and 73 (1945), that Pound's work proved consistent with more usual convention: in this case, the poet speaking for his cause in time of war. In the writings that followed Pound's arrest and incarceration, he worked more fiercely than ever to undermine the traditional models of historical and cultural reflection.

5
Unpacking Münch's Satchel: Musical Notation and the Defiance of *Pisan Cantos*

> Poetry is a long hesitation between sound and sense.
> —Michel Butor, "Repertoire"

"The Poetry Breaks Off"

In the winter of 1968, in the last public interview he ever gave, Pound rose to the defense of his poetic method. That he should do so after an eight-year public silence punctuated only by such expressions of dejection as his lament to Grazia Livi that "everything I touch I spoil," or his insistence to Daniel Cory in an earlier interview that *Cantos* is "a botch," is remarkable.[1] That he should do so in the final moments of an interview in which he had reiterated his own belief that "I have not succeeded" is even more so. It was not that Pound had suddenly recovered the brash zeal of his youth; nor was he simply expressing long-repressed belief in his own work. Pound's defense took fire from a continuing concern with how different discourses interact, and it can provide a dramatic opening into the most opaque moment of his much celebrated *Pisan Cantos*.

David Anderson, who transcribed and translated this interview from a tape of its Italian broadcast, reconstructs its sometimes confusing negotiations.[2]

---

1. Recorded in Noel Stock, *The Life of Ezra Pound*, expanded edition (San Francisco: North Point Press, 1982), 457. The interview with Cory was conducted in October of 1966.
2. David Anderson, "Breaking the Silence: The Interview of Vanni Ronsisvalle and Pier Paolo Pasolini with Ezra Pound in 1968," *Paideuma* 10 (Fall 1981): 331–45.

Originally set up by the Sicilian poet Vanni Ronsisvalle, the interview was filmed over a number of morning sessions. The first sessions were conducted between Pound and Ronsisvalle, according to a fairly controlled format. As Anderson explains: "To avoid slips in Italian, Pound followed the conventional practice of asking for a list of Ronsisvalle's questions some days in advance of each session. He prepared brief answers in English which he then translated into Italian. Olga Rudge wrote out the Italian texts in large letters on cardboard sheets which were then held up at a distance from Pound during the interview. . . . He either read the answers directly onto the record, or based his answer on the prepared text." From the start, then, this session mixed discourses—English and Italian, prepared script and improvisation—but the mixture was well-tempered by comparison with what developed on the final day of interview. Whether or not, as Olga Rudge speculated, Ronsisvalle and his friend Pier Paolo Pasolini had agreed beforehand to "share" the interview, Pasolini appeared that last day unannounced and in Ronsisvalle's place. Once there, Pasolini interjected his own questions among those Ronsisvalle had previously submitted in writing. Pasolini's questions ("inconsiderate," Rudge thought) altered the nature of the interview in several ways. To the prior mixture of prepared and extemporaneous elements was now added a spontaneity to which Pound sometimes had difficulty responding. Pasolini's questions denied Pound the opportunity to think his answers through in English and then translate them. More upsetting still, Pasolini's questions were not (as had been Ronsisvalle's) those of a disciple, but of a poet-critic and communist activist interested in rehabilitating the reputation of an unrepentant fascist. Consequently, even when he was not bridling at Pasolini's questions, Pound's answers often crossed purposes with them.

Indeed, it was not Pasolini's criticism but his attempted defense of the *Cantos* that provoked Pound. Pasolini had supposed that Pound's combinatory principles respected how "intelligent people say things to one another . . . at random" (337). Unimpressed by Pasolini's perception that his verse was so like the language of random experience, Pound immediately objected that he had tried to give his poems coherence, but had not succeeded. But Pasolini would not let the matter rest, and continued with his inference of "randomness." The result was that Pound undertook to save himself from Pasolini's help, and countered with a defiant avowal of his poetic, his first in nearly a decade:

PASOLINI: Literary critics all agree that your poetry is extremely vast. It is as if your poetry covered an immense poetical territory. And it's true, for quotation after quotation . . .
POUND: Chosen at random . . .
PASOLINI: Chosen at random? What? The critics or the quotations?
POUND: They say they are chosen at random, but that's not the way it is. It's Music. Musical themes that meet each other. (338)

Pound's outburst responded, not to Pasolini's immediate speech, but to Pasolini's repeated imputation of randomness. This sudden discursive shift left Pasolini uncertain of the very meaning of the word he had introduced into the conversation, and both he and Pound dropped it. Pound, however, returned in the final moments of the interview to the idea of music as a kind of relation and quoted a critic who had written that "Pound chooses to compare his poetry to sculpture and to music, and he has never shown a particular interest in painting." Almost as if desiring to demonstrate the vitality of Pound's notion of musical association, Pasolini responded by reciting the opening lines of Canto 75, commenting "and here the poetry breaks off and is followed by a musical score."

Pound's insouciant rejoinder, that he had included "only the first lines of the piece of music, not all of it," seems not only to grant Pasolini's perception of discontinuity, but even to sharpen it by pointing to additional "breaks" within the score itself. But if Pound did not address Pasolini's comment, he did respond to something Pasolini said: the mention of the musical score reminded Pound of the physical, typographical difficulty of including it in his poem. Pasolini had once again hoped to suggest the randomness of discourse, Pound the difficulties of combining unlike generic elements. The interview itself illustrates Pound's concerns and suggests an analogy for many of the generic exchanges in the *Cantos*.

Pound's interview with Pasolini also suggests the defiance that Canto 75 shares with the rest of *Pisan Cantos*. Since the praise of the Bollingen committee in 1948, the Pisan sequence has commonly been regarded as the most successful in the *Cantos*—successful meaning most traditionally lyric and politically unobtrusive. There is much in *Pisan Cantos* to support such regard: the "dove sta memora" passages of Canto 76; the "beauty is difficult" passages of Canto 80; or the justly praised "what thou lovest well remains" and "pull down thy vanity" passages of Canto 81. But each of these long cantos contains other elements, very different in kind, for which the first ten lines of Canto 74—the first ten lines of the sequence, might stand as example:

> The enormous tragedy of the dream in the peasant's bent
>   shoulders
>   Manes! Manes was tanned and stuffed
>   Thus Ben and la Clara *a Milano*
>   by the heels at Milano
> That maggots shd/eat the dead bullock
> DIGONOS, Διγϕνϕσ, but the twice crucified
>   where in history will you find it?
> yet say this to the Possum: a bang, not a whimper,
>   with a bang not with a whimper,
> to build the city of Dioce whose terraces are the color of the stars.

Pound's emphasis in these lines falls not on the historical, but on the ideal, the dream which remains forever outside history. What is disturbing here is that Mussolini is remembered only as a defeated dreamer—who at least went down fighting. The motif of the "twice crucified," which Pound had used in Canto 72 with reference to Marinetti, ironically parallels the model of Christ or Dionysius "Digonos"—twice born. Pound's mythopoeic enlargement on the public humiliation of the corpses of Mussolini and his mistress suggests that the victorious powers were not content merely to destroy the physical embodiment of the dream, but sought to strike through it and destroy the dream itself. As in the infinitive of purpose, "to build the city of Dioce . . . now in the mind indestructible," *Pisan Cantos* affirms the futility of such attempts to crush the human spirit. In this way, *Pisan Cantos* enacts its defiance in a way consonant with the praxis of earlier cantos, by mythopoeic displacement. It exemplifies Pound's determination to "include" history precisely as it works to transform detail into symbolic event. But because of the increased presence of his own autobiography, Pound's manner of including history is easily mistaken for a confessional project akin to the work of younger American poets like Snodgrass, Lowell, or Berryman. For whatever confessional elements it contains, *Pisan Cantos* respects an older tradition. It is a poetry interested not in the personal relations of the poet, but in the totality of the cultural-historical relations that inform the poet's apparent political failure.

The Legacy of Pater: Eliot, Lewis, and the Idea of Music

> The stagnation in music publishing is due, in part, to the decades wherein music has been a separate interest, not an integral part of the most active intellectual life.
> —Ezra Pound, "Another Chance" (1938)

Pound's last interview defended the inclusion of musical notation in his poetry because he was less interested in music per se than he was in its relations to a larger cultural totality. Pound saw music as "an integral part of the most active, intellectual life"; but to consider the nature of that integrity he resolved first to distinguish it from the other elements with which it interacted—chiefly, poetry itself.

For Pound, and for his self-consciously "modern" cohorts, the issues surrounding the idea of music were largely inherited from late-nineteenth-century figures like Walter Pater and Arthur Symons. Although French writers like Mallarmé or Verlaine were of seminal importance, it was Pater, Symons, and others like Wilde, Johnson, or (slightly later) F. S. Flint, who more immediately made French notions of musical form current for an English audience. But the French "symbolists" were themselves developing densely laden historical assumptions, the weight of which can be seen in the changed significance of musical terms commonly used in nonmusical ways. "Rhapsody," for example, was during the Enlightenment a term of mild censure, denoting "an effusion marked by extravagance of ideas or expression without connected thought or sound argument" (*Oxford English Dictionary*). Subsequently, those same qualities also came to mean ecstatic flight and elevated feeling. And so, as John Hollander has noted, although poets have long discussed their craft in musical terms, such discussions have turned on changing and often competing ideas about the music that is in poetry.[3]

In an essay on Robert Browning's interest in music, Penelope Gay describes how music ceased to be considered as the expression of laws and numbers and came instead to be discussed as their transcendence.[4] Gay points out that by the late eighteenth century, *the* idea of music had given way to

---

3. See John Hollander, *The Untuning of the Sky: Ideas of Music in English Poetry, 1500–1700* (1961; reprint, New York: Norton, 1979).
4. Penelope Gay, "Browning and Music," in *Writers and Their Backgrounds: Robert Browning*, ed. Isobel Armstrong (London: G. Bell & Sons, 1974), 211–30.

"two, or perhaps three attitudes" that "competed for authority." Even in their differences, however, these attitudes were commonly disposed to drive open the sovereign grip of reason. The oldest among them had been promulgated by the French encyclopédistes, who sought to refine a science of music to the point where music might be used to provide exact expression of emotion. Charles Avison's "Analogy between Musical Air and Grammar" (1766), for example, later held great interest for Browning. But the continued rationalism of this view emerges clearly when compared with the romantic conviction "that music expressed the inexpressible, that it in some way echoed the structure of the organic universe; or that, conversely, it expressed nothing but its ineffable self" (217, 226). This latter position was extended to radical conclusions by such writers of the next generation as Schlegel (1772–1829) and Schopenhauer (1788–1860), so that, by the time of his 1836 lectures, Hegel (1770–1831) could conclude that music was the "central" art. Hegel believed, however, that music was "neither as spiritual as poetry nor as sensuous as paintings," and found in that centrality a sign of the imperfection of his age (219). Later writers would reconsider Hegel's hierarchy and elevate the importance of music; but after Hegel music remained a "cultural" issue, and claims made about it frequently carried totalizing implications.

Still, as Gay cautions, this new aesthetic "was to have almost no impact on England until the 1870s." Through the first half of the nineteenth century, English poets formulated musical explanations of their work only infrequently. Wordsworth had admitted a fondness for "tracing the resemblance between Poetry and Painting," but showed little interest in discussing music.[5] Fifty years later, William Michael Rossetti, brother to the painter-poet Dante Gabriel, asked of Robert Browning: "In speaking of the adaptation of style to conception. . . . Are the versification strong, the sound sharp or soft, monotonous, hurried, in proportion to the requirements of sense; the illustrative thoughts apt and new?"[6] Rossetti's question indicates a continued preference for visual over musical explanatory models for poetry. He regarded the question of "sound" as contingent to "the requirements of sense." It is, accordingly, important to see that Pater's essay "The School of Giorgione," added to *The Renaissance* with the publication of the third

---

5. William Wordsworth, "Preface to the Second Edition of *Lyrical Ballads* (1800)," in *Lyrical Ballads*, ed. Jack Stillinger (Boston: Riverside Editions, 1965), 451.

6. W. M. Rossetti, review of *Christmas Eve and Easter Day*, by Robert Browning, *The Germ: The Literary Magazine of the Pre-Raphaelites* (1901; reprint, Oxford: Ashmolean Museum, Oxford and Birmingham City Museum and Art Gallery, 1979), 191.

edition in 1888, accomplished a revision of Wordsworth's or Rossetti's critical precepts. Pater proclaimed that

> *All art constantly aspires towards the condition of music.* For while in all other kinds of art it is possible to distinguish the matter from the form, and the understanding can always make this distinction, yet it is the constant effort of art to obliterate it. That the mere matter of a poem, for instance, its subject, namely, its given incidents or situation—that the mere matter of a picture, the actual circumstances of an event, the actual topography of a landscape—should be nothing without the form, the spirit, of the handling, that this form, this mode of handling, should become an end in itself, should penetrate every part of the matter: this is what all art constantly strives after, and achieves in different degrees.[7]

Far from asking if a poet's use of sound matches "the requirements of sense," Pater claimed that it is the purpose of art to "obliterate" rational categories, to fuse sound and sense in a way that thwarts ordinary intellect.

Pater's phrase "the mere matter of a poem," which works to subordinate questions of content, was soon imitated by enthusiastic disciples like Arthur Symons. When describing Verlaine's deep suspicion of words, Symons celebrated Verlaine's ability to paint with pure sound, to write "*romances sans paroles*, songs almost without words, in which scarcely a sense of the interference of human speech remains." The denotation of speech seemed to him, as it did to Pater, an "interference." So, Symons affirmed that "with Verlaine the sense of hearing and the sense of sight are almost interchangeable: he paints with sound, and his line and atmosphere become music."[8] The implication of Pater's aesthetic, that art should carry the perceiver beyond the limits of reason to a more intense mode of perception, became dogma for Symons. To say that Verlaine "paints with sound" does not simply assert the supremacy of music as form; in its synaesthetic formulation it already treats language in a "musical" manner. Sense is an obstacle, and the poet's first task is to overcome it.

Dissociating the music of poetry from its sense, late Victorian writers

---

7. Walter Pater, *The Renaissance* (London, 1910; reprint, Chicago: Pandora Books, 1978), 135. Italics Pater's.
8. Arthur Symons, *The Symbolist Movement in Literature*, rev. ed. (London, 1919; reprint, New York: E. P. Dutton, 1958), 48.

departed dramatically from earlier discussions of the subject. This conception of music, with its sustained devaluation of sense, prompted Eliot and Pound to try to reconceptualize the nature of music in poetry, and Wyndham Lewis to assert—angrily—that music has no place whatsoever in poetry. For all of these writers, the idea of music involved serious issues, the solutions to which they regarded as central to the task of poetry in their time. Nevertheless, Pound, Eliot, and Lewis each presented quite distinct arguments about the relations between music and poetry, and—surprisingly—both Eliot and Lewis pursued more extreme courses than did Pound.

Eliot's antagonism toward Paterian identifications of music and poetry was evident early in his career, and sometimes took unlikely form. In "Kipling Redivivus" (May 1919), Eliot claimed that the lack of critical attention to Kipling had less to do with Kipling's imperialism than with the inability of "poetical" coteries to recognize any talent not of their own prevailingly "aesthetic" stripe. Invoking Flaubert precisely as Pound was wont to do—as a cultural critic—Eliot imagined that "the admired creator of Bouvard and Pécuchet would not have overlooked Kipling's *dossier*." Then, from among those poets more in vogue, Eliot chose the one most conventionally regarded as Kipling's antithesis and argued that Kipling "has an affinity to Swinburne, even a likeness. There are, of course, qualities peculiar to Mr. Kipling; but several of the apparent differences are misconceptions, and several can be reduced to superficial differences of environment. Both are men of a few simple ideas, both are preachers, both have marked their styles by an abuse of the English Bible." In Eliot's view, both Kipling and Swinburne advocated moral positions: "Both are preachers." Moreover, Eliot continued, Kipling and Swinburne were

> alike even in a likeness which would strike most people immediately as a difference; they are alike in their use of sound. It is true that Swinburne relies more exclusively upon the power of sound than does Mr. Kipling. But it is the same type of sound, and it is not the sound-value of music. Anyone who thinks so may compare Swinburne's "songs" with verse which demands the voice and the instrument, with Shelley's "Music when soft voices die" or Campion's "Fairy Queen Proserpina." What emerges from the comparison is that Swinburne's sound like Mr. Kipling's, has the sound-value of oratory, not of music.

Both poets, Eliot submitted, create a "poetry of oratory" whose music is "music just as the words of the orator or preacher are music; they persuade, not by reason, but by emphatic sound."[9]

Eliot concluded that "Swinburne and Kipling have, like the public speaker, an idea to impose; and they impose it in the speaker's way, by turning the idea into sound, and iterating the sound." The importance of "Kipling Redivivus" lies in Eliot's treatment of sound as a kind of "sense" rather than as a vehicle for its defeat. He described as "oratory" the Swinburnian obsession with sound that Pater would have taught us to regard as the antithesis of such special pleading. Eliot sought to reduce sound to a rhetorical "instrument," a way "of stimulating a particular response in the reader." He granted that music may not be "rational," but insisted on its subservience to rational purpose.

This determination stiffened with time. In March of 1928 Eliot attacked the effort of L. C. Martin to win a popular audience for the work of Richard Crashaw by likening it to that of Shelley and Keats. Juxtaposing lines from "The Weeper" and "The Skylark," Eliot wrote that "I doubt whether the *sound* of two poems can be very similar when the *sense* is entirely different."[10] Eliot did not explain how it is that the sense of a line alters its sound, but his subsequent deprecation of Shelley's poetry reiterated his belief that poets must work with sound and sense together. Shelley's poem "The Skylark" contains, Eliot charged, "no brain work." It is "the first time perhaps in verse of such eminence [that] sound exists without sense." In this case, Eliot's inveterate abuse of Shelley stemmed from the fact that Eliot shared Martin's desire to advance Crashaw's reputation, but believed Martin sought to do so by appealing to the very attitudes that had led to Crashaw's neglect. Eliot thus resubmitted the concerns that had prompted "Kipling Redivivus." He found Martin guilty of pandering to a popular craving for the irrational, a craving that Eliot identified as created by the romantics and grossly whetted by the generation of Pater, Swinburne, and Symons. Two years later, in "Thinking in Verse" (12 March 1930), he warned again against the indiscriminate combination of music and poetry. Positing "two kinds of 'music' in verse," the one exemplified by Campion and the other by Donne, Eliot averred that "the song of Campion is as simple in content as possible; its merit

9. "Kipling Redivivus," *Athenaeum*, no. 4644 (2 May 1919), 297–98.

10. T. S. Eliot, *For Lancelot Andrewes* (New York: Doubleday, Doran, 1929), 134. Compare Eliot's charge to Pound's remark in "The Serious Artist" (1913) that "Shelley's 'The Sensitive Plant' is one of the rottenest poems ever written, at least one of the worst ascribable to a recognized author. It jiggles to the same tune as 'A little peach in the orchard grew'" (*LE*, 51).

lies in its delicate, irregular metre responsive to the music. Donne's music has a similarly skillful irregularity; but the metrical beauty is so closely associated with the thought, that if it were sung, the sense would be lost."[11] This distinction not only attempts to put sound and sense on an equal footing, but also enforces a kind of segregation. It was yet another move against what Eliot felt to be the prevailing celebration of "music." He turned the explanatory categories of his opponents to his own purpose: the development of a poetic not designed to overpower rational order.

By the time of *Four Quartets*, the constructions of which trade heavily on analogies with music, Eliot's program had become even more explicit. In "The Music of Poetry," a lecture delivered in February of 1942, Eliot reasserted the relation of sound and sense. Once again, although Eliot continued to invoke Paterian terms, his lecture systematically reconceived them. While Pater or Symons argued that music accomplishes the stupefaction of rational cognition, Eliot identified music as a coming together of intelligible, sensible relations:

> The music of a word is, so to speak, at a point of intersection: it arises from its relation first to the words immediately preceding and following it, and indefinitely to the rest of its context; and from another relation, that of its immediate meaning in that context to all the other meanings which it has had in other contexts, to its greater or less wealth of association. . . . This is an "allusiveness" which is not the fashion or eccentricity of a peculiar type of poetry; but an allusiveness which is in the nature of words, and which is equally the concern of every kind of poet. . . . The sound of a poem is as much an abstraction from the poem as is the sense.[12]

This lecture completed Eliot's programmatic revision of late-century conceptions of "music," for here, Eliot defined "what the music of a word is" without even mentioning its sound. By "music" he meant a principle of intelligible association, the way the use of a word in one context inevitably recalls previous uses elsewhere. "There is an allusiveness which is in the nature of words," he wrote, and it was this allusiveness that he here identified with poetic "music." Interestingly enough, Pound had attacked just this

---

11. "Thinking in Verse: A Survey of Early Seventeenth-Century Poetry," *Listener* 3, no. 61 (12 March 1930): 441–43.
12. *On Poetry and Poets* (1957; reprint, New York: Farrar, Strauss & Giroux, 1979), 25–26.

identification of poetic music with semantic "associations" almost thirty years before: in "Status Rerum" (1913) Pound had called such activity "subjective" and linked it to the looseness of "symbolism." But Eliot's formulation carried a similar design; it sought to diminish the appeal of what he regarded as the siren call of Verlaine—the call that Symons and his generation had found so exciting—that "*de la musique avant toute chose; de la musique encore et toujours!*"[13] Sympathetic with Eliot's valuations, John Hollander has characterized Verlaine's "exhortation to divide sound from sense and to choose the sound" as "abandoning both poetry and music to the shadow of the irrational."[14] Eliot would, no doubt, have applauded Hollander's description. His own insistence that "the sound of a poem is as much an abstraction from the poem as is the sense" was, above all else, a rejoinder to claims for the primacy of the irrational in aesthetic experience.

Eliot's strategy was to admit the importance of music in poetry, but to link the term "music" to poetic features different from those to which it had hitherto been applied. It was a most "intellectual" strategy. Lewis, however, delivered a contentiously sensational argument for the importance of sense in poetry. Significantly, Lewis's arguments for the continued commitment of poetry to sense came in the form of an attack on Pound. In "The Revolutionary Simpleton," published but twelve years after he and Pound had ended their collaboration on *Blast* (July 1915), Lewis recalled: "I was informed [sometime around 1924] that the good Ezra was breaking out in a new direction. He was giving up words—possibly frightened, I thought, by the widespread opposition to *words* of any sort—words, idle words, and their manipulators. He was taking to music—a less compromising activity. For in music the sounds *say* nothing. (M. Paul Valéry, like Ezra Pound, would prefer to believe that they *say* nothing in poetry either. But in spite of these musical dogmatists, *still they speak*. Pound shows his appreciation of this by turning to music.)"[15] Besides his sarcastic implication that Pound took up music because he was unable to make of words much besides "antiquarian" expressions of Tennysonian "divine despair" ("tears, idle tears, I know not what they mean"), Lewis made an important distinction: "in music the sounds *say* nothing," in poetry "still they speak."

The calm with which, forty years later, Pound heard Pasolini observe that

13. Symons, *Symbolist Movement*, 47.
14. Hollander, *Untuning of the Sky*, 11.
15. "The Revolutionary Simpleton" originally appeared in the first volume of Lewis's short-lived *The Enemy*, January 1927, 25–192. I cite the reprint of this essay as the first part of *Time and Western Man* (1927; reprint, Santa Rosa, Calif.: Black Sparrow Press, 1993), 39.

in Canto 75 sense "breaks off" and is followed by pure sound suggests the soundness of Lewis's belief that Pound saw music as the antithesis of speech. Less certain is Lewis's polemic charge that Pound's experimentation was motivated by a fear of insisting on sense. In "The Revolutionary Simpleton," Lewis denounced the Bergsonian glamorization of sensation in an analysis not unlike Eliot's. In Lewis's account, the attempt to make sensation the "exclusive fact" of our existence threatened to engulf "western man" in the darkness of solipsism, to cut off one man's recognition of the reality of others and even to banish within that "all *individual* continuity" (13). Just as Eliot submitted that "the sound of a poem is as much an abstraction as the sense," Lewis denied the primacy, the "exclusivity" of sensation. To posit sensation as the "exclusive fact" of our existence is to surrender, he believed, the possibility of "true value," for either the individual or society.

Lewis's diagnosis points to the consequence of regarding "music" as the model for human consciousness. In describing the situation he piled up appositional phrases, gave dominance to participles over finite verbs, anaphorically intoning "the same . . . the same" to expose the utter vapidity produced by a society bent on achieving a state of constant "emotional tension" (23).[16] Lewis's syntax apes, in a deliberately sermonic fashion, the ceaseless "drumming on the top note" which he felt characterized the twentieth-century world of "the advertisement." The metaphor of music served Lewis as a way of demonstrating the collapse of distinctions between "art" and "mass" or "jazz" culture. Music provided a means of delivering his charge that the clamorings of the avant-garde were no less informed by a relentless attempt "to startle into credulity" than were the ubiquitous slogans of the marketplace. Instead of the world of heightened sensitivity such rhetoric promised, Lewis foresaw endless monotony. Even more than Eliot, Lewis was convinced that the valuation of the musical "moment" threatened moral and artistic sensibility; like Pound and other inheritors of Ruskinian thunder, Lewis refused to privilege the aesthetic over the moral.

Yet Lewis chose Pound as one of his major exemplars of the writer guilty of "straining merely to outwit and to capture momentary attention." In the

16. Lewis believed that art should be "a stronghold . . . of the purest human consciousness," but saw in modernist art the infection of modern society: an incessant "emotional tension, the same spurious glamour, in which no one believes, but which yet arrests belief from settling anywhere—extracting, as it were, the automatic reaction from it without desiring, even, a more conscious, or deep-seated response; the same optimistic air, suggestive of a bad conscience, or a vulgar self-congratulation; the same baldly shining morning face; the same glittering or discreetly hooded eye of the fanatical advertiser, exists in the region of art or social life" (23).

very phrase that would forty years later spark Pound's rejoinder to Pasolini, Lewis objected to Pound's tendency to "break off" from his subject. But Lewis used the phrase critically, repeating it often, and sometimes mimicking Pound in the process: "in his verse [Pound] is always 'breaking off.' And he 'breaks off,' indeed, as a rule, twice in every line" (70, see also 72). Ranging beyond Pound's discussions of music to what he regarded as the implications of Pound's poetic, he derided Pound's tendency to "break off" as an example of "the repetitive hypnotic method," a deliberate subversion of reason.

For Lewis, Pound's verse was musical, all too musical, an ultimately self-defeating flight from sense. Referring immediately to Pound's work on his operas, Lewis charged that Pound was "lost halfway between one art and another" and suggested that "Pound's desertion of poetry for music may mean that music is really his native art; and having been misled early in life into the practice of an art in which he had nothing whatever to say, he is now painfully attempting to return to the more fluid abstract medium of musical composition" (111). It was not Pound's attempts at opera in themselves that disturbed Lewis, but his cultivation of musical effects in his poetry. "Lost halfway between one art and another," Pound must, Lewis submitted, choose one or surrender for good his hopes of achieving anything in either.

Writing in 1927, Lewis could not have forseen the direction Pound's writing would take. In retrospect, he seems a little silly in his charge that the writer of the usura canto, or of *Jefferson And/Or Mussolini*, was "frightened" by potential public "opposition to words of any sort." Nevertheless, for all his excess, Lewis remains to this day nearly alone in his perception that Pound's interest in music can tell us something important about his poetics. Lewis's criticism remains seminal in that it finds in materials that formalist critics have deemed marginal the central historical issues raised by Pound's combinatory procedures.

Both Eliot and Lewis were more systematic in their treatment of music than was Pound, for whom it yet constituted a more central concern. Between his early studies of the troubadours, his work on his two operas, and his late inclusion of music in the *Cantos*, Pound's concern took many forms. Nevertheless, in one conviction he remained constant: "Music is not speech."[17] For all of his concern that, in song, the music should "grow out of" the language, he steadfastly distinguished between them. Once again his position was beleaguered from the start: it seemed as reactionary to the

---

17. From "George Antheil (Retrospect)," originally published in the *Criterion*, March 1924; reprinted in *EPM*, 271.

aesthetes perpetuating Paterian synaesthesia as it did to those of his "modern" cohorts, such as Eliot, who contrived to identify music with sense.

"Gettin Round to a Few Formulations"

In his exacting analysis of what he calls Pound's "new syntax of the eye," Vincent Sherry demonstrates Pound's "tendency to conceive of musical sound as the material medium in which the shape-tracing powers of the eye may operate."[18] For Pound, Sherry explains, the idea of music was infected by Bergsonian visions of mass politics—the stupefaction of intellect and the empathy of the crowd. Thus in the *Cantos*, the "oral muse of epos gives way to the next syntax of the eye" (77). Certainly, the features of oral discourse that figure in the *Cantos*, especially with and after *Eleven New Cantos*, are not "sonorous" in kind. Sherry's work amplifies the distinctions we have made above. Despite the attraction to musical empathy evident in early lyrics like "Mesmerism," music became for Pound a means of aiding rather than overcoming intellectual discrimination.

This precise purpose suggests the futility of R. Murray Schafer's protest that "the fact that actual music does make an appearance in the *Cantos* should surprise no one" (*EPM*, 20–21).[19] No other part of Pound's work developed more antagonistically to popular genres, or sought more energetically to upset popular expectations. Indeed, readers have been as unsettled by how Pound included music as by the fact of the inclusion itself. Or inclusions: besides the deliberate separation of sound and sense in Canto 75 (Fig. 1), Pound's other inclusions of "actual music" all raise unique issues: in Canto 81 a section of the poem is indicated as being a "libretto," but no musical notation is included; in Canto 91, musical and metrical notations are joined together. Pound's inclusions of music in the *Cantos* do not share any single signification. Music, like all the interpolated materials of the *Cantos*, must be understood in terms of specific generic mixtures. In each case, the manner of Pound's inclusion derives both from arguments about music, and from his comprehensive ambition to reconstitute cultural totality.

---

18. Vincent Sherry, *Ezra Pound, Wyndham Lewis, and Radical Modernism* (New York: Oxford University Press, 1993), 181–82.
19. Like any study of Pound's interest in music, my work is indebted to Schafer, even though I am not chiefly interested in the lyricality of the *Cantos*, or in explaining Pound's formal experiments in "organic" terms.

Oᴜᴛ of Phlegethon!
out of Phlegethon,
Gerhart
art thou come forth out of Phlegethon?
with Buxtehude and Klages in your satchel, with the
Ständebuch of Sachs in yr/ luggage
—not of one bird but of many

Fig. 1. From Canto LXXV.

Music, as Schafer proposes, "played a strong part in convincing Pound of the necessity of the reforms he was initiating," the "investing [of] English poetry with new rhythmic life" (*EPM*, 15). But in working to establish Pound's genuinely serious concern with music, Schafer sometimes risks aestheticizing what Pound had tried to free from just that consignment. Pound's sense of music was informed by his determination to expand the subject matter of poetry. In a letter of 1933, for instance, a period when he was caught up in economic and political activity, Pound told an aspiring poet that he doubted there was "any chance" that "*any* yng. feller" could make "a dent in the pubk. [public] or highly select consciousness by means of pomes writ in the style of 1913/15." The date "1913/15" was no allusion to his old "Georgian" rivals, but to imagism and vorticism, and Pound assessed its continued effectiveness with an eye to popular as well as elite audiences. "There are," he concluded, only "two roads." The first was "the old man's road (vide Tom. Hardy)—CONTENT, the INSIDES, the subject matter." The second was "music. And I am slowly gettin round to a few formulations, shocked largely by the god damn ignorance in which I have lived, and which wuz inherited from the generation of boobs who preceded me" (*SL*, 248–49). Two roads leading to the same end: it is crucial to see that although Pound distinguished music from subject matter, he did not then describe it as leading to a poetry removed from social struggle. Instead, the subject provoked Pound into further declamations against inherited "ignorance." Here and elsewhere, Pound mixed musical with political issues.

In *Guide to Kulchur*, after fulminating that "no man free of mental lice wd. tolerate the bank racket or the taxing system," Pound asserted that "the function of music is to present an example of order, or a less muddied congeries and proportion than we have yet about us in daily life" (*GK*, 255). The inclusion of music in the *Cantos* resulted from this kind of association, and we can find its traces in his early contention against Paterian synaesthesia: in his 1912 protest that "song demands now and again passages of pure sound, of notes free from the bonds of speech" (*EPM*, 34); or in his (rather conventional) complaint in 1917 that Debussy merely wrote program music—"it is no mortal use trying to play his music as if it were 'pure,' as if it were simply 'sound' arranged into time and pitch patterns for the expression of emotion" (*EPM*, 61–62). By 1918 Pound had condensed such concerns to the dictum "music is not speech" (*EPM*, 86), and smugly distanced himself from literati who considered music in purely aesthetic terms: "We recall a period when Pater and Fiona McLeod wrote long purple paragraphs about music," a period redolent of the "backparlour with heavy curtains, probably puce-covered" (*EPM*, 73). This was no fond indulgence of nostalgia, but an attempt to embarrass those who still carried the aesthetic candle. Pound accepted the Paterian valorization of music as the primary art, but denied that it could serve as a model of poetry. At the same time, he saw much to be gained from their intersection. His interest was not in synthesizing different forms, but in combining them in a way that preserved and highlighted their different integrities.

For Pound, the force of semiotic combination always depended on the prior recognition of differences in kind.[20] To talk, then, of Pound's combinations of music and poetry is to talk of something beyond traditional discussions of the "music" contained in poetic diction. After *Eleven New Cantos* Pound included music as an actual, structural component of his poem. This manner of inclusion is to be distinguished from what Leon Surette has called "the poetry of inference," a poetry whose "structural key . . . was provided by the framing device of allusion." Although Surette rightly observes Pound's desire "to incorporate all important aspects of modern thought into his epic," Pound in fact "incorporates" not just ideas but the genres in which those "thoughts" or "ideas" find expression: actual bits and pieces of other texts, fragments of conversation, even nonlinguistic sign systems—such as musical notation.[21] This is not "allusion," although Pound engaged in that also, but inclusion. Richard Sieburth has called this process "the art of quotation," and cautioned that it "should not be confused with mimesis: it is a mode not merely of copying or reflecting [or alluding, I would add] but of including the real—much as a cubist collage includes a metro ticket or a newspaper headline."[22] Insofar as it might convey the sense of concrete inclusion without an accompanying sense of inevitable changes, hermeneutic and material, the analogy of collage can be misleading. But as a means of "including the real," Pound's inclusion of music in the *Cantos* intersects his political and economic concerns. This intersection has been discussed before, but without sufficient sense of how "Pound's music" carries such content. Clarke Emery, a critic much concerned with Pound's politics, has proposed that "Canto 75, which seems to say little or nothing,

20. In his discussion of Pound's "Vorticism," Reed Way Dasenbrock draws a similar conclusion; see *The Literary Vorticism of Ezra Pound and Wyndham Lewis: Towards the Condition of Painting* (Baltimore: Johns Hopkins University Press, 1985), 15–19.

21. Leon Surette, *A Light from Eleusis: A Study of Ezra Pound's Cantos* (Oxford: Oxford University Press, 1979), 25 and 18.

22. Richard Sieburth, *Instigations: Ezra Pound and Remy de Gourmont* (Cambridge: Harvard University Press, 1978), 121.

does in reality suggest a good deal to the student of Pound's prose." In it, Emery finds commentary

> upon the dangers of divisiveness (e.g. in poetry, of dividing words from music); upon the virtue of a writer's giving *the thing* instead of a reference to it (as Pound, in Canto 38, instead of giving an abstract of Douglas' Social Credit Theory gives Douglas speaking in his own voice); upon the durability (recurrent vigor) of the excellent, the substance of which maintains its validity regardless of a change in its accidents; upon the importance, therefore, of conserving the tradition; upon the value of the ideogrammic method in the criticism of the arts; and upon the need, in criticism and elsewhere, to make dissociations.[23]

Emery connects Pound's uses of music with political concerns; but his is a centrality very different from that which I am proposing. Canto 75 "comments" on none of the issues Emery names; the musical notation doesn't "comment" on anything at all. Pound's separation of sound and sense is, in this instance, precisely the point.

Pound could sometimes argue that words were an encumbrance on music. He wanted music that would, without violating these precepts, do more than "illustrate verbal qualities." As he explained to Mary Barnard in 1934: "thing is to cut a shape in time. Sounds that stop the flow, and durations either of syllables, or implied between them, 'forced onto the voice' of the reader by nature of the 'verse' " (*SL*, 254). In other words, music was a way of guiding the reader's performance or interpretation of language, a means of "forcing" the observation of relations that were in "the nature of the verse," as opposed to relations that were merely the product of interpretation. It supported his claim that he could alter the texts he was including in the *Cantos* without violating their meaning, and could manipulate the responses of his own readers.

Pound's concern with "sounds that stop the flow" bears a different relation to problems of sense than does Eliot's conception of poetic "music." Pound regarded music as a means to "slow up" the poetic line and concentrate the attention of the audience on single words. Music became for him another means to change how poets handled words. In other words, "mu-

---

23. Clark Emery, *Ideas into Action: A Study of Pound's Cantos* (Coral Gables: University of Miami Press, 1958), 137.

sical" principles had for Pound less to do with qualities of rhythm than they did the organization of discourse: "music" functions in these discussions in opposition to notions of rational syntax. Music would not "replace" syntactical organization in the *Cantos*, but its very presence indicates Pound's interest in developing less discursive combinatory models. This impatience with discursive organization differed from the vision of ecstatic experience that Pater had identified with music—even though his 1924 essay "George Antheil (Retrospect)" had engaged to prove music *the* art of the machine age, and to ordain Antheil as the leading creator of machine music. Pound did not want music to overpower sense, but to empower it. The essay on Antheil exemplifies Pound's sense of music as an intersection of discrete elements:

> Prose is perhaps only half an art. The medium of poetry is words, i.e. human symbols, conventions; they are capable of including things of nature, that is, sound quality, timbre, up to a point.
>
> They have interior rhythm, there can be rhythm in their arrangement, even tone leadings, and these with increasing precision; but you can not get a word back into the non-human.
>
> It is redundancy, and therefore bad art, to use it where a less conventionalized humanised means will serve. Words are superfluous for certain things and inadequate for others. (*EPM*, 260)

Strangely enough, given Pound's fiery reputation, this was a more cautious, and yet more characteristically fin de siècle formulation than that of either Eliot or Lewis. Eliot, in order to resist claims for the primariness of the irrational, had sought to reunite music with sense. Fighting the same threat of unreason, Lewis had insisted on the distinctiveness of each of the arts, and refused even to consider the inclusion of musical features in poetry. Pound, however, unlike Eliot, accepted the identification of pure sound with the primary irrationality of nature; and despite his assertion that "you can not get a word back into the non-human," Pound argued against Lewis that the power of poetry comes from its ability to "include things of nature . . . up to a point." The question of inclusion was not for Pound a matter of "similarities." Pound himself said that "the thorough artist is probably more sensible to the differences between his own art and other arts, than to their resemblances." The inclusion of features from one art in another does not deny difference, but asserts it: words can include sound quality and timbre— "up to a point." As we have said, Pound sought combinations in which "one art interprets the other." Pound was persuading himself that an art will only achieve "horizontal" breadth by building on prior differences; and so it was that he proposed that what makes "any work of art permanent" is an "ideograph" of "admirable compound-of-qualities."

Pound did not argue that the "sound" or "music" in poetic language itself, as Lewis put it, "speaks." Neither did he equate music with sense. Interested in the "allusiveness which is in the nature of words," and in how words can enact simultaneously many different functions, Pound cultivated the potential heterogeneity, the "compound-of-qualities" made possible by bringing different uses of words together. This was not a matter of setting words "free," but of placing them in less discursive patterns of association. Music, "a less conventional humanised" art than words—less so but still "conventional"—was at once for Pound beyond language and a part of it. As such, it was a conception of music very different from that which Lewis attributed to him during the twenties. Pound too felt the inadequacy of the Paterian cultivation of music, but rather than leveling the distinctions between poetry and music, he hoped to use music to stimulate a signification not limited to a linear and strictly rational conception of "sense."

Making "Sense" of Pound's Musical Notation

Music represents the problem of a semiotic
system without a semantic level (or content
plane).
— Umberto Eco, *Theory of Semiotics*

The deliberate separation of the musical and metrical notations of Canto 75 poses a now notorious critical difficulty, evident not so much from critical protest as critical neglect. The twenty-three staves of Münch's score do little, for example, to further Wendy Flory's claim that the *Cantos* is a record of personal struggle. And Eugene Paul Nassar must surely be right in omitting Canto 75 from his discussion of those "certain passages" that "have always been appreciated by the poet's readers": musical notation in this context hardly lends itself to arguments for the primacy of "visionary experience," or of the "lyric mode." On the other hand, in a book devoted solely to *Pisan Cantos*, Anthony Woodward does not even mention Canto 75. The point here is not specific, but general and methodological: all explanatory models necessarily determine what is or is not amenable to analysis. Canto 75 is of particular interest precisely because it has consistently been relegated to a position of secondary critical interest. The structure of *Pisan Cantos* suggests that Pound himself thought otherwise: Canto 75 is the shortest canto in not only the Pisan sequence, but in the entire poem. Its brevity underscores its significance.

In Canto 75 the determination of modern criticism to isolate *meaning* confronts its limits. Taxed to make sense of its combination of musical and metrical notation, leading critics have responded by laboring to translate that notation into something else.[24] Christine Brooke-Rose, Hugh Kenner, and Daniel Pearlman, for example, treat the score as a kind of ideogram. For these critics, the score constitutes a primarily visual and thematic feature, and Pound's extraneous references to the score seem to encourage such an approach. He had discussed the music in "The Recurring Decimal" chapter of *Guide to Kulchur*, and in a letter to Louis Dudek, Pound recounted its long history:

> the carry through: Arnaut whom I don't mention.
> Janequin whom Münch don't mention (vide his handwriting)
> Francesco da Milano who set it for lute whom I don't mention.
> Four times was the city rebuilded.
> les Oiseaux having been thar fer some time in the "first" place.[25]

---

24. Christine Brooke-Rose, *A ZBC of Ezra Pound* (Berkeley and Los Angeles: University of California Press, 1971), 183, unreservedly maintains that the song of the birds in Canto 75 "like all of [Pound's] ideograms," emphasizes "the unity, now lost, of poetry and music." Daniel D. Pearlman, *The Barb of Time: On the Unity of Ezra Pound's Cantos* (Oxford: Oxford University Press, 1969), 261, explains that "the bird canzone is an elaboration of the idea represented by the [Dantean] rose-symbol and an intimation of the artistic synthesis Pound's contrapuntal oscillations are yet to achieve." The score, Pearlman proposes, "presents in musical terms . . . the theme of memory as an active force surviving time." Forrest Read, *'76 One World and the Cantos of Ezra Pound* (Chapel Hill: University of North Carolina Press, 1981), 324, describes the "textual-visual duality of LXXV." Hugh Kenner, *The Pound Era* (Berkeley and Los Angeles: University of California Press, 1971), 250–51, relies on Pound's reference in Cantos 79 and 82 to the random combinations of birds perched on the barbed wire that surrounded the detention camp outside Pisa. Kenner's reading purports to reenact the "inspiration" that brought Pound to use Münch's violin setting. That process, Kenner suggests, is "like" that first remote act of invention inspired by birdsong, just as it is "like" each of its subsequent settings. Each of these readings avoids the obvious inadequacy of Loisann Oakes's early attempt (1964) to treat the music as music: Oakes sought to explain the relation between the words and music of Canto 75 by contriving to show that the music in fact "set" the words which preceded it.

25. Louis Dudek, ed., *DK/Some Letters of Ezra Pound* (Montreal: DC Books, 1975), 63.

The Provençal poet Arnaut Daniel had written a song "out of"—as Pound says in *Guide to Kulchur*—bird song, which the Renaissance composer Clement Janequin reset as a choral motet; da Milano, a contemporary of Janequin's in turn reset it for solo performance—this time on lute; nearly three hundred years later Gerhart Münch rediscovered the piece in the unpublished papers of the musicologist Oscar Chilesotti and in 1936 transcribed it for violin (*EPM*, 328). Pound further amplified this process of transmission, a series of metamorphoses of an "ideal" beauty in which each instance exemplifies a perfect relation between the timeless "patterned energy" within and its form without, by associating it with the work of Frobenius. Forbenius had discovered a site in Africa where four successive civilizations had been built each on the ruins of its predecessor. Each city differed from the others, but each seemed to Frobenius to stand in perfect harmony with its environment. He called the place "Wagadu," and its story became one of Pound's familiar *leitmotifs*. "Four times was the city rebuilded" is Pound's quotation from Canto 74 (444–45):

> 4 times was the city rebuilded, Hooo Fasa
>   Gassir, Hooo Fasa dell' Italia tradita
> now in the mind indestructible
>
> . . . .
>
> Hooo Fasa, and in a dance the renewal.

Pound gave frequent expression to this fascination with "the carry through," and it relates closely to his interest in "culture possessed and forgotten." But Pound's discussions of this music comprise different generic instances, and unlike the music itself are not included in Canto 75. The invitation to understand the musical notation in other terms is attractive simply because it makes sense of what is beyond sense. By contrast, accepting the integrity of Pound's generic combination means accepting hermeneutic limits.

Pearlman, Kenner, and others have been quite right to address themselves to the striking appearance of Münch's score on the page. But the contrast between musical and metrical notation is not the only visual disjunction in the canto.[26] The text of Canto 75 also interrupts the regular type of the

---

26. The "shock" of such a combination can be overemphasized, although both poets and novelists have found it enticing. To name but a few examples: Browning's "Pietro of Abano" (1880), Apollinaire's "Venu de Dieuze" (1915), Joyce's *Finnegan's Wake* (1939), or Zukofsky's *A* #24 (1968).

metrical notation by reproducing, and reducing in scale, Olga Rudge's hand-copy of Münch's score.[27] This typographic break is amplified by the reduction of Münch's score to a nearly unperformable scale. Pound's acceptance of this risk might appear to confirm the thesis that the score is a strictly visual-perceptual phenomenon. Other evidence suggests a contrary conclusion. Pound's observation to Pasolini that "there's too much" to include beyond "the first lines of this piece of music" bespeaks his determination to get the music into the poem. Were Pound interested only in recalling how birds on a barbed-wire fence "look like" notes on a stave (as Kenner—drawing on Cantos 79 and 82—has suggested), any one or two bars would have sufficed. Pound's concern to include as much of the score as possible suggests that he wanted the actual music rather than merely an allusion to it.[28] Pound includes the score as "a whole slab of the record"; and his interest in its transmutations reflects his Frobenian convictions about the "perfected form" of folk-culture "as an inheritance from remote ages." Pound did not want to suggest or "allude" to music. He wanted to "include" or reproduce "the evidence." He expected that his readers would (as he explained in "Another Chance") derive pleasure merely from reading the score, however "far from the nearest musical instrument" they might be. The microphotography of Rudge's copy, then, associates the score with informal and oral history—with the popularization of scholarship.

Pound's reproduction of "Les Chants des Oiseaux" was informed by "extra" and even "anti" poetic concerns, antipoetic not in any dadaist fashion but in the sense that Pound was working to rejuvenate the power of art by removing it from the constricted and rarefied "aesthetic realm." By the time he was preparing Canto 75 for print, Pound had spent some fifteen years trying to excite popular interest in microphotography. Here again we find Pound the popularizer. Pound had high hopes for this process; recognizing how greatly it could reduce printing costs, he saw it as a means of making hitherto rare texts available for a mass audience. As Rudge wrote in an essay

---

27. Note that the musical notation included in Canto 83, too, is striking in its visual presentation. Interestingly, in an interview with Thomas Cole in June of 1949, Pound claimed the music was his own creation. See Thomas Cole, "Ezra Pound and Imagi," *Paideuma* 16 (Winter 1987): 56.

28. In *One World*, 320n, Read quotes a letter from Pound to Eliot, dated 1 June 1940: "I spose Faber will give me a FEW musical illusions in next Vol? One fer Canter XX. shall want I think four in whole poEM." It is important here not to confuse "illusion" with "allusion." This is not a minor quibble. When critics like—to cite yet another example—Stephen Adams, "The Soundscape of the Cantos," *Humanities Association Review* 28 (Spring 1977): 167–88, propose that "music is . . . one of the many subordinate motifs in a thickly woven tapestry of allusion," they are missing the single most innovative feature of the *Cantos*: its ambitious inclusiveness.

that followed the printing of another of her holograph transcriptions of Münch's score in 1938, "the invention of this micro-photographic process should prove as important a discovery for the history of music as that of the printing press for letters."[29] Rudge's optimism suggests what Philip Furia has called Pound's major enterprise: his hope that in transmitting "the lost documents from our past, he could help transform his age just as medieval Europe was reborn when a flood of long-lost classical documents was channeled through the new technology of printing."[30] Microphotography in Canto 75 advertises what the new technology can do for modern efforts to popularize serious scholarship.

Canto 75 is a highly uncertain experiment, a distinctive application of the political and poetic principles from which Pound generated the greater part of the *Cantos*. Its generic mixture is reproduced nowhere else in Pound's work. And yet, it is not unique. It shares with other cantos thematic and generic features and, more fundamentally, Pound's combinatory procedures. The musical notation of Canto 75 suggests both a principle of organization, as Pound answered Pasolini, and a further rejection of narrative order.

Janequin's "chant" exemplified for Pound an early instance of the "pattern" or "horizontal" music he sought to champion in his own time. "Pattern" in Pound's sense is antinarrative. The motifs of a perfectly repeated pattern in themselves "mean" nothing. Pattern is not meaning, but a principle of organization that unfolds in several directions simultaneously, creating meaning by variation and violation. Generally, Pound contrasted "horizontal" or contrapuntal music with "vertical" or harmonic music, "pattern" with melody. Janequin did not "represent" the sound of birds by creating the melody of a birdsong, he reproduced the sound of many different birds in the trees at once. In addition to choosing other words carefully for their sound, Janequin used many words that are simply ono-

---

29. Olga Rudge, "Music and a Process," *Townsman*, January 1938, 21; the version published here was a different copy, but essentially the same score. This was the first issue of the *Townsman*, and the importance Pound attached to the microphotographic process can be inferred from how he thought information about it would be a dynamic way to help Ronald Duncan launch his journal. Stephen J. Adams has also discussed Pound's interest in microphotography. He observes that "one of the Rapallo concerts (5 February 1938) was given to a demonstration of the process, and Pound began to advertise it frequently in articles, notes in little magazines, and correspondence." Adams infers as well that "this economical process is one of the points of the Janequin music in Canto LXXV."

30. Philip Furia, *Pound's Cantos Declassified* (University Park: Pennsylvania State University Press, 1984), 4.

matopoeic. At several places in the chant, the voice of the "minstrel" is silent, melody is dropped, and the thronging songs of the birds are heard all at once: "friam, teo, to, coqui, oy, ty, trr, tu, huit, teo, frian, fi, ti, trr, huit, tar, turri, quiloi." This meaningless libretto conveniently exemplifies Pound's assertion that there is but "one subject matter that music can properly represent, namely sound." Such music, he thought, "flowered in Janequin," and "Gerhart Münch has written it into a violin part."[31] Three years earlier, in *ABC of Reading*, Pound explained: "Clement Janequin wrote a chorus, with words for the singers of the different parts of the chorus. These words would have no literary or poetic value if you took the music away, but when Francesco da Milano reduced it for the lute, the birds were still in the music. And when Münch transcribed it for modern instruments the birds were still there. They ARE still there in the violin part" (*ABCR*, 54). What Pound admired was Münch's ability to recover the original, firsthand perception of the birdsong: the recovery of a prelinguistic experience.

In fact, as Schafer remarks, Münch's transcription is really, more than a "transcription," a "quite elaborate reconstruction" (*EPM*, 328). Münch's score substitutes for the contrapuntal question and answer of Janequin's chanson a pronounced interest in melody that is without parallel in the Janequin. Nevertheless, Münch endeavored to preserve—by giving new form to—what Pound called Janequin's "poetic atmosphere," his "clever registration of the sounds of nature," by means of two techniques unique to a stringed instrument. Pound commented on both. First, the use of pizzicato (plucking instead of bowing the violin strings), of which Pound said in 1936: "The beauty of the staccato section in the violin solo of Münch's Janequin transcription resides in his use of the lower strings of the instrument, coinciding approximately with the sound of the medieval *viel*" (*EPM*, 392). The vielle does not figure in Janequin's choral music: Münch impressed Pound by his ability to write music that sounded medieval without resorting to an archaeological reproduction of Janequin's techniques. Second, Münch's text calls for the use of double-stopping (bowing two notes simultaneously), the effect of which Pound thought exceptionally successful. As he wrote to Louis Dudek, "itz the double stopping for the fiddle that makes leZWoiseaux the FINAL product. (to date)." Münch uses both techniques to convey the sense of "hearing" more than one bird sing at once. The pizzicato sections approximate roughly the purely onomatopoeic passages in Janequin's chan-

---

31. "Ligurian View of a Venetian Festival," *Music & Letters*, vol. 18 (January 1937); reprinted in *EPM*, 416. Pound repeats this argument in *Guide to Kulchur*, 152–53.

son, and introduce a rhythmic variation that corresponds to those sections. The double-stopping, especially of fourths, has a slightly jarring effect in a melody line that, save for the pizzicato passages, is otherwise simple and pellucid. Pound believed these techniques preserved the pattern, the sound of not "one bird but of many," in Janequin's original, even though he knew that Münch did not try, any more than had da Milano before him, "to preserve Janequin's text philologically" (*EPM*, 348).

Pound's praise of Münch's resetting of Janequin's music reveals much about his own resetting of Münch. Pound's use of Münch's score both included actual music and gave, yet again, new form to the "registration" in that music of prelinguistic experience. Pound's notion of "musical themes that meet each other" was, more than simply a way of supplanting discursive organization with nondiscursive, a way of emphasizing multiple associations that may not result in a single unified experience.

It is in keeping with his appreciation of "pattern" music that Pound subscribed to Dolmetsch's view that "music didn't begin with Bach, it ended there." But Pound's concern with pattern did not derive immediately from Renaissance and baroque music; that the idea of "pattern" registered in the way it did owed a great deal to the futurist manifestos of Marinetti—who first visited London some four years before Pound met Dolmetsch.[32] In his "Technical Manifesto of Futurism" (1912), for instance, Marinetti called for the destruction of syntax ("scatter nouns at random"), the avoidance of finite verbs, the abolition of conjunctions and punctuation, and the use of "an ever-vaster gradation of analogies." In a manifesto of 1922, Marinetti declared: "Before us, men had always sung as Homer did, with narrative sequence and a logical catalog of events, images, and ideas. . . . Our free-word tableaux, on the other hand, finally distinguishes from Homer

---

32. According to Humphrey Carpenter, *A Serious Character: The Life of Ezra Pound* (Boston: Houghton Mifflin, 1988), 257, Pound was first "taken to the Dolmetsch home at Haslemere by Alvin Langdon Coburn." Pound wrote to his father in October of that year to say that he had "commissioned a clavicord." Pound's response to Marinetti was complicated. He had been excited by Marinetti's manifestos in 1913. But, under the jeering influence of Lewis, who wanted an explicitly English revolution, Pound soon became an outspoken opponent of futurism. In the late 1920s, after half a decade in Italy, Pound again reversed his position and began to hail Marinetti as the inventor of "modernism." Canto 72, the first of the two Italian cantos, begins with a long apostrophe to Marinetti—although apostrophe is not a wholly accurate description: what happens in Canto 72 is much more like the meeting of spirits that Blake described in his "Milton"; Marinetti's spirit comes to Pound and asks for the use of his body, or at least his voice, in order to continue fighting for the fascist cause. Pound's debt to Marinetti has also received attention from Redman, *Ezra Pound and Italian Fascism*, 199–20.

since they no longer contain narrative sequence, but rather the simultaneous polyexpression of the world."[33] "Musical themes that meet each other," or musical association, were phrases with which Pound explored his own sense of "the simultaneous polyexpression of the world." It is the simultaneity that informs Pound's "'new' historic sense," his insistence in the *Guide* that "we do NOT know the past in chronological sequence." Pound's opposition between simultaneity and sequence, another version of the culture-mechanism duality, was thus an argument about how we know the world. Canto 75 associates Münch's "pattern music" with the recovery of that process of knowing.

Canto 75 enacts the process of rejuvenation. While imprisoned in the six by six-and-one-half-foot "death cell" Pound had suffered a physical and mental breakdown and experienced a loss of memory. The echoed exclamation that opens the canto alludes to Dante's description (*Inferno*, Canto 12) of a river of boiling blood wherein flounder the souls of the violent. There, the river is both instrument of justice and emblem of crime. In Canto 75, "Phlegethon" refers to the hardly stilled fury of the Second World War, but the allusion to Dante suggests that world war will prove as endless as the torment of the damned. Dante had feared that his mind could not withstand the witness of all required of him; Pound's exclamation in Canto 75 was one of relief at the endurance of his sanity. In part, the opening of Canto 75 continues from the concluding lines of Canto 74:

> out of hell, the pit
> out of the dust and glare evil
> . . . .
> we who have passed over Lethe.

Pound thus characterized his personal inferno as a confluence of violence and mnemonic oblivion. Lethe is the river of forgetting. "Out of Phlegethon" is a cry of recognition at the sudden remembering of an old friend, and of joy upon discovering that his memory, and hence his poetic power, have survived the ordeal of the death cell. By a "metonymic" process of "association" (no matter that Pound would have rejected both terms),[34] Pound recalls Münch's transcription of a chanson in which the trouvère calls upon "the

---

33. Marinetti, "The Free Word Style," trans. Arthur A. Coppotelli, in *Marinetti: Selected Writings* (New York: Farrar, Straus & Giroux, 1972), 164.

34. In "Affirmations III," *New Age*, 21 January 1915; reprinted in *A Memoir of Gaudier-Brzeska* (New York: New Directions, 1970), 97, Pound attacked the notions of "association" and "me-

sleeping hearts" of men and women to "rouse from their stupor" and answer the "summons of the god of love." Like Janequin's motet, a celebration of the "miracle" (his word) of spring, Pound's canto is a cry of rebirth and reawakening.

This "theme" of rebirth makes for an interesting and dramatic story. But while it can be argued that it is "authorized" by the further allusions in Cantos 79 and 82 to birdsong and to the shifting positions of birds on the camp wire, it cannot be said to be "the story" of Canto 75. Canto 75 is not a story. Strictly thematic readings of this or of any canto can be compelling, and there are good reasons for presenting them. They may indeed be inevitable in the interpretation of a work whose compositional principles are antinarrative. But these critical constructions achieve their sense—even in so short a canto as 75—at the price of excluding intractable or unproductive features. Although it is true that any critical account privileges certain associations, in this case conventional constructions of sense have explained away the single largest constituent feature of the text, substituting critical narrative for the intractable antinarrative features of the canto. Where the provision of local sense is the predominant goal, this kind of substitution is understandable; but here let us defer the making of sense from the musical notation itself to Pound's deliberate inclusion of that which is beyond sense.

The seven lines of poetry in this canto combine epic and lyric features on structural as well as thematic levels. Although Pound associates his young friend with Dante's river of fire, or juxtaposes that river with birdsong, he does so in dactylic and trochaic feet. This latter mixture suggests in part an attempt to combine epic scope and lyric intensity. But it participates too in Pound's desire to expand the English poetic tradition. As he wrote in Canto 81, "to break the pentameter, that was the first heave":

> Out of Phlegethon!
> Out of Phlegethon,
>   Gerhart
>   art thou come forth out of Phlegethon?
> With Buxtehude and Klages in your satchel, with the
> Ständebuch of Sachs in yr/luggage
>   —not of one bird but of many

---

tonymy." But what Pound objected to was association that was mechanical and overly discursive—hardly the textual process of Canto 75.

Both of what D. S. Carne-Ross has called "the two major innovations in Pound's metric" are evident in these lines: "the use of falling rhythm (. . . dactylo-trochaic) rather than the familiar English rising (or iambic) rhythm; and a much more extensive use than had been common in serious English verse of trisyllabic feet."[35] Indeed, Massimo Bacigalupo finds the relation of "Gerhart-art-forth" with "thou-out" to be "a fine counterpoint" that, coupled with "the ecstatic dactylic measure of the *Cantos* (art thou come forth out of Phlegethon)," makes for "what is indeed a noble bit of music."[36] Bacigalupo's sense of the "ecstatic" and "noble" reflects his interest in demonstrating how Pound transforms lyric elements into epic. However, the contents of Münch's satchel, indeed the very presence of the satchel, comprise other features neither lyric nor epic, and not susceptible to such attractively grand descriptions.

Like Malatesta's post-bag, Münch's satchel contains documents that resist the romance of storytelling. Besides Münch's transcription of the Janequin—or rather da Milano—canzone, the contents of the satchel include: a score of Buxtehude's music (probably organ music and most likely church music); a book by Ludwig Klages, a German writer of anti-intellectual, antipositivist, and anti-Semitic tracts "to whom Münch addressed several letters"—a man so vituperative that even Pound referred to him as a "buzzard" and declined Münch's attempts to interest him in Klages's opinions.[37] Equally "unlyrical" and "unepic" is the "standebuch" or book of trades that Pound incorrectly attributed to Hans Sachs—a text for the rising bourgeois of the sixteenth century, describing and illustrating the occupations open to a man of industry.[38]

To be sure, Buxtehude, Klages, and Sachs figure only as allusions and are of secondary importance to the musical transcription of Münch, which is an integral part of the canto. But the associational structure of the canto makes them a necessary part of the process by which that music is remembered. Consider the last phrase Pound unpacked from Münch's satchel: "not of one bird but of many" exemplifies Pound's understanding of the music of poetry.

---

35. D. S. Carne-Ross, "New Metres for Old: A Note on Pound's Metric," in *Ezra Pound: A Critical Anthology*, ed. J. P. Sullivan (Harmondsworth: Penguin, 1970), 347–49.

36. Massimo Bacigalupo, *The Forméd Trace: The Later Poetry of Ezra Pound* (New York: Columbia University Press, 1980), 115.

37. Eva Hesse, "Klages in Canto 75/450: A Positive Identification," *Paideuma* 10 (fall 1981): 295–296. Until Hesse made this identification, it was generally assumed that "Klages" referred to the nineteenth-century French guitarist.

38. Walter Baumann, "Gerhart . . . Standebuch," *Paideuma* 10 (winter 1981): 589–94.

It refers not just to Münch's comment that in "reading Janequin's music transposed" he heard the voices of "a lot of birds, not one bird alone" (*GK*, 153), but to all the associations that accompany Pound's memory of Münch. The phrase participates in several genres at once. It was first uttered in private conversation. But it is also an instance of musical criticism; and when Pound used the phrase in *Guide to Kulchur* and elsewhere, it became explicitly so, as well as being a part of a broadly directed didactic tract. In Canto 75, Pound altered the phrase for metrical purposes, and by isolating it suggested its power to describe his own poetic. The phrase here refers not simply to the original birdsong, but to the work's accumulation of other voices through time: Buxtehude, Klages, Sachs, Münch, even Pound himself. "Pattern" moves in many directions simultaneously: "musical themes that meet each other."

Pound's resistance to a controlling story is further evident in the repetition of the phrase "out of Phlegethon." In line 1 it is an exclamation; in line 2 it is a statement; and in line 3 it is a question. Here is anaphora with a difference. Rather than the amplification or development of litany, each successive repetition makes the force of the phrase more problematic by confusing generic expectations. The confident cry of line 1 is by line 4 neatly reversed, transformed into an interrogative as it is moved from a position on the left margin to one on the right. "Gerhart," the figure to whom these lines refer, is named in a line by himself, midway between the extremes of elation and uncertainty: just as he functions at once as the object of Pound's revived memory, and of Pound's quickly following uncertainty whether the man himself has survived the war. Both of these themes "meet" in the cryptic reference to "Gerhart," a one-word line that resolves neither of them. Anaphora has a related function in lines 5 and 6: the repetition of "with" is placed at the end of line 5 rather than at the beginning of line 6, mitigating what emphasis might have rested on the figures mentioned in line 5 and emphasizing instead the continuing process of multiple association. Other formal elements contribute to this process: the repetition of rhythmic units ("Phlegethon"/"Buxtehude"/"Standebuch"); the use of internal rhyme, usually near rhymes and, except for instances of homeoteleuton, no end rhymes ("Gerhart"/"art", "Klages"/"luggage," "satchel"/"Sachs"); the use of alliteration ("bird"/"but," "forth"/Phlegethon," the heavy use of *g* sounds in "Klages"/"luggage"/"Gerhart"/"Phlegethon," and the use of *s* sounds in lines 5 and 6); and the use of assonance ("thou"/"out," "Standebuch"/"Buxtehude," and the frequent use of slightly varying *o* sounds).

All of these elements create patterns of sound, but as Lewis would say, the words still speak. Indeed, Pound's text here exemplifies how overdetermination can create ambiguity rather than limit it. The verbal density of this canto develops still further resonance by virtue of Pound's exploitation of typographical convention. His spacing of words on the page heightens their polysemic multiple relatedness. He told Michael Reck, who visited him at St. Elizabeths in 1950, "ALL typographic disposition, placings of words *on* the page, is intended to facilitate the reader's intonation, whether he be reading silently to self or aloud to friends. Given time and technique I might even put down the musical notations of passages or 'breaks into song.'"[39] That Pound spoke of "*breaks* into song" implies heterogeneity of content, not all of the *Cantos* is song, but promises that there will be songs. His use of typographic disposition was another instance of a practice with both visual and aural functions: the visual function of setting off a word or group of words with others not necessarily part of the same syntactic unit, and the aural function of facilitating the placing of emphasis. Six of seven lines in Canto 75 begin at a unique point of indentation, and the score begins at a seventh. These varied margins exemplify Lewis's complaint that Pound "is always breaking off . . . indeed, as a rule, twice every line." But a break in sense need not imply a structural break, not an attempt to "escape" sense. Pound's manner of structuring his lines should be understood in conjunction with his loose syntactical structure. There are no conjunctions between lines; Pound relies instead upon a prepositional structure, so that the canto unfolds by means of association: there are ten prepositions in seven lines. "Buxtehude and Klages," "Sachs," and Münch's score do not constitute a sequence. Pound's construction strains to make all simultaneously present with the invocation "Gerhart." Despite the exclamation mark at the end of line 1, or the question mark at the end of line 4, there are no truly end-stopped lines. It may not be accurate to say that the seven lines of metrical notation constitute a single syntactical unit, yet we can say that each line participates in a single associational unit or pattern. This is the informing principle of the post-bag or satchel. It is, moreover, the kind of technique to which Pound's combination of musical and metrical notation points. Although it is not "contrapuntal" in the usual sense of that term, "counterpoint" was Pound's way of conceiving of the simultaneous unfolding of several distinct themes or concerns.

While campaigning with Lewis to distinguish "vorticism" from "postim-

---

39. Michael Reck, *Ezra Pound: A Close-Up* (New York: McGraw-Hill, 1967), 200.

pressionism," Pound had identified this process of formal combination as the "musical conception of form." "The musical conception of form," Pound explained, involved the recognition that one "cannot pretend fully to express oneself unless one expresses instinct and intellect together." It meant, he believed, the "understanding that you can use form as a musician uses sound, that you can select motives of form from the forms before you, that you can recombine and recolour them and 'organise' them into new form."[40] His notion there of joining "instinct and intellect" anticipated his later turn to folklore as a repository of culture; his conceiving of the recombination and reorganization of formal aspects as "musical" was only a few short steps from the association in *Guide to Kulchur* of music with the establishment of "hierarchies of value" for his own time.

Pound included Münch's score in much the same way he handled other texts: seeking to preserve the "sense of" the work as a whole even as he found it impractical to include more than parts. But here too Pound emphasized passages presenting multiple voices at once—the sound "not of one bird but of many": precisely the effect cultivated in much of the *Cantos*. The combination of musical and metrical notations provided a means of foregrounding textual processes that were crucial to his historical program. Even more than in such earlier sequences as *The Fifth Decad of Cantos*, in *Pisan Cantos* Pound was concerned to find in natural processes a model for human conduct. This concern, which Pound felt with a new urgency after the collapse of what he had taken to be a millennial regime, betrayed a closer affinity with Enlightenment attitudes toward nature than it did with those of the more immediate romantic past. Pound's use of Münch's score, for this reason, ought not to be taken as a Wordsworthian or Keatsian "epiphanic moment." Music for Pound connoted measure, not ecstatic excess. And yet, his association of both music and memory with instinct was a distinctly romantic legacy.

As usual, the relations among Pound's various motifs are not easily resolved. His interest in creating a poem whose chief bid for greatness lay in an unprecedented inclusiveness often produced highly unstable mixtures in which warring ideological precepts are found side by side. His identification in Canto 75 of music with memory and instinct, and of the natural processes in which he hoped to discern a model for human government, is but one example. This complex association he carried over into the opening of Canto 76:

40. "Affirmations II," *New Age*, 14 January 1915, 278.

> And the sun high over horizon hidden in cloud bank
> > lit saffron the cloud ridge
> > > dove sta memoria
>
> "Will" said Signora Agresti, "break his political
> but not economic system"

"The musical conception of form" was among Pound's most important explanatory metaphors, and yet it seriously undermined his attempts to create anything as stable as a "hierarchy of values." Pound's combinatory procedures followed from his assumption that issues of genres bore no necessary relation to the generation of what he abstracted as "value." Genre, it seemed, was as dispensible as other forms of historical context. The *Cantos* sought a less contingent coherence, an epic coherence that made its appeal on the basis of the absolute and total unity that Ruskin had identified with "culture" itself. Much of the trouble that vitiates the *Cantos* comes from Pound's supreme confidence that, by creating new, overdetermined contexts he could appropriate elements from any variety of texts without fear for their integrity. After *Pisan Cantos*, Pound renewed more resolutely than ever his attempts to "take a totalitarian hold on history."

6
"These are the Histories, OR":
Narrative in the Benton Cantos of
Section: Rock-Drill

The History That Is in the *Cantos*

There has been [among historians] an inclination to cling to narrative as being least
easily convertible into generalization; to hug
events rather than engage with their patterns; to resign the economic aspects of history to economists rather than include them;
to ignore the results of ethnography on the
external ground that they were dateless and
therefore non-historical; to allow the history
of the great Asiatic civilizations to settle behind watertight bulkheads; to view any
larger culture history askance; to emphasize
the mechanics of documentation as evidence
that history, too, was objective and scientific.
   —A. L. Kroeber, *The Nature of Culture*

In the midst of recording the rise and fall of dynasties and empires in Canto 61, Pound asserted that "litterati fought fiercer than other men." The phrase

---

Both epigraphs in this chapter are from Kroeber's *Nature of Culture* (Chicago: University of Chicago Press, 1952), a book he made from "those papers and selected parts of my professional writings that might be of most general interest" (vii). Although not precisely an instance of "popularized scholarship," *The Nature of Culture* was an effort to present to a wider audience his "theory about the kind of thing culture is." It is interesting that Kroeber, theorizing within the discourse of culture at approximately the same historical moment as Pound, came to inveigh against set academic circumscriptions in terms analogous to Pound's.

carries a portentous ring, but the "story" or narrative of which it is a sign does not figure in Pound's text. In this regard the line exemplifies a persistent generic feature of his historical writing, an antinarrative presentation from which he departed but once anywhere in the *Cantos*. That experiment came late, in the "Benton" cantos of *Section: Rock-Drill*, and although anomalous derives from Pound's characteristic combinatory procedures.

Pound had been working with historical texts and "documents" since *A Draft of XVI Cantos* (1925), and been devoting serious attention to histories in particular since *A Draft of Cantos 17–27* (1930). But such sources as *The Book of the Council Major* (Canto 25) were not primarily narrative, and Pound's treatment of them did not purport narrative continuity. The generic features of the Benton cantos need also be distinguished from the extensive historical attentions of *Cantos LII–LXXI*. Especially in the China cantos (Cantos 52 through 61), these latter constituted in themselves a significant generic experiment, though one that depended on an inherited "orientalism" of a quite common kind.[1] Although the structure of *Cantos LII–LXXI* as a book equates what Pound saw as the lessons of Chinese history with those lessons he found in the papers of John Adams, Pound in fact saw no development or change, but pattern. In *Guide to Kulchur*, completed immediately before the composition of *LII–LXXI*, he had explained "THE LESSON of Chinese history": "As I can have no pretense to 'potting' it here, might nevertheless be of two kinds. By implication, we might more despise and suspect the kind of education which we (my generation) received, and we might acquire some balance in NOT mistaking recurrence for innovation" (*GK*, 274). Pound's remarks make clear his continuing dedication to popularizing specialized knowledge. But they also exemplify his desire to locate enduring pattern within mere chronology. Chinese history appears in the *Cantos* before sustained treatment of a Western history precisely because Pound presumed the "Orient" to be changeless. The sudden proliferation of ideograms in *Cantos LII–LXXI* bespeaks the same concern. No ideograms had previously appeared in the *Cantos* except the "cheng ming," which concludes Canto LI—the last canto of *Fifth Decad*.[2] The repeated inclusion of ideograms in *LII–LXXI* stems not so much from Pound's usual impulse to

---

1. See Edward Said's groundbreaking *Orientalism* (New York: Vintage Books, 1979).
2. See Barbara Eastman's account of Pound's retrospective inclusion of ideograms into earlier cantos in *Ezra Pound's Cantos: The Story of the Text, 1948–1975* (Orono, Maine: The National Poetry Foundation, 1979).

capture the sound of his sources as from a new boldness with an old idea; it was from Fenollosa's notebooks that Pound had learned twenty years before to see ideograms as representations of pattern.

The orientalism of Pound's Chinese history is hardly singular. But in Pound's case it merits attention because he proposed to use oriental history as a model for understanding the West, and indeed human history in general. And so, just as *Cantos LII–LXXI* divide between Chinese and American sources, so too do the cantos of *Section: Rock-Drill*, composed some fifteen years later. Cantos 85 and 86 are dominated by materials drawn from the *Shu Ching*, a Chinese history that reconstructs the past on the basis of Confucian models. The ellipsis with which Canto 87 opens refers us back to previous condemnations of usury, after which the next motif, repeated from *Guide to Kulchur*, seems all the more significant: Mussolini's one question to Pound—

"—perché si vuol mettere—
your ideas in order?"
Date '32
(Canto 87/583)

Pound read much into Mussolini's banality, and praised him out of the conviction that Mussolini shared his sense that the creation of order was the principle task facing modernity.

Such are the materials that set up Pound's work in Canto 88, the fourth of the cantos of *Rock-Drill*, but the first of Pound's cantos ever to take up a single historical narrative and treat it in a sustained manner. The narrative itself was but a small part of a larger narrative—a chapter from Senator Thomas Hart Benton's *History of the Workings of American Government . . . from 1820–1850 or Thirty Years' View*.[3] Pound used Benton's narrative not only to open Canto 88 but also to conclude it, and he returns to Benton's *View* throughout Canto 89. Thus the "Benton" diptych contains both the most sustained narrative in the *Cantos* and also, as Peter Nicholls observes, Pound's "last extended excursion into modern history."[4] But although the two Benton cantos share many thematic concerns and quote extensively from Benton's text, Canto 89 includes Benton's language only in short phrases or passages, and is more characteristic of Pound's manner of treating

---

3. The passage Pound uses is found in *Thirty Years' View* (New York: D. Appleton, 1854–56), 1:70–77.
4. Peter Nicholls, *Ezra Pound: Politics, Economics, and Writing* (London: Macmillan, 1984), 202.

historical texts. This is not to say that the problems it raises are uninteresting, or that its procedures are wholly unlike those of Canto 88. But the sustained narrative of Canto 88 distinguishes it from anything Pound had written since *A Draft of XXX Cantos* (1920–30); and the manner of its inclusion distinguishes it even from such explicitly narrative cantos as Canto 1.

It is therefore precisely because Pound treated it in so sustained a manner that that part of Benton's narrative which opens Canto 88 affords an exceptional opportunity to examine what the presence of history in the *Cantos* really means. Consider the first eighty lines of Canto 88. It is difficult poetry, and the reasons for its difficulty involve Pound's most central procedures. Aside from exceptional lines where Pound condenses long passages by a paraphrastic use of particular words, the language of this sequence does not deviate from Benton's, and yet Pound did not succeed in preserving Benton's meaning. In part, inadvertent changes in meaning stem from Pound's frequent omissions from Benton's account: sometimes one or two words from a sentence, sometimes entire pages between sentences. But these omissions are not the most fundamental source of change.

Pound's inclusion of Benton's narrative met resistance that originated, principally, from three factors: differences in generic composition, differences arising from their respective historical conditions, and differences between their conceptions of history and how those conceptions informed their separate projects. Pound adhered, for the most part, to Benton's language, accepted Benton's valuations of honor and heroism, and was excited by Benton's tendency to regard monetary issues in moral terms. But Pound's perceptions notwithstanding, this last tendency is not to be identified with Ruskinian principles of cultural organism. Benton's historical view turns on profoundly different assumptions about historical relations; a more analytical reader than Pound might even have found Benton's writing—in both its thematic and its generic features—antithetical to the discourse of culture within which Pound inscribed his work. Benton's *View* was a late development of an older, Enlightenment model with which Ruskin's work was soon to compete. Pound's text "includes" Benton's, but its inclusion is not accomplished without change: some features of Benton's text are preserved, some are dropped, and some features alien to it are added. It is finally by the manner of this inclusion, rather than by the nature of the included material itself, that we know that Pound's totalizing, "cultural" vision has replaced Benton's analytical view of the "workings" of government.

The Underpinnings of Benton's *View*

Senator Thomas Hart Benton was a Jacksonian Democrat who represented the state of Missouri between 1821 and 1851. One recent historian has described him as a man "convinced that moderation was the normal human state of mind, [and he] was willing to work for and settle for this without insistence upon outright approval."[5] Although moderate in many of his political positions, including the issue of states rights, he was an ardent fiscal conservative: a precarious mixture, given his slave-holding, western constituency. Eventually, Benton's hard-money policies—never popular in the specie-poor west—and his increasingly isolated battle against sectionalism cost him his seat. *A History of American Government . . . from 1820 to 1850 or Thirty Years' View* (1854–56) was written in an attempt to carry on his efforts for the ill-fated cause of compromise. The part of Benton's narrative that Pound included at the beginning of Canto 88 concerned a duel fought in 1826 between Senators John Randolph and Henry Clay.

According to Benton, the origins of the duel lay in a series of misunderstandings. Randolph had delivered a speech when Clay was absent from the Senate, attacking Clay and John Quincy Adams for supporting a treaty with the newly independent states of Latin America. A distorted version of Randolph's speech (Congress as yet kept no detailed written records of its debates) reached Clay, who heard that Randolph had not only attacked him personally, but held himself accountable for all he said. When Clay demanded an explanation, Randolph demurred, answering that "he denied the right of any person to question him out of the Senate for words spoken within it." Clay challenged Randolph to a duel, and with each of them clinging so obdurately to a (different) point of principle, their seconds proved unable to mediate their resolve. They met, exchanged fire, and survived only due to poor marksmanship and Randolph's decision not to return Clay's second shot.

This synopsis is a convenience—no more. It cannot represent either Benton's narrative or Pound's adequately because it glosses over formal characteristics whose importance to our understanding of what Pound's inclusion of history really means will become evident as we discern what happens when they are changed. Pound, having proposed to create "a poem including history," aimed to avoid summary or paraphrase and sought

---

5. Elbert Smith, "Thomas Hart Benton: Southern Realist," *American Historical Review* (July 1953), 806.

instead to include the material itself. Benton's "view" of thirty years of history is by definition synoptic, but in accordance with a carefully arranged hierarchy of generic features.

The notion of "view" was central to Benton's thinking and writing about history, and Benton showed himself to be keenly aware of that centrality. The principle function of his introduction—his "Preliminary View"—was to propose the advantages gained in writing history as a "view," and throughout his narrative Benton seldom referred to his work as anything else. Indeed, Benton used the word repeatedly, so that readers would not mistake his purpose in raising inflammatory issues at a time of heated political passions. Benton worried, in other words, that his "view" might be mistaken for a polemic, a mistake all too likely given that *Thirty Years' View* was published only four years before southern troops fired on Fort Sumter.

Although Benton's notion of "view" was tied to his political aims, and although autobiography is one of the important generic constituents of *Thirty Years' View*, Benton recounted his participation in events infrequently. But he recalled his perspective at the time events unfolded with care and precision. Most often, Benton depicted himself as a calm and rational observer, even when describing his own sometimes impassioned orations. He wrote of himself in the third person and described his activities as author with passive constructions: "Mr. Benton addressed himself mainly to Mr. Webster's position, confounding insolvency and bankruptcy, as taken at the previous session; and delivered a speech of some research on opposition to that assumption—of which some extracts are given in the next chapter" (2:234). Benton's continual concern with perspective and his tendency to translate his own actions into perspectival terms are part of his argument for the value of his own conclusions. These tendencies emerge more clearly still in Benton's short "Autobiography," included in the front of some editions of *Thirty Years' View*. Here again, Benton was interested in his own story only insofar as it intersected with the larger movement of history. Citing Macaulay's approbation of historians who offer no other "qualification for writing history" than that they "had spoken history, acted history, lived history," Benton affirmed his own impartiality: "I was in the Senate the whole time of which I write—an active business member, attending and attentive—in the confidence of half the administrations, and a close observer of the others—had an inside view of transactions of which the public only saw the outside, and of many of which the two sides were very different—saw the secret springs and hidden machinery by which men and parties were to be moved, and measures promoted or thwarted—saw patriotism and ambition at their respective labors, and was generally able to discriminate between them." We can understand why Benton's wish for "harmony and concord among all the States" prompted this incessant attention to perspective by recognizing his participation in Enlightenment tradition. Benton expected that observation, if elevated by reason above the enthusiasms of partisanship, could discern "the true relation" between human events.

In this confidence that historical narrative could produce from the welter of particular facts a "whole truth," he was relying upon a conceptual pattern deriving from the epistemological premises of John Locke. Benton hoped that by taking a broad "view" of the workings of American government, by looking back over thirty years and beyond the anger of the moment, he could demonstrate a long pattern of factions working together, even if only for their own benefit. Benton's argument is essentially that difference need not lead to dissolution or war. The difference between Benton's notion of "view" and Pound's conception of "vortex" suggests that Pound did not hold the same confidence. Where the vortex implies the suddenness and violence of change around a still center, Benton's notion of "view" expected that change developed over time, and so could be anticipated and prepared for gradually. This belief in the value of perspective, in the need for understanding to follow from observation conducted with the equanimity of reason, points to the epistemological underpinnings of Benton's work. His notion of "view" was not merely a rhetorical gesture, a claim for impartiality, but a Lockean way of thinking inseparable from his composition.

The language of "view" implies, all the same, a political attitude. Benton was explicit on this point: "I do not propose a regular history, but a political work, to show the practical working of the government, and speak of men and events in subordination to that design, and to illustrate the character of Institutions . . . upon the fate of which the eyes of the world are now fixed" (1:v). By classifying his narrative as "a political work," Benton intended to dissociate it from a self-serving antiquarianism that would merely celebrate the glory or "interest" of the past. Benton was less interested in how the federal government had developed than in how it would continue beyond 1850. He desired, not to be the annalist of thirty years of government, but to show to a troubled time a past that had kept the faith of its fathers. He offered detachment when the public was clamoring for commitment, and counseled calm when "daily newspapers and periodicals all more or less involved in partisan warfare" were anticipating action (1:692). His work was "political" in that its purpose was to suggest policy, it was a "view" in the way it sought to achieve that policy.

Thirty Years' View was a complex mixture of different kinds of writing: political, historical, personal, detached. The particular chapter that Pound used in Canto 88 was no exception. Benton had vowed to "speak of men and events only in subordination" to his political design, and his narrative of the duel between Senators Henry Clay and John Randolph observed that vow implicitly. The duel narrative follows Benton's account of "the Panama Mission": a controversy surrounding an invitation to the United States from the newly independent states of Latin America to join a mutual defense league against the monarchies of Europe. The invitation fired the imaginations of many Americans, and members of Congress like Clay argued that it amounted to little beyond a formalization of the Monroe Doctrine. But a minority that included Benton and Randolph maintained that the United States had best preserve its "old policy" of avoiding the "entanglements" of foreign alliances. The invitation occasioned such strident debate in Congress that although both houses narrowly approved the mission, no action was ever taken. Benton's closing comments on the issue are calm, yet pointed: "No question, in its day, excited more heat and intemperate discussion, or . . . ever cooled off, and died out so suddenly and completely. And now the chief benefit to be derived from its retrospect—and that indeed is a real one—is a view of the firmness with which was then maintained by a minority, the old policy of the United States, to avoid entangling alliances" (1:69). Exploiting the tension generated by the preceding narrative, Benton's conclusion enabled him to frame his narrative, to establish a "view" of it as a closed chapter in the larger story of the workings of the American government. Benton saw two points here: first, that after a serious trial our government preserved its "old policy" (a conservatism that Pound too would admire); and second, that federal government continued working largely by virtue of the firmness with which a minority maintained principle, a victory Benton believed repeatable in his own day.

It is this latter motive that led Benton to tell at length the story of the Clay-Randolph duel. Significantly, Benton defended this particular attention to "men and events" in the same language that he defended all his undertakings—in the language of point of view: "It is in that point of view that I dwell on circumstances which might seem trivial, but which are not so, being illustrative of character and significant to their smallest particulars" (1:71). The central task of Benton's *View* was to propose a model for the resolution of factionalism. A "novelistic" treatment of character provided one means of doing so. To say that Benton's narrative included at certain points some features of novelistic discourse is to invite misunderstanding. Benton's *View* is not a novel, but makes use of features ordinarily associated with the novel. He was as attentive to the connections between events as to the events themselves. He took care to relate the situation surrounding events, speeches, or conversations, as well as to indicate when and whom he was quoting and to preserve in all cases a distinctiveness of voice. In fact, Benton's apology really functioned by drawing attention, not to the strength of Randolph's character, but to the fairness of his own depiction of it.

Benton's narrative was designed to minimize, if not eradicate, the intrusion of the unexpected. He related a succession of difficult problems that arose gradually and were made subject to the ordinary workings of government, rather than a succession of crises that so upset those workings that they overturned familiar procedures. Benton traced the cause of the Clay-Randolph duel to a series of misunderstandings—some accidental and some the result of third-party machinations, initiated when words spoken on the Senate floor by Randolph were taken out of context and misrepresented to Clay, who had not been in attendance that day. Benton concluded by closing his "story" with a "moral"—just as he had ended the previous chapter.

> But enough. I run into these details, not merely to relate an event, but to show character; and if I have not done it, it is not for want of material, but of inability to use it. . . . It was about the last high-toned duel that I have witnessed, and among the highest-toned that I ever witnessed, and so happily conducted to a fortunate issue—a result due to the noble character of the seconds as well as to the generous and heroic spirit of the principals. Certainly dueling is bad and has been put down, but not quite so bad as its substitute—revolvers, bowie-knives, blackguarding, and street-assassinations under the pretext of self-defense. (1:77)

Benton was no less self-conscious about form and style than any "literary" author, and believed meaning and method inseparable. No more exacting test of that belief could be devised than Pound's inclusion of his text in Canto 88.

"Whole Slabs of the Record": Pound's Poetics of Inclusion

> I see narrative as incidental rather than as essential to the method of history in the wider sense. Recognition of quality and of organizing pattern seems much more important.
> —A. L. Kroeber, *The Nature of Culture*

As Nicholls demonstrates, Pound so tended to translate political, economic, and ideological issues into questions of method that the latter constituted one of his most typical forms of discourse.[6] In the late twenties, Pound began to turn his methodological discussions to the problem of historiography and—of specific pertinence here—to the problem of "including history" in the *Cantos*. Increasingly informed by his vision of cultural organism, such discussions culminated in 1938 with the publication of *Guide to Kulchur*: the major effort of Pound's career to expound his historiographical method, but also, as he himself professed, his "totalitarian treatise." These two aspects of the book cannot be separated. And since the "guidance" Pound offered was no appeal to reason but an inflammatory polemic, both aspects of the book have been widely misunderstood.

Pound designated his technique of stripping away to bring out the "gists and piths" of his sources (*ABCR*, 92) the "taking of a totalitarian hold on our history" (*GK*, 32). Demanding that a poem be a "'ONE PRINCIPLE' text," Pound called for a "'new' historic sense" that would "carry a principle through concrete and apparently disjunct phenomena and observe the leaves and/or fruits of causation." "We know," Pound proclaimed, that "history as it was written the day before yesterday is unwittingly partial; full of fatal lacunae, and that it knows next to nothing of causes." And causes, Pound sternly continued, are always "economic and moral; we know that at whichever end we begin we will, if clear headed and thorough, work out to the other" (*GK*, 31).

There is no mistaking that the "totalitarianism" Pound advocated retained many of its more usual connotations: Pound quite explicitly located in the "accustomed . . . loose waftiness of demoliberal ideology" the type of "lazy" thought he most abhorred (*GK*, 36). Pound adopted both the tone and the first-person plural of the manifesto pamphleteer, offering definitions that, under the guise of precision, willfully exchanged evenhandedness for

---

6. Nicholls, *Ezra Pound*, 94.

boldness. His language became immoderate and often offensive, evincing the shrillness characteristic of an ideologue without an audience. For all the attention that has come to his writings since, Pound never found the audience for which he was working. He wanted an audience with some education, but whose curiosity was not structured by the "received wisdom" of the academy. He wanted an audience willing to take important social and economic issues out of the hands of professionals and rethink them in no-nonsense, common language. He wanted to reintegrate political, poetic, and popular discourses; and to do that he needed readers who demanded to "see for themselves."

Pound's failure to find or create that kind of audience might be measured by the neglect of his call for a "totalitarian" treatment of history. He meant his notion of totalitarianism to indicate an attention to causation so relentless that it would shatter what he saw as the usual compartmentalization of experience: the categories of obscurantists who are "ever trotting out minor issues to obscure the main and basic." Totalitarianism was Pound's term for the "habit" of analyzing "*any* act or thought" in terms of how it connects or correlates with some "main principle"—by which Pound meant "economic and moral" causes.[7] No other part of Pound's work was more ambitious than his hope that he might, by taking hold of other texts, open them up to reveal an unchanging basis for moral judgment. Undimmed by the postwar collapse of his immediate political aims, this hope informed Pound's appropriation of Benton's narrative. "These are the Histories," he proclaimed midway through Canto 88, and by their study Pound aspired to erect "'a throne,' something God can sit on/without having it sqush."

That same hope lay behind the programmatic claims of *Guide to Kulchur* that "poetry is totalitarian in any confrontation with prose. There is MORE in and on two pages of poetry than in or on ten pages of any prose save the few books that rise above classification as anything save exceptions" (*GK*, 121). Pound's descriptions of the process of including historical texts in his poem turned repeatedly on the language of struggle—whether of "confrontation" or of "the taking of a totalitarian hold on our history." No doubt this reflected his perception of the difficulty of breaking clear of the "minor issues" in history in order to reveal "the main and basic." But it is important that Pound located this activity at the very heart of his project. Everything else—the recognition of luminous detail or the "totalitarian" pursuit of a

---

7. From "Prolegomena," originally published in the *Exile*, autumn 1927; reprinted in *Impact: Essays on Ignorance and the Decline of American Civilization* (Chicago: Henry Regnery, 1960), 221.

single principle—followed on the prior presentation of "concrete phenomena." This presentation comprised Pound's central historiographical premise. We could call it dogged yankee empiricism. But Pound—here as elsewhere—preferred to trace his premises back to Confucius, who, Pound claimed, "demanded or commended a type of perception, a kind of transmission of knowledge obtainable only from . . . concrete manifestation. Not without reason" (*GK*, 28).[8] "Not without reason"—produce the bases of your conclusions fairly, Pound argued, and you can leave the conclusions out. They will be self-evident. Without such immediate, firsthand perception, one risked dependency on hearsay or, worse, deliberate deception. So in *ABC of Reading*, just before defining an epic as "a poem including history," Pound offered his reader advice that carried with it the criteria making that definition important: "And the quicker you go to the texts the less need there will be for your listening to me or to any other long-winded critic" (*ABCR*, 46).

In Canto 88 this belief found overt expression in Pound's quotation of Confucius's solution to the problem of style: "Get the meaning across and then quit"—or in Pound's more elaborate rendering of Canto 80/513–14:

>   to take the sheep out to pasture
>   to bring your g.r. to the nutriment
>   gentle reader   to the gist of the discourse

This belief about learning, and about the poet's responsibility, informed Pound's inclusion of Benton's narrative in Canto 88. For believing that historical knowledge was, like any other, "obtainable only from concrete knowledge," he came to attempt the inclusion of history in a quite literal way. In "The New Learning" section of *Guide to Kulchur*, Pound wrote that "the 'new' historic sense in our time demands whole slabs of the record." This "sense" was not to be regarded as wholly "new." It was, he proposed, only a revival of an ancient but neglected tradition, and he pointed to other artists and writers whose work exhibited a method similar to his own: there was George Antheil, who Pound averred, rather than merely representing

---

8. This is not to say that Pound turned solely, on this or on any other issue, to Confucius for intellectual warrant. As Ian F. A. Bell has noted, Pound often joined Louis Agassiz to Confucius as "an imparter of knowledge." Agassiz asserted that facts are "stupid things until brought into connection with some general law." See Bell's book *The Critic as Scientist: The Modernist Poetics of Ezra Pound* (New York: Methuen, 1981), 53 and 121.

musically the sounds of modern life, demanded "bits of solidity" and included such things as airplane engines in his compositions. Then too there was Guillaume Apollinaire who "lifted," Pound said, "large chunks of the Congo collection from the Musee de Trocadero" and placed them in his work. Like these cohorts, but unlike the historical novels and poems of the nineteenth century, the *Cantos* would include actual history. It would not only draw on, it would incorporate histories and historical texts.

Pound's talk of including "slabs" of the record, of lifting "chunks" from the museum into his poem, indicates how literally he took the idea of "concrete manifestation." If Pound's explanatory language was here colloquial, it reflected no casualness, but his ambition to make history available to any curious mind, and not just to the educated or scholarly. And yet it reflected as well the limitations of his conception of history. If Pound's notion of "a poem including history" indicates that he regarded history as but one element within a matrix of other elements, it also indicates that he imagined that larger matrix in ahistorical terms. That is, he believed the historical element of his poem to be restricted to the historical texts that he included, to be something apart from his own combinatory procedures. Pound did not regard form itself as inherently historical but felt that he could alter form without altering meaning.

It was not just that Pound treated nonliterary texts as "documents"; in handling "literary" or poetic texts he characteristically treated parts as wholes, and whole texts as part of his larger text. He had done so as early as his *Passages from the Letters of J. B. Yeats* (1917), continued to do so throughout the *Cantos* and such later anthologies as *Profile* (1932), and eventually did so even with his own work in *Selected Cantos* (1967). In other words, although his sense of concrete inclusion was resolutely literal, his sense of "wholeness" was not.[9] Other explanatory figures that Pound employed in the *Guide* suggest this latter aspect of his procedures more immediately than the phrase "whole slabs" can: he submitted, for example, that "whole beams and ropes of real history have been shelved, overclouded and buried" (*GK*, 30). "Beams and ropes" are also "concrete" images, but these suggest continuities that connect the "whole slabs" of Pound's description, and not the "slabs" themselves. Slabs, beams, ropes: Pound's proliferation of metaphors

---

9. We encounter here another of Pound's peculiar inconsistencies, made all the more striking by his celebration in *Profile* of that poetry in his time (he named Williams as an example) which had achieved "a new sort of unity," in which "the parts are more definitely 'of' the entirety than they had been in earlier sorts of poem which could be taken piecemeal or in quotation." See Ezra Pound, ed., *Profile: An Anthology Collected in MCMXXXI* (Milan: Giovanni Scheiwiller, 1932), 127.

can be exasperating, but are consistent in terms of his "totalitarian" poetics. These figures reflected Pound's purpose "to carry a principle through concrete and apparently disjunct phenomena." As he added shortly after the exposition we have been following: "I am not being merely incoherent. . . . I need more than one string for a fabric." Pound's ropes or strings, or in other descriptions "axes," were not so much "whole" texts as the parts of many texts excised from their original contents and collected together. And of course, for Pound, these parts were those which could convey the force and truth of the whole—those which observed the "economic and moral . . . leaves and/or fruits of causation."

In sum, Pound's image of "whole slabs" did not imply that works purporting to include history must include historical texts in their entirety, but rather that certain features must never be omitted. A "true" history would uncover the moral and economic causes of war, peace, famine, or prosperity. Pound's equation of history with a knowledge of moral and economic foundations was the meaning behind his proclamation, in the midst of a broad digest of monetary policies from antiquity to the twentieth century, "That these are the Histories." In Canto 89 that equation made for a polemic opening: "To know the histories [*Shu*]/ to know good from evil / [*Ching*] / And know whom to trust." More than metaphoric hyperbole, Pound's attempt to shift our usual sense of wholeness as a quality belonging to single texts to one formed by parts of many texts is a programmatic part of his combinatory praxis. Pound's notion of wholeness is not to be identified with Wimsattian notions of unity, but with his description of *Guide to Kulchur* as "a totalitarian treatise."

Pound's enduring faith that "art and humanity remain ever the same" developed in defiance of Continental historicism. Here again at odds with modern attitudes, Pound sought in history the kind of mirror theorized by the Victorians.[10] It is no accident that Pound's China looks so much like his Renaissance Italy, or that there are in the *Cantos* so many Odysseus figures. The variegated historical scenery of the *Cantos* ultimately provides little more than backdrops, before which are reenacted a finite number of dramas. For all the color they add to his work, Pound's historical settings are interchangeable. His notion of "wholeness" responded to what he saw as the

---

10. See A. Dwight Culler, *The Victorian Mirror of History* (New Haven: Yale University Press, 1985). Culler explains the "habit of mind among the Victorians to perceive analogies between their own day and various historical epochs in the past and then to use these analogies in conducting their controversies" (3).

needless division of history into periods whose distinctiveness dissipated when their cultural life was considered in terms of "the main and basic issues." Recognizing no "progress" in history, he rejected "narrative" as a reliable form for writing it.

Pound's aversion to narrative form did not derive solely from arguments about the philosophy of history; he felt, on more aesthetic grounds, that narrative sacrificed too many words in order to reach one climatic point of interest. But Pound felt that the writing of history as a narrative encumbered understanding. After his exposition in the *Guide* of "The Recurring Decimal," Pound counseled that "there is no use in trying to 'understand' history as a mere haphazard list of events arranged chronologically. You can on the other hand read almost any biography with some interest if you have some sort of provisionary scaffold, hat-rack, or something to work from" (*GK*, 260). Pound imagined that even the most particular and enclosed narratives (biographies) might serve his "totalitarian" ends, if read with an eye to the "main and basic issues." Nevertheless, he was persuaded that narrative form restricted awareness of historical "causes" and was therefore inimical to what he defined in the *Guide* as "Zweck or the Aim":

> We do NOT know the past in chronological sequence. It may be convenient to lay it out anesthetized on the table with dates pasted on here and there, but what we know we know by ripples and spirals eddying out from us and from our time. . . .
>
> You can write history by tracing ideas, exposing the growth of a concept.
>
> You can also isolate the quality or direction of a given time's sensibility. That means the history of an art. . . .
>
> But the one thing you shd. not do is to suppose that when something is wrong with the arts, it is wrong with the arts ONLY. (*GK*, 60)

Since Pound hoped that his "'new' historic sense" would usher in a modern renaissance, there is more than a little irony in his turn of Eliot's phrase "anesthetized on the table." "Zweck or the Aim" offers a constellation of Pound's ideas about history: his resistance to chronological narrative, his preference for the tracing of particular axes ("ideas" or "concepts") through disjunct phenomena, and his determination to integrate the examination of artistic with politico-economic problems. We can characterize Pound's project no better than to consider these proclivities in conjunction with his empiricist insistence on the need for "concrete perception"; the end result of their interaction was that Pound's "poem including history" called for "whole slabs and columns of histories and works of reference" (*GK*, 33) rather than the presentation of historical narrative.

Despite the catastrophes of war and incarceration, and despite his subsequent work on the more meditative *Pisan Cantos*, the position Pound outlined during the thirties regarding the inclusion of history in his poem remained fundamentally unchanged. But Pound's historiography was not always consonant with his practice. His expositions of method cannot account for many of the consequences of his actual handling of Benton's narrative, or of many of the other texts that he included in the *Cantos*, because the historiography on which he based so much was undermined by the radical discontinuity of his poetics. Pound's confidence in causality played an important part in the shaping of the Benton cantos—but it did not play the part which he had anticipated.

There remains, moreover, the resistance that Pound encountered from Benton's text. In many respects, Benton's procedures were antithetical to Pound's. Where Pound ignored perspective, Benton privileged it. Where Pound worked to conflate national and cultural distinctions, Benton proudly restricted himself to that which was singularly American. Where Pound was interested in timeless patterns, Benton was concerned "to illustrate the character of Institutions which are new and complex—the first of their kind, and . . . still believed by some to be an experiment" (1:v). Benton believed that history is a progress. Pound recognized only Benton's forebodings and understood much of Benton only in part. Yet it would be unjust to say that he missed Benton altogether. One need not invoke Harold Bloom's oedipal notion of misreading to grant that one writer's partial understanding of another stimulates much of the writing we think of as literature.

View and Vortex

Exchanging questions of "essential" differences between history and poetry for questions of their function makes more interesting still the study of those passages where Pound continued to use Benton's words. Since he did not consistently do so, Benton's words—even where preserved—change in significance, and change significantly. More than any other detail, Pound's omission of Benton's conclusion to the narrative of the Clay-Randolph duel illustrates the effects of his inclusion. Like most nineteenth-century narratives, Benton's story of the duel moved slowly toward the "climax" of the encounter, and "fell off" swiftly thereafter into a conclusion that attended to all the loose ends. Pound, on the other hand, interrupted Benton's account, and then broke off from it at precisely that moment to which all narrative logic tended.[11]

>   He and the seconds took carriage,
>   I followed on horseback.
> His (R's) stepfather
>   brought out a "Blackstone"   (a.D.1804)
> The place was a thick forest in which a little
>   depression or basis.
> Bellum perenne:

Pound's departure from Benton's story was in fact implicit in his presentation of Benton's opening lines. Pound did not simply exploit the mounting tension of Benton's story to carry his readers to a new and different conclusion, but from beginning to end resisted narrative order. Christine Froula has argued that after Pound's early and frustrated efforts "to discover and explore fundamental structures in human history," he eventually came to see the "necessity . . . of learning to conceive history apart from the certainty of story and the closure of form."[12] A guiding thematic aim of Pound's treatment of Benton's narrative, and of histories in general, was such a resistance to "story." But the rhetoric of liberation misses the point. Canto 88 is not free from "the closure of form." Rather, inclusionary principles implement formal features that are not conventional in historical writing. In large part, Pound's resistance to narrative involved the substitution of visual-perceptual elements for syntactic ones.

These substitutions affected Benton's text in numerous ways. Consider the differences between how Pound and Benton introduce the story of the Randolph-Clay duel:

---

11. The allusion to "His (R's) stepfather," George Tucker, is Pound's interpolation. What Tucker "brought out" was an edition of *Blackstone's Commentaries* on the Federal Constitution (1803). The interpolation suggests the importance of clarifying principles by getting, as Pound wrote in Canto 96, "some laws written down." It exemplifies Pound's attempts to open up Benton's text to "larger" issues.

12. Christine Froula, *To Write Paradise: Style and Error in Pound's Cantos* (New Haven: Yale University Press, 1984), 152–53.

> It was Saturday the 1st day of April, toward noon,
> the Senate not being that day in session . . .
> 	came to my room at Brown's asking was I
> Mrs. Clay's blood relation?
> 						(Canto 88/591)

> It was Saturday, the first day of April, towards noon, the Senate not being that day in session, that Mr. Randolph came to my room at Brown's Hotel and (without explaining the reason of the question) asked me if I was a blood-relation of Mrs. Clay? I answered that I was, and he immediately replied that that put an end to a request which he had wished to make of me; and then went on to tell me that he had just received a challenge from Mr. Clay, had accepted it, was ready to go out, and would apply to Col. Tatnall to be his second. (1:70)

In *Thirty Years' View*, Benton was principally concerned with the workings of government. He began his *View* in 1820 not merely because that was the year in which began his own senatorial career, but also because that date enabled him to take as his subject a government that had already survived early challenges to its survival, demonstrated its adaptability, and achieved a relative stability. Pound's treatment of Benton's opening sentences illustrates the radical difference of his concerns. Where Benton emphasized the ability of government to take in hand extraordinary events and subject them to normal constitutional process, Pound sought out the violence of such events. Benton's first sentence endeavors to lessen the shock of Randolph's disclosure even while presenting it, providing the circumstances to help us understand Randolph's appearance at Benton's door in the middle of the day, and hence suggesting Randolph's attempt to keep his private quarrel with Clay distinct from government business. But Pound's lines work toward a very different end. Pound sought to amplify the startling effect of Randolph's news.

Pound's elision of the subject of Benton's sentence suggests that it was "the Senate" that came to Benton's room. An immediate thematic function of this suggestion is to introduce one of Pound's recurrent themes: the insidious violation of the "borderline between public and private things" (*GK*, 192 and 194).[13] But more broadly, Pound's use of ellipsis here and elsewhere exemplifies a characteristic feature of his handling of Benton's

---

13. See also "Prolegomena," 221.

narrative. An ellipsis indicates discontinuity: in its first seven lines alone Canto 88 admits three of them. That the primary function of these ellipses is not to indicate omissions is plain from how the second of them occurs in a place where nothing has been left out, whereas after line 4, 184 lines of Benton's prose drop out with no indication whatsoever. Of Pound's first three ellipses, two occur as line endings, which position amplifies the sense of disruption. Rather than being designed to join together previously separated material, Pound's ellipses disrupt continuity.

The discontinuity built into Pound's line requires no other description than Lewis's complaint that Pound "'breaks off,' indeed, as a rule, twice in every line." What does require attention is the effect of such a poetics on imported materials that had previously depended on syntactic clarity and continuity. For Pound's use of ellipses is not an isolated phenomenon, but a feature executed in keeping with his larger praxis. He used line breaks and irregular margins, Chinese ideograms, even other sorts of scholarly apparatus, in ways similar to how he used ellipses. By isolating words and breaking up narrative flow, he drew from Benton's words significance where it was not previously found. Consider the fourth line of Pound's canto: "Mrs. Clay's blood-relation?" Breaking the iambic rhythm of Benton's prose, Pound's trochees fell heavily and ominously on the word "blood." "Relation" makes a feminine end-rhyme with "session," further intimating Pound's thematic concern with the "boundary line between public and private things." Its brevity after three longer lines, its long right-hand margin, and the fact that Pound tells us neither its answer nor why it was asked bring to the question further weight. The result of such incremental changes is that these words will be perceived very differently in Pound's text than in Benton's. Small, hardly perceptible changes, often introduced inadvertently, compound with analogous changes in every line of the canto. Even where Pound adhered to Benton's language, the placing of his narrative prose into the irregular poetic line of the *Cantos* initiated significant change.

In a very real sense, the meaning of Pound's canto cannot be separated from its appearance on the page. Pound's interweaving of print and blank space affects our perception of his words. The language that moved lucidly and predictably in Benton's narrative looks on Pound's page to be riddled with discontinuities. This new visual-perceptual element itself changes expectations and responses. And it is, moreover, joined with other innovations in kind. Abbreviations like "1st" or, later, "wd/" or "shd/" may not "depart" from Benton's words, but they alter both his text and how we perceive it. Pound's abbreviations contribute to his systematic transformation of the polite and formal writing of Benton's narrative into the more casual language of verbal exchange. They add to the sense of "hurriedness" so marked in Pound's treatment, but so incompatible with both the formal reserve of Benton's narrative and the function of his "view" to describe the "course" of history as a process of gradual developments.

The apparent "hurriedness" of Pound's treatment of Benton is more than a matter of Pound's having wanted to get through a "mass of verbiage" and on to the "salient points" of his source, although such anxiousness undoubtedly played its part.[14] It stems from his belief that "we do NOT know the past in chronological sequence." Pound's concern with achieving the "concrete manifestation" of history led him to attempt the "effect" of being caught up in the whirl of events that Benton described. Consequently, Pound strained on every front Benton's narrative order: for the ideal of equanimous detachment of Benton's "view" Pound systematically substituted the force and movement of "vortex." It is in this regard that we can understand Pound's interest in transforming the polite balance of Benton's prose "back" into verbal discourse. Pound wanted, literally, to have the "sound" of Benton's speakers in his poem, wanted his readers to be able to "hear" them firsthand.

For this reason, Pound's treatment of Benton's narrative resembles his handling of the many other sources quoted or included in the middle section of Canto 88. That section of the canto is something of a set piece for Pound's lifelong conviction that "all ages are contemporaneous" (*SR*, 6 and 157). Aristotle "speaks" with the same immediacy as Confucius, St. Ambrose, or the fascist official Delcroix; and all of these figures appear to affirm, if not the "same thing," at least compatible values. But the cumulative effect of these "repetitions" depends on our prior perception of wide differences in voice. In the *Cantos* Pound included many phrases in their original language: Italian, Chinese, Latin, Greek, Renaissance English. Moreover, he sought to cultivate differences of social station and dialect: the voices range from the language of kings and emperors, to Pound's friends and relatives, to peasants and Negro slaves. The earnestness of Pound's interest in the sound of spoken words can further be seen in the many means by which he sought to guide pronunciation: phonetic spelling ("Waal," "tol'," etc.), metrical

---

14. The description of Pound's eagerness to get through "verbiage" is Michael Harper's; see "'Truth and Calliope': Ezra Pound's Malatesta," *PMLA* (January 1981): 6. Pound's rejection of "chronological sequence" is in *GK*, 260.

patterns, the frequent use of upper-case to denote emphasis, even in his specific identification of the ideogram *ching* ("in the fourth tone").

This interest in voice, this use of sound quite apart from sense to generate meaning, was not compatible with the designs of Benton's narrative. Benton included voices other than his own only in an explicitly subordinate manner, and he relied on careful introduction and explanation to minimize the discontinuity inevitable in the interactions between several voices. Pound's inclusions destroyed that subordinating structure. Indeed, the very inclusion of Benton's text as but one document among many, one group of voices among a welter of voices, altered the integral logic of Benton's *View*. Benton's citational distinctions served to limit the connotations of the words quoted and, hence, to clarify his "view" of their significance; Pound's merely emphasized the verbal nature of the discourse. Pound sought to recover the confused verbal discourse from which Benton had formed his narrative. It was a step in keeping with his "totalitarian" project: an attempt to open texts up in such a way that they would reveal the "real" history underneath them, an attempt to demonstrate how failure to be mindful of "main principles" leaves the realm of human action vulnerable to the power of accident and fortune. Hence the playing-card emblems that close the canto. My concern, however, is not with the history that Pound sought to evoke, but with the text he developed from Benton's narrative. On this level, Pound seems more interested in using the sounds of Benton's words to create a "sense of" controversy than in conveying in detail their sense.

Pound's one-word line "('blackleg')" is a case in point. Of a speech which Benton recorded in its entirety, a speech whose spurious imputation to Randolph Benton took care to establish, only this single word, still in quotation marks, remains. The parentheses are Pound's significant addition. Benton wrote, "That a letter from General Salazar, the Mexican Minister at Washington, submitted by the Executive to the Senate, bore the ear-mark of having been manufactured or forged by the Secretary of State, and denounced the administration as a corrupt coalition between the puritan and the blackleg; and added, at the same time, that he (Mr. Randolph) held himself personally responsible for all that he had said" (1:73). Clearly, "effect" is not synonymous with explanation. Pound seized on the oral nature of the report of Randolph's words that reached Clay. The very care with which Benton set off and presented these words gives them a stability and clarity they may never have had. To say that Pound's one-word line condenses that speech to a single slur is to miss the way that what it does characterizes Pound's larger usage. "Blackleg" is not the "sum" of this "speech" but a rendering of what was already a misrepresentation of Randolph's words. What Pound saw in Benton's account is the instability of oral discourse, and its susceptibility to change in repetition.[15] This is why he recorded what Benton discussed as "a report [to Clay] of words spoken—a verbal report" as but "vague report." Pound's line—"('blackleg')"— exemplifies how contextual omission transforms truth into falsehood. Pound's line conveys the sense that someone surreptitiously called someone a "blackleg," but indicates no responsibility for either the slander or the report. This, Pound's construction would suggest, is how rumor works. He strove, not to explain the circumstances or sense of the "report," but the "sense of" unchecked rumor.

The phrase "sense of" comes from *Guide to Kulchur*, where Pound described his unsuccessful attempt to produce a "stageable" version of *Agamemnon*. Explicitly offered as a model for other translators, the account also bears on the *Cantos*. "I twisted, turned, tried every ellipsis and elimination," he wrote, but "by the time you had taken out the remplissage, there was no play left on one's page." However, "there was magnificence; there was SENSE of play" (*GK*, 92–93). One can edit, Pound maintained, and yet retain a sense of wholeness, providing that sense of wholeness is figural and configurative.[16] As literally as he took his notion of including "slabs" of history, he could not have expected to be able to include long histories "whole"—in their entirety. It was the "force" of historical experience that Pound hoped to include undiminished. His pursuit of "effect" was no compromise of his inclusionary principles. It owes to the same idealist convictions that drove *Fors Clavigera*, the same confidence that wholes can be divined from parts, or that the *Cantos* could include "whole slabs of the record." But, as the example of "('blackleg')" demonstrates, Pound's attempts to locate the "sense of" Benton's prose in a single line, phrase, or even word attenuate Benton's sense.

---

15. That Pound carried over Benton's case for the value of written records may seem uncharacteristic, given his own poetic procedures. But although Pound was always capable of inconsistency, his point about law differs from his arguments about history, as well as from his valorization of folk wisdom and oral tradition. The *Cantos*, especially after *Section: Rock-Drill*, celebrates the codification and recording of law. See, for example, Canto 96/666: "Rothar got some laws written down."

16. Pound's sense of form resembled, in this sense, nineteenth-century conceptions against which he railed so energetically. As Thomas McFarland explains, "the doctrine of organic form," insofar as it develops from the recognition that "an organism is no singleness but rather a manifold," presupposes "that perfect wholeness, which must be a singleness, tends to lie outside the fact—to become as it were a hypothetical construct." See *Romanticism and the Forms of Ruin* (Princeton: Princeton University Press, 1981), 41.

One crucial reason for this is that Pound's "sense of" Benton's prose usually involves a substitution of visual-perceptual structures for syntactic ones. In Benton's text, for example, the proper attribution of speaker—whether Clay or Randolph—and the exact words spoken were explicitly an issue. Pound presented this exchange as follows:

> By which time it had become "forgery"
> (Jessup to Tatnall)
> "Forged or manufactured"
> (Tatnall quoting his principle: Charlotte jury
> Wd/ find presumptive strong likeness
> "in points of style" to other papers,
> Not proof but suspicion, for which he declined to offer
> explanation

It is difficult to tell from Pound's construction whether "(Jessup to Tatnall)" belongs with the line above it, or the line below. Moreover, the parenthesis begun to distinguish Tatnall's speech from that of Jessup (in Benton both of these were *written notes*) is never closed. This open-endedness is a deliberate device that Pound employed frequently. Canto 88 alone contains three other instances where Pound began a quotation that he never closed, and one where he "closed" a quotation whose beginning he had never marked. Examples proliferate in other cantos.[17]

Pound's broken parentheses are not casual, but another means by which he opens up Benton's narrative. Like his interest in contrapuntal poetic "music," they contribute to his effort to compel his audience to "read ALL the words on a page," to read slowly, as opposed to the tendency of narrative to propel one along "at ten pages a minute."[18] Pound took the occasion of his Rome radio broadcast for 21 May 1942 to elaborate on the importance of this technique. Chewing out his words in the cracker-barrel voice of his "yankee" persona, and exemplifying the point at hand, he supposed that "Old Henry James worried his European readers to death by his parentheses. They are an American habit, they mean something to us and for us as Americans. They mean something more than the one track mind. But they do NOT imply deviation or lack of direction. They are a desperate attempt,

---

17. See, for example, Canto 87/585, 589, 590.
18. "E. E. Cummings Examined" (21 May 1942), in *Ezra Pound Speaking: Radio Speeches of World War II*, ed. Leonard W. Doob (Westport, Conn.: Greenwood Press, 1978), 143.

no not an attempt, a DEVICE, to avoid leaving out something NEEDED, some part of the statement needed to set down, to register the direction, and meaning." Pound's parentheses "register" meaning by slowing down the process of reading, and those left open do so even more effectively as they trouble the eye to search for a closure never delivered. This same pause might seem an unlikely way of registering "direction," especially since Pound often does not return to the matter which had prompted the parenthesis. But by "direction" Pound did not mean narrative direction—"one track mind"— but indications toward what he thought of as "the main and basic issues." Here again, he was moving toward a poetry that was less discursive, and a poem that was totalizing in its scope.[19]

Lines 169–81 of Canto 88 further exemplify this function, and its interaction with other characteristic Poundian techniques:

    Ile des Pinqouins,
So that Perry "opened" Japan.
Use of foreign coin until 1819.
  Exception Spanish milled dollars,
every dealer occupied in exporting them,   page 446
their exclusion an unconstitutional fraud . . .
A currency of intrinsic value FOR WHICH
  They paid interest to NOBODY

               page 446
               column two

   ("Thirty Years", Benton)
Is suppressed in favour of fluctuation,
  this country a thoroughfare.

With these lines, after the ninety-line digest of monetary and political wisdom and outrage that he called "the Histories," Pound returns to Benton's text. The return actually comes with the third line, but the previous two lines illustrate how Pound manipulates context in order to generate, or

---

19. In his practice, Charles Olson turned the Poundian exception of the late cantos into the rule. Denying that the technique of opening parentheses stemmed from any desire to startle or discomfit, Olson defended it in "natural" terms—rather like those which Pasolini attempted to apply to the *Cantos*. Olson said: "Opening, and then not closing a parenthesis is merely the way that one does parenthesize, actually: true to feeling (don't let the other convention trouble you, for its only conventional)." See Charles Olson, *Charles Olson and Ezra Pound: An Encounter at St. Elizabeths*, ed. Catherine Seelye (New York: Grossman Publishers, 1975), x.

"register," meaning. The first line is the title of Anatole France's satirically fabulous parody of academic history, the end of which draws the spectacle of endless wars being fought merely for the sake of opening new markets. France's parodic history underscores the irony of Pound's subsequent allusion to Commodore Perry. Although Pound quoted William Elliot Griffs in Canto 103 to the effect that the American version of that episode— that Perry "opened" Japan to foreign markets and hence to civilized "progress"—was "colossal conceit," in Canto 88 Pound provided no further clue than the inverted commas. Nevertheless, Pound aimed to transform Benton's account of an episode in the Bank War into evidence—once again—of a much larger war: the struggle of the nations against the power of what Pound saw as an international economic oligarchy. Together, the France and Perry motifs telescope much of what Pound had recorded in "the histories" and condition the reader's response to the Benton material that followed.

However, where Pound had previously seized on a story-like narrative, here (370 pages later in *Thirty Years' View*) he lit on what Benton called a "narrative of facts." Benton was not being metaphorical. This chapter recounted the opposition of Benton and others to the scheme of the National Bank to replace foreign coins with paper money. It included, like other chapters, accounts and excerpts of Benton's speeches and histories of legal developments; but it also included factual tables of monies collected at various times and places. This kind of documentation greatly appealed to Pound, and the constructions of these lines in Canto 88 strive to give "the sense of" a rich welter of fact. These constructions remain distinct from his practice in *Thrones* a few years later, where he included raw statistics in profusion. But even here Pound's documentation came in different forms from Benton's: Pound disassembled Benton's narrative, working to create shard-like fragments. He was, in other words, using Benton's narrative itself as his documentary evidence. He included Benton's words and "evidence" of Benton's testimony.

The results of this manner of inclusion can be seen by comparing Benton's "factual narrative" with the "facts" of Pound's canto:

> He [Mr. Benton] denounced this exclusion of foreign coins as a fraud, and a fraud of the most injurious nature, upon the people of the States. The States had surrendered their power over the coinage to Congress; they made the surrender in language which clearly implied that their currency of foreign coins was to be continued to

them; yet that currency is suppressed; a currency of intrinsic value, for which they paid interest to nobody, is suppressed; and a currency without intrinsic value, a currency of paper subject to every fluctuation, and for the supply of which corporate bodies receive interest, is substituted in its place. He objected to this suppression as depriving the whole Union, and especially the Western States, of their due and necessary supply of hard money. Since that law took effect, the United States had only been a thoroughfare for foreign coins to pass through. (1:446)

The parenthesis "('Thirty Years', Benton)" epitomizes the changed function of this material in Pound's canto. In one sense, it simply "documents" Pound's source, testifying to his inclusion of "bits and chunks of real history." Yet Pound's construction suggests that it is the suppression of *Thirty Years' View* itself that enabled dangerous "fluctuations" in the value of money. Benton had been concerned with the bank's suppression of "foreign," but hard and "intrinsically valuable" foreign coinage in favor of paper money.

The new context Pound created dramatically altered the significance of Benton's narrative. In Pound's handling, the precise facts of Benton's case no longer matter, or are subordinate to the mere fact that they are, as Pound would say, "on record." The function of this parenthesis, like that of the earlier references to France and Perry, is to connect particular suppressions of civil rights with what Pound regarded as the ancient crime of suppressing history itself. Its "registration" of direction is confirmed five lines later with Pound's allusion to Tocqueville: "may pass *in Europe* for American history." For Pound, Tocqueville's work typified the "loose waftiness" of most history. By propagating insignificant arguments, it manages a more insidious "concealment" of "real history" than outright attempts to destroy the record, which at least can be recognized for what they are (*GK*, 264).

Pound's use of parentheses represents then another of the various means by which he supplanted syntactical and narrative order. Yet unlike the lines that began the canto, lines 169–81 reconstruct no narrative. Drawn from Benton's account of one of his own speeches, Pound here reproduces little more than isolated phrases, and Benton's tone of indignation and outrage. In this case, readers seeking Benton's sense really must look up Pound's page references to *Thirty Years' View* to understand what was being said and why. And yet even in this example, Pound is not merely alluding to Benton's book; the material included is not coincident with its function in *Thirty Years'*

View. With the literally "whole" inclusion of this material being both impossible and undesirable ("dichten = condensare"), Pound sought to achieve depth on the very basis of what he omitted.

> In England, salt tax overthrown.
>   Andy vetoed the Maysville Road bill . . .
>   unconvertable paper . . .
>   mines now yielding . . .
> Prospects, as Peru, now ½ million per annum
> and what is still better, have exports.
>   (Canto 88, lines 187–92)

Pound's technique in these lines shows an extreme development of his tendency to "break off" in every line; it was unquestionably in keeping with Pound's repeated injunction to historians to leave spaces for what they don't know—to "have a respect for the unknown."[20] But the "sense" of this kind of writing is not to be had strictly from the kind of perseverance and learning embodied in Carroll F. Terrell's *Companion to the Cantos*. One must, once again, consider how this information is included.

Not all of the *Cantos* is composed like lines 169–81 of Canto 88. Indeed, some fifty lines later in that canto, Pound includes two long excerpts from Benton's final speeches against the Bank, and includes them with the same close attention that characterized his account of the Clay-Randolph duel. But lines 169–81 exemplify the controversial difficulty that characterizes much of the middle cantos, and most of the late ones. In the twelve lines cited above, Pound's omissions arguably are still "on the page," albeit in trying and unfamiliar ways; his omissions surround isolated words, hover at the ends of his open quotations and parentheses, and lie just under his documentary apparatus. These techniques push Pound's notion of concrete inclusion to the limits of credibility, and it is arguable whether in certain cases he is not more "allusive" than "inclusive." And yet if the techniques are allusive, then we must call it Pound's failure; for even in these passages where his notion of "wholeness" is most obviously attenuated, he aspires to make historical texts an integral part of his poem.

With his own fundamental principles militating against literal or narrative wholeness, Pound came to rely increasingly on techniques whose play we have only begun to describe here. Eventually they brought him to the limits

---

20. See, for instance, *GK*, 26, 127, 357.

of intelligibility, and so to crisis, since Pound had long considered his historical task to be "popularization." Running out of time, Pound attempted technical innovation in characteristic fashion—by experimenting with new mixtures of generic features. And yet this last experiment, among the most daring of Pound's career, proved the narrowest of his conceptions of what it meant to write "a poem including history": an attempt to include within the language of the lyric the archaeological discourse of numismatic history.

7

"Nummulary Moving Toward Prosody": The Del Mar Cantos of *Thrones*

"The Main Interest Is Not in Aesthetics"

One afternoon in 1924, Pound spent an hour in conversation with Arthur Griffith, the founder of the militant Sinn Fein brotherhood and a man dedicated to revolution. The topic of the day was one already grown too familiar to Pound's old friends, and one that would in the coming years frequently discomfit others who had admitted Pound expecting to discuss art or literature. After having listened to Pound urge upon him the necessity of joining economic to political reform, Griffith, shrewd enough to sense that Pound was not to be put off easily, extricated himself by granting that "all you say is true. But I can't move 'em with a cold thing like economics."[1] Pound's readers have, on the whole, proven the wisdom of Griffith's observation; most have probably wished that Pound had discovered in it something more than ironic grist for the *Cantos*. Pound, however, fully understood that Griffith was speaking plainly. He later praised Griffith as "a great man" precisely because of "the sincerity and frankness of his reactions" (*GK*, 105). Pound recognized in Griffith's remark the inherited aversion that his project must anticipate. To carry on discussions of economics in the ways that had, he thought, characterized those discussions for centuries would accomplish

---

1. Recounted in "The Central Problem," *Townsman* 4 (March 1941), 13–14. Pound was long fascinated with Griffith's remark, although his memory of it was subject to change: the version he repeated in Canto 19, published only a few months after that memorable conversation, differs slightly; he repeated it again in *ABC of Economics* (*SP*, 239); again in *Jefferson and/or Mussolini* (New York: Liveright, 1935), 27; and again in Cantos 78, 97, and 102. Marcella Booth has recorded that, especially during his last years in St. Elizabeths, Pound "often teased [his pupils] by reciting Griffith's [phrase]. He didn't," she says, "in the least believe it." See "Through the Smoke Hole: Ezra Pound's Last Year at St. Elizabeths," *Paideuma* 3 (winter 1974), 334.

little, because those discussions were doomed to reach an audience limited to the professionals currently propagating a rotten system. True still to his early belief that "the ultimate goal of scholarship is popularization," Pound sought to bring his sense of the issues to the masses. He was convinced that although radicals like Griffith underestimated what a popular awareness of economics could accomplish, those in a position to fix and exploit international monetary policy did everything in their power to perpetuate the popular misconception of economics as a technical science, of interest only to experts. Pound concluded therefore that the precondition for reform was to change what people took economics to be.

More than fifteen years separated Pound's first published cantos from the publication of cantos in which economics figured prominently. Thereafter, economics came, like the other constituent elements of the *Cantos*, to be included in a variety of ways—the manner of which cannot be explained on the basis of his supposed "conversion" to Social Credit in 1919. What Pound realized by the thirties was that economics was, in important ways, a kind of writing: its particular sense of "science" was tied to particular discursive norms. To change how economics was written and presented was to change the "science" itself. So, in 1934, Pound remembered that his own "economic study" dated from the 1919 "union" of Orage and Douglas. He did not mean that he had been swayed by Douglas's assimilation of elements from Orage's Guild Socialism but that, as he later told Wallace Martin, "Orage taught Douglas how to write."[2] Readers of Douglas's work might find this statement puzzling, since Douglas's writing never displayed, even at its tortuous best, a "literary" style. But it was not "literariness" to which Pound was referring, but Douglas's improved consciousness of the importance of rhetoric and method to his cause. Orage, Pound believed, showed Douglas how to join the various planks of his platform and place his facts before the reader.

The more closely one examines "how" economics is presented in the *Cantos*, the less "Pound's economics" resembles that of Douglas or Gesell. Some of his divergences from them may have been inadvertent; some, as Nicholls makes clear, derived from his own changing concerns, but a good many reflect Pound's intuition that to change the way the thing was written was to change the thing itself.[3] Pound introduced economics into various

---

2. Wallace Martin, *The New Age under Orage* (Manchester: University of Manchester Press, 1967), 271.

3. See Richard Godden's account of Pound's iconographic view of language, "Icons, Ety-

generic mixtures, within the *Cantos* and without, to demonstrate the multivalent relations of economics with other discourses. For these reasons, I shall have little to say about what Earl Davis has called Pound's "economic theme," or about the ethical status of the economic ideas to which Pound was attracted. My examination focuses on Pound's methods for interrelating "economics" with poetry.

Most of the growing number of studies dedicated to explicating or evaluating the function of economics within the *Cantos* have done so by treating economics either as "poetry" or as "ideas."[4] Despite their different interests, both strategies gloss over the presence of economics in the *Cantos* as changeable discursive features, translating it, on the one hand, into some broadly humanist discourse and, on the other, into "ideas" then extractable from the text as historical "background." Richard Sieburth's "In Pound We Trust: The Economy of Poetry/The Poetry of Economics" constitutes a recent exception.[5] Interestingly enough, Sieburth's essay opens by turning to the same instance considered here: Pound's use in Canto 97 of Alexander Del Mar's *History of Monetary Systems*.[6] "Canto 97," Sieburth justly observes, "is an extreme example of Pound's poetry of money." Canto 97 is *the* extreme example, and Sieburth submits that "unless we are specialists in numismatology, or unless we have a copy of Del Mar at our side, we have little choice but to read this text as a mosaic of signifiers without signifieds (or, more precisely, of signifiers treated *as if* they were signifieds)." But Sieburth draws conclusions quite different from mine; he speculates that "Pound seems to have willfully withdrawn his poem from circulation and deposited

---

mologies, Origins, and Monkey Puzzles in the Languages of Upward and Fenollosa," in *Ezra Pound: Tactics for Reading*, ed. Ian F. A. Bell (Totowa, N.J.: Barnes & Noble, 1982).

4. See, for example, Earle Davis, *Vision Fugitive: Ezra Pound and Economics* (Lawrence: University Press of Kansas, 1968); Kenneth Elzinga and William Breit, "Ezra Pound and the GNP★," *Southern Economic Journal* (January 1980); Dennis Klinck, "Pound, Social Credit and the Cantos," *Paideuma* 5 (fall 1976); David Murray, "Pound-Signs: Money and Representation in Ezra Pound," in Bell, *Ezra Pound: Tactics for Reading*; Peter Nicholls, *Ezra Pound: Politics, Economics, and Writing* (London: Macmillan, 1984). Other studies of Pound that consider the relations between poetry and economics include Robert Casillo, "Troubadour Love and Usury in Ezra Pound's Writings," *Texas Studies in Literature and Language* 27 (summer 1985); Andrew Parker, "Ezra Pound and the 'Economy' of Anti-Semitism," in *Postmodernism and Politics*, ed. Jonathan Arac (Minneapolis: University of Minnesota Press, 1986); and Jean-Michel Rabaté's *Language, Sexuality, and Ideology in Ezra Pound's "Cantos"* (Albany: State University of New York Press, 1986).

5. Richard Sieburth, "In Pound We Trust: The Economy of Poetry/The Poetry of Economics," *Critical Inquiry* 14 (autumn 1987), 142–72.

6. Alexander Del Mar, *History of Monetary Systems* (Chicago: Charles H. Kerr, 1896; reprint, Orono, Maine: National Poetry Foundation, 1983).

its signs in a secret account whose arcane dividends are accessible only to the initiate" (143–44). By contrast, I argue that Pound's inclusion of Del Mar stemmed, ironically, from a rather desperate bid to attain a circulation wider than he had ever before managed. It is precisely its extremity that makes Canto 97 so valuable an opportunity to understand the relations between poetic fragmentation and Pound's long-held Ruskinian vision of totality. My concern is to examine neither "the economy of poetry" nor "the poetry of economics," but how economics enters the *Cantos* as a kind of writing.

Carpenter has observed that for a full four years after completing *Pisan Cantos*, Pound showed "not the slightest inclination to produce any more." That hiatus ended only when "around 1950 he discovered the writings of the nineteenth-century American economic historian Alexander Del Mar." Almost immediately Pound began to describe Del Mar "as America's greatest writer of history, comparing him to Frobenius as a master in the 'art of collecting and arranging a mass of isolated facts, and rising thence, by a process of induction to general ideas.' (As usual with his enthusiasms he did not make clear what Del Mar had actually contributed to knowledge.) This new interest seems to have prompted him to begin work on the *Cantos* again."[7] Carpenter's assertion is provoking, but not as illuminating as his parenthetical complaint about Pound's "enthusiasms" taking their usual course. Pound preferred to celebrate Del Mar's style rather than his matter because the "what" of his work was vastly less important to Pound than the "how" of it. In a letter to Robert Creeley, Pound thus proclaimed Del Mar "a great historian, gt/historiographer."[8] It was Del Mar's method that returned Pound to the *Cantos* and proved consonant with Pound's assumptions of both cultural totality and the necessary "totalitarian" method. But the nature of Pound's interest in Del Mar presented its own problems. Del Mar's numismatics involved the study of irreducible concrete fragments of the record. Pound's work involved textual evidence and semiotic displacements.[9] For all his admiration, it took Pound another six years to find a way

---

7. Humphrey Carpenter, *A Serious Character: The Life of Ezra Pound* (Boston: Houghton Mifflin, 1988), 798.

8. Robert Creeley, "Selections from Ezra Pound's Letter to Robert Creeley, March 1950 to October 1951," *Agenda* (October/November 1964): 19.

9. Nicholls makes much the same point in *Politics, Economics, and Writing*, 216, he writes that "the redaction of the *Eparch's Book* has an antiquarian feel which is due not only to historical distance but also to an absolute divergence between language and material practice." In "*Res* and *Verba* in *Rock-Drill* and After," *Paideuma* 11 (winter 1982): 383–94, Donald Davie considers Pound's late treatment of words as "things" in terms more general than and quite different from mine.

to appropriate Del Mar methodologically: Del Mar was not to figure in the *Cantos* until *Thrones* (1959).

Numismatics and the Discourse of Cultural Totality

Del Mar's *History of Monetary Systems*, original and unorthodox, stubbornly empiricist yet totalizing in its claims, was nothing less than an attempt to retell world history on the basis of changing monetary systems. Del Mar's subtitle gives some indication of his ambitions, a "record of actual experiments in money made by various states of the ancient and modern world, as drawn from their statutes, customs, treaties, mining regulations, jurisprudence, history, archaeology, coins, nummulary systems, and other sources of information." That all of this lay under the apparently simple and self-enclosed subject of monetary systems was precisely Del Mar's point. It is not difficult to imagine Pound's excitement on first looking into Del Mar, for under Del Mar's scrutiny, a coin became a kind of "luminous detail" from which the historian could very nearly reconstruct an entire culture. Moreover, the very nature of numismatics lent itself to Pound's project. Here was a historical method that used, quite literally, bits and chunks of "real history"—a method that seemed to offer an incontrovertible check on the written word, and so a weapon in Pound's battle to undermine academic history. Pound's understanding of Del Mar informed his inclusion of source materials throughout *Thrones* and, less consistently, in the cantos of *Drafts and Fragments* (1969), such as Canto 111, written while he was in St. Elizabeths.

We must be careful to distinguish between Del Mar's numismatics, or even his subject matter, and the generic features of his own richly heterogeneous text. A principal generic constituent of *History of Monetary Systems* is, for example, historical narrative. However, Pound systematically omitted this aspect of Del Mar's work and concentrated on nonnarrative features unique to Del Mar's nummulary "record": tables or ratios, excerpts from legal codes, or such devices as epigrams or coin mottoes. Pound's interest in the nature of coins and coinage led him to emphasize Del Mar's statistical apparatus. But such features as tables or epigrams, once in Pound's text, serve more to signify an intention, an insistence on the concrete, than discretely quantified information. These features are the trace of Pound's attempt to carry over ways of ordering material, as well as a manner of presenting that ordering. Still, Pound's ordering of Canto 97 cannot be explained by the structural analysis of Del Mar's *History of Monetary Systems*. By isolating and extending aspects of Del Mar's treatment of numismatics, Pound changed them.

The study of Canto 97 often encounters problems analogous to those examined in Canto 88. Pound's work in Canto 97, or in any of the cantos in *Thrones*, presents no radical discontinuities with his previous cantos. It developed in perceptible ways from his practice in *Rock-Drill*, or in *Cantos LII–LXXI*: so much so that at least one reader has seen in *Thrones* little more than elaborations of Pound's earlier principles. Peter Makin, commenting that *Thrones* is the "product of the same phase in Pound's life" as *Rock-Drill*, argues that "the progression in poetics between them is relatively small," and Carpenter draws a similar conclusion.[10] Yet the differences that seem small to some readers will appear large and disturbing to others; a long succession of critics have found, with Scott Eastham, that the cantos of *Thrones* are the most opaque cantos of all.[11] Davie regards *Thrones* as evidence of Pound's psychological collapse: "One cannot read *Thrones* without remembering that the author had spent twelve years in a hospital for the insane." Nicholls finds that *Thrones* reveals the extent to which Pound had lost touch with his audience: "Pound's handling of sources in *Thrones* . . . is marked by a concern for linguistic nuance which is often arid and unilluminating."[12] In fact, evidence can be found to support contentions of either sort. By developing techniques used in earlier cantos, Pound carried on his promulgation of a "'new' historic sense"; but, we might say, by overdeveloping certain of those techniques Pound changed them and so changed the combination of his historical materials.

While Pound seemed often to doubt his sense of mission, the manner in which he used Del Mar testifies to its late endurance. The publication of

---

10. Peter Makin, *Pound's Cantos* (London: George Allen & Unwin, 1985), 252; Carpenter, *Serious Character*, 854.

11. Scott Eastham, *Paradise and Ezra Pound: The Poet as Shaman* (Lanham, Md.: University Press of America, 1983), 252; Donald Davie, *Ezra Pound: The Poet as Sculptor* (New York: Oxford University Press, 1964), 240; Nicholls, *Politics, Economics, and Writing*, 214.

12. Davie, *Poet as Sculptor*, 214. In arguments related to Davie's, other critics note with C. David Heymann that "early in 1959 Pound's health began to deteriorate and with it his resolve to go on" (*Ezra Pound: The Last Rower, a Political Profile* [New York: Viking Press, 1976], 266). In less than five years after his publication of *Thrones*, Pound publicly capitulated, and resigned the *Cantos* to what he then assumed would be the inexorable judgment of posterity. These arguments would explain away the difficulties presented by *Thrones* by pointing to its temporal proximity to Pound's penitential silence. I propose, by contrast, that his explicit confessions later on should not initiate hunts for earlier implicit ones, but bring us to accept his enduring (if shaken) sense of mission while working on *Thrones*.

Thrones, coincident with the anniversary of the attack on Pearl Harbor, and the publication a few months later of *Impact: Essays on Ignorance and the Decline of American Civilization*, testify to the same purpose. Pound was at this time as anxiously aggressive as ever, and he used every means available to state his case plainly. This is especially true of Canto 97, whose original publication in the *Hudson Review* (Autumn 1956) was accompanied by an impatient prolepsis: "To put Monsieur Butor out of his misery, let us say that this Canto deals with the different rates of exchange between gold and silver, as in imperial Rome and the Orient, and to ease his despair about there never being a new paideuma, several Americans of the younger generation would already understand this without the (let us hope temporary) need of this note." However much his defensiveness revealed his own uncertainty, thirty years after *Guide to Kulchur*, Pound was still proclaiming the advent of a new "paideuma."[13] He was also, as we see here, still fighting a losing battle against the "aesthetic" criteria insisted on by the New Criticism.

Thirty years after the publication of *Thrones* the New Criticism may no longer be called "new," and it may no longer be consciously invoked, but its strictures continue to affect interpretations of the *Cantos*. We find, for example, George Kearns, in his *Guide to Ezra Pound's Selected Cantos*, concluding that "the *Thrones* cantos are largely ineffective as poetry." Too often, Kearns says, Pound "sounds like a teacher":

> He sends us away from the poem to investigate a variety of subjects—exciting investigations to be sure . . . [but], for poetry, the method is fatal: Pound has not lived long enough with his materials to have developed a sure feeling for them (although he is convinced they are important), and his talent for selection of "luminous detail" often fails him. . . . The hundreds of fragments Pound has arranged for his paradisal mosaic in praise of Justice are often witty, interesting, dazzling—but seldom moving. Aristotle (*Poetics* 3.1) warned epic poets against choosing "an action which, though one, is composed of too many parts." In *Thrones*, Pound has not discovered a structure suitable for his epic subject.[14]

---

13. Ezra Pound, "Canto XCVII," *Hudson Review* (autumn 1956): 1.
14. George Kearns, *A Guide to Ezra Pound's Selected Cantos* (New Brunswick: Rutgers University Press, 1980), 222–25. Another reader's guide presents an interesting contrast to Kearns's on the subject of *Thrones*. William Cookson, in *A Guide to the Cantos of Ezra Pound* (New York: Persea Books, 1985), 123, argues that "in the late cantos, Pound has found a form that weaves the lyrical,

Kearns's argument displays a cluster of assumptions that need to be examined, not because Kearns is unique in holding them but because he has written a reader's guide: a work that avoids (at least in most any but Pound's own) controversy for a safe and accessible way "into" difficult material. As with most "guides" of this kind, we can expect that even where Kearns diverges from popular conclusions he continues to answer popular questions. He finds fault with Pound for being too concerned with extraneous ideas ("subjects") that take away from the "poetry." He submits that what was wrong with those ideas was that Pound did not have "a sure feeling" for them; and so even where those ideas are "interesting," they are not "moving." This critique reinscribes a New Critical definition of a "poem": a serious work of high feeling, not paraphrasable into ideas, that achieves a unity and an autonomous status vis-à-vis other discourses.[15] The enabling assumptions of such a definition are from the start antagonistic to the kind of poem that Pound was writing. The antididactic criteria of high feeling and unity would deny to him much that he most hoped to accomplish.

Although quite distinct from the prose-laden textures of the cantos of the thirties, *Thrones* is nevertheless resolutely didactic. It enacted, more precisely, a calculated experiment that risked, and often lost, sense in a quest for compression and precision. This is not to say that the Del Mar materials provide the principal thematics for the whole of *Thrones*. In fact, the sequence introduces a variety of new sources, materials, and motifs: from the *Wen Li*, the Na Khi materials, the legal writings of Sir Edward Coke, and Waddell's *Indo-Summerial Seals Deciphered*. Indeed, even Cantos 96 and 97 draw heavily from other sources, such as Jacques Paul Migne's nineteenth-century edition of the eighth-century *Historia Langobardum*, or the ninth-century *Edicts of the Eparch*. But the Del Mar materials are especially significant because their methodology fascinated Pound even where Del Mar's ideas about money contradicted the fiscal precepts that had motivated him for over thirty years.[16] One suspects that at this point Pound was willing to welcome confirmation that economic exchange informed the totality of human relations from almost any quarter. It was, finally, less Del Mar's ideas

---

factual, anecdotal and didactic into a single texture, so there are none of the dry stretches that we get in some of the middle sections of the poem."

15. *Thrones* seems a strange place to complain that the *Cantos* lacks unity of action—it demonstrates no such unity in any of the previous sections. But what should really be questioned here is the value of trying to define any modern work of art in strictly Aristotelian terms.

16. See Nicholls on this topic, in *Politics, Economics, and Writing*, 202ff.

about money than his conviction that money could provide a key to everything else that inspired Pound. In a career marked by departures and false starts, the attempt to appropriate the numismatic model would be his last radical venture.

Pound did not adopt the model successfully. He proved unable to control the discursive intersections on which the didactic aims of *Thrones* depended. What checked him, however, was not ineptitude but the incompatibility of his poetics with his historical and political aims. Struggling for health and running out of time, Pound possibly came to realize this, for the final published fragments return to the more traditionally "lyric" textures of *Pisan Cantos*. Del Mar's *History of Monetary Systems* is not, then, included in the same manner as other kinds of economic discourse, like the litanies against usury (Cantos 45 or 51), the verse expositions of Douglas's "A+B Theorem" (Canto 38), or of Gesell's attempt to battle inflation with "shrinking money" (Canto 28). It differs from these even though its inclusion reflects the same conviction that economic understanding can illuminate cultural totality. In *Thrones*, numismatics becomes the dominant presence in a complex mixture, a presence that shapes how other materials appear.

In *The Economy of Literature*, Marc Shell submits that despite Pound's relentless adjurations to study economics and its relation to culture, his sensitivity to the shaping force of economics seldom went beyond a thematic interest. He quotes Stock's opinion that Pound tried to reform the canon around poets who could be shown to have had an interest in economics and that Pound's "opinion of a writer sometimes depended on whether that writer mentioned money."[17] Later, but again touching on Pound only in passing, Shell goes further still, accusing Pound of misunderstanding the relation between economics and language. Shell's suggestions have been considered by Peter Nicholls in his penetrating study *Ezra Pound: Politics, Economics, and Writing*. Nicholls grants that Shell's proposition seems, "on the face of it,"

> adequate since Pound stresses that, in a just system, money must function only as a sign. What should give us pause for thought, though, is the striking absence of the analogy between money and discourse in most of Pound's own writings. In fact those critics who have argued for some sort of homology between money and language in his theory have been hard pressed to cite concrete examples

---

17. Marc Shell, *The Economy of Literature* (Baltimore: Johns Hopkins University Press, 1978), 2.

of it in either his prose or verse. It thus needs to be emphasized that a remark such as the following one is extremely rare in Pound's writing: "Money and language exist by being current. The acceptance of coin as of value; of words as having meaning, are the essence of currency and of speech." (191)

Nicholls's resistance to facile analogies is well considered, but he does nevertheless mistake the kind of statement Shell was making. For Shell, who is not really concerned with Pound, the homologies between money and language exist whether or not a writer consciously exploits them. Shell mentions Pound only to exemplify what he would regard as an inadequate view of the relation of economics to the arts. His object is only to highlight the departure of his own from previous positions on the subject. Nicholls's caution that Shell's position should not be confused with Pound's is thus unnecessary. As for those critics "who have argued for some sort of homology between money and language in [Pound's] theory," Nicholls adds in a footnote that they usually "find themselves driven to quoting Allen Upward ('Words are, like money, a medium of exchange')."[18] Relevant examples are, Nicholls rightly protests, scarce in Pound's own writings. And yet he is hasty in dismissing both the importance of Upward's ideas for Pound's thought, and the seriousness of Shell's efforts to ground literary practice in cultural practice.

In their different ways, the arguments of both Upward and Shell are concerned to make issues of writing a central concern for new and broader audiences, and that concern is one which Pound would have appreciated. It need not take the form of arguing for a totality behind the apparently random fragments of experience—as it often did with Pound. It can suggest the variegated relations between diverse forms of cultural life. Although his beliefs precluded contact with the Marxian model of base and superstructure, Pound yet maintained the fundamental importance of economics for "culture." But one of the values of Shell's analysis is that it demonstrates how economic exchange can itself be informed by cultural myths and values. Pound could sometimes regard the vulnerability of "culture" to economic forces as indicative of its secondary vitality. As we have noted, Pound expected that the investigation of history—at least when pursued by "the new learning"—would turn up "causes" that were inevitably moral or economic, and that these just as inevitably turned one into the other. Pound's

---

18. Nicholls, *Politics, Economics, and Writing*, 251 n. 22.

growing interest in numismatics, coming especially after an incarceration which had isolated him more than ever from his audience, stands as testimony to such a concern: the hope that he might, after all, recover for the arts their ancient centrality.

But Pound's determination to win readers to his cause bespeaks awareness that he was failing to do so. As Eastham has observed, Pound's self-justification in the first canto of *Thrones*—"if we never write anything save what is already understood, the field of understanding will never be extended"— would never have been included by a poet fully confident in his method.[19] Those doubts were anything but allayed by the public response to *Thrones*. Donald Hall has said that by the time of his 1960 interview with Pound, Pound's tone was growing self-accusing, although he affected to seem "jaunty as he tried out the notion that a man could admit his errors and even survive them."[20] Yet even then, Pound insisted that the title *Section: Rock-Drill* "was intended to imply the necessary resistance in getting a certain main thesis across—hammering." In *Thrones*, the motif of "litterae nihil sanantes" alternated with similar assertions about the sociopolitical power of art. Pound suggests, for example, that it was no coincidence that a mere thirty-three years separated Shakespeare's death from the beheading of Charles I. (Pound believed that Shakespeare's history plays presented objections to the idea of unlimited monarchy that quickened the popular unrest which eventually brought revolution.) Pound's doubts pressed him. But his didactic impulse was more urgent still, and compelled him so long as he continued to write.

Discussing Pound's economic concerns of the late thirties and forties, Nicholls submits that his "main reason for attending to this now forgotten body of writing is to show how the deformation of Pound's thought, his anti-semitism, his irrationalism, his pseudo-mysticism, was closely linked to his conception of money."[21] Nicholls believes that Pound's economic thought will lead us to the margins of Pound's achievement, as it seems to have led Pound to the margins of society, and even sanity itself. Significantly, this most darkly driven period of Pound's interest in economics was accompanied by almost no work on the *Cantos*, as Nicholls himself observes. Only

---

19. Scott Eastham, *Paradise and Ezra Pound*, 119. This statement closely recalls Pound's protest to Harriet Monroe in 1913 that "if one is going to print opinions that the public already agrees with, what is the use of printing 'em at all? Good art can't possibly be palatable all at once" (*SL*, 12).

20. Hall's *Paris Review* "Interview: Ezra Pound," in *Remembering Poets: Reminiscences and Opinions* (New York: Harper Collins, 1978), 222–44.

21. Nicholls, *Politics, Economics, and Writing*, 158.

in his final years did Pound experience a comparable period of inactivity. Between these two periods came a period of intense activity, activity informed by altered but deeply earnest economic concerns. In a very real sense, when Pound surrendered his economic struggle, he surrendered writing. But before that surrender came his final outpouring: the same obsessions that had brought his work on the *Cantos* to a halt proved once more the way back into the heart of his enterprise.

Prophet and Profit

No other part of *Thrones* provides a better opportunity to examine the intersection of economic and lyric discourses than Cantos 96 and 97, precisely because critics have almost unanimously regarded them as among the most "arid" (to use Nicholls's term) of Pound's later compositions. Certainly these cantos fail as "lyrics": at least as we have, more or less in the romantic tradition, come to value that term. But I propose to consider these cantos in terms for which a rigorously "lyric" model cannot serve. Leon Surette's judgment of *Thrones* conveniently illustrates the difference between these two projects: "It is possible to distinguish between the didactic and visionary aspects of the later cantos. And it is in the visionary portions of the poem that we find poetry achieving rhetorical success comparable to the *Pisan Cantos*. Here the subjective lyric voice once again comes into its own because its subject is appropriate to its rhetoric, as the subject of the principles of good government is not."[22] Surette's discriminations are perfectly consistent with his initial premises: he is interested in "the subjective lyric voice" and its "visionary" flights. Such interests necessarily leave Surette disinclined to discuss "principles of good government" or economics. A more historical understanding would, however, inquire why and how Pound combined the "didactic and visionary aspects of the poem."

Consider the eight lines which open Canto 97:

> Melik & Edward struck coins-with-a-sword,
> "Emir el Moumenin" (Systems p. 134)
>   six and ½ to one, or the sword of the Prophet,

---

22. Leon Surette, *A Light from Eleusis: A Study of Ezra Pound's Cantos* (New York: Oxford University Press, 1979), 236.

> SILVER being in the hands of the people
> "and for the first time in my life
> "I had thousand $ bills in my hand-bag"
> (Princess A.)
> after the 27/75 Spew Deal wangle
> (682)

Pound's opening does not mix economic with more traditionally poetic elements, it conflates them. Although not the only kind of intersection Pound attempts in these cantos, the mutual infection of discourses here is a sort of showpiece to introduce the serious concerns of the canto. The first line offers at least three readings. According to Del Mar, Melik (or "Habdimelich" in *History of Monetary Systems*) was the first of the Omayyad caliphs to coin gold in defiance of Byzantine authority; Edward III of England was among the first European monarchs to do so. A primarily denotative reading of this line, or at least a reading which most respects Pound's hyphens, suggests that these monarchs minted coins with swords on them. This was as much as Del Mar said, although he indicates that the swords on the coins symbolized the authority which enabled the coining of gold. But at the same time, Pound's line makes other significations, and these arise from the polysemic interplay of "struck" with "sword." By writing "coins-with-a-sword" rather than, say, "sword-bearing coins," Pound placed considerably more stress on the word "sword" than it carried in its original context of Del Mar's *History of Monetary Systems*:

> In A.H. 67 (A.D. 686) Abd-el-Melik, being at that period involved in civil war with the Mardaites, bought peace of Justinian II (afterwards called Rhinotmetus) by the payment of a tribute of 1,000 gold solidi or dinars per annum for ten years. Down to this time these coins were struck by Abd-el-Melik, with Roman emblems and legends upon them. Six years later, the Arabian caliph, having disposed of the Mardaite trouble, determined to assert his independence of Rome, and by a token understood of all the world. He struck gold coins with his own effigy, holding a drawn sword, as afterwards did Edward III, when he renounced the same dread authority. Abd-el-Melik's dinars bore this challenging legend: "The Servant of God, Abd-el-Melik, Emir-el-Moumenin." These coins Justinian refused to receive, because, says Zonaras, "It is not permitted to stamp gold

coins with any other effigy, but that of the emperor of Rome. Whereupon a war was declared by Justinian. (134)

Del Mar goes on to recount how Abd-el-Melik substituted the Oriental ratio of exchange between silver and gold of six and a half to one for the Roman of twelve to one. After explaining that in the provinces the Muslims took from Rome, silver was primarily in the hands of the people, whereas gold was in the hands of their rulers, Del Mar theorized that because this revaluation doubled the value of the people's silver it facilitated the Moslem conquest.

To turn from Del Mar's prose to Canto 97 is to be struck by how forcefully Pound's dactylic and trochaic lines alter Del Mar's meaning. Pound's phrase "coins-with-a-sword" suggests Melik's cutting of the monetary ratio in half, and lends as well a kind of battlefield valor to his assumption of the sovereignty to mint coins. Pound's first line, then, describes coins, monetary reform, and a factive or heroic deed. His third line continues this integration of the economic and the lyric by making the motto "the sword of the Prophet" an appositive to Melik's ratio of "six and ½ to one," and so synonymous with the sword on Melik's coins. But where the end place of line 1 went to "sword," in line 3 it is "Prophet" that receives Pound's emphasis. Line 4 plays out a further association with "sword of the Prophet," as it concludes with the parallel syntactical structure "hands of the people." In so doing, Pound puns on "prophet/profit," thus associating the prophet with a Confucian-like character who believed good ethics get things done. This last association completes Pound's transformation, as it links Del Mar's ambitious and crafty caliph with Pound's Ruskinian belief that "you can not make good economics out of bad ethics."[23]

The above is a generous reading, in the sense that it brings a great deal to Pound's text, being informed by knowledge of his source materials. Yet the multiple meanings generated by each phrase are a necessary part of Pound's construction, an overdetermination designed to facilitate his "totalitarian" reading and to compensate for the reader's unfamiliarity with the source texts. But what I have said so far risks substituting thematic summary for the chiseled phrases of Pound's writing. My point is that Pound's construction works to thwart attempts to disjoin the visionary and the didactic, prophet and profit. Pound's idea was not just to make the didactic more attractive, but

---

23. Ezra Pound, "The Individual in His Milieu" (1935); reprinted in *Impact: Essays on Ignorance and the Decline of American Civilization* (Chicago: Henry Regnery, 1960), 244.

to transform the visionary into something useful—into writing, as Orage said, that would "be not only action itself, but the cause of action."

These aims inform even such passages where didactic and visionary elements remain distinct. In Canto 96, for instance, an essentially unelaborated list of European kings, from Migne's *Historia Langobardum*, is followed by a traditionally lyric outburst:

> Cedwald, Architriclin
> From the golden font, kings lie in order of generation
>   Cuningpert elegant, and a warrior . . .
> de partibus Liguriae . . . lubricus
> Aripert sank, auro gravatus, because he was carrying gold.
> Who shall know throstle's note from banded thrush
> by the wind in the holly bush[24]

The natural imagery, end rhyme, and characteristic substitution of trochees for iambs call attention to the sudden shift to pastoral lyric element. But the lyric question here is meant to problematize the confidence with which we make distinctions and pass judgments. Take, for example, "Cuningpert" and "Aripert." Two Lombard monarchs, one whom the Church regarded as a dangerous heretic, but who gave his people their first written code of law; the other who defended the faith, but was so avaricious that he drowned from the weight of the gold about his body while crossing a river. Which of these was the better king? Pound's construction does little to help answer the question, and much to make it more difficult. Even the names of the kings sound alike to the English ear, and Pound, concealing more than he reveals, offers for each king only scant detail. Epithets such as "elegant, warrior" or "lubricus" do not in fact tell us about these men, but serve as "signs" for them. This treatment of the language of his source, like the treatment of Del Mar that opens Canto 97, transforms individual words into coins, and so introduces the more extreme appropriations of "numismatics" to come.

Another passage from Canto 96 exemplifies this further direction: those lines where Pound first turned to the *Eparchikon Biblion*. *The Eparch's Book*, or *The Edicts of the Eparch*, was written by the Byzantine emperor Leo the

---

24. Canto 96/666–67. Pound took these lines from Jacques Paul Migne's nineteenth-century edition of the eighth century *Historia Langobardum*, by Paul the Deacon; see Carroll Terrell, ed., *A Companion to the Cantos of Ezra Pound* (Berkeley and Los Angeles: University of California Press, 1984), 2:590–91, 594 n. 36, and 607 n. 271.

Wise to govern the relations among the various guilds of his domain. Its inclusion by Pound within the context of Del Mar's treatise on monetary systems indicates Pound's concern with the relations among authority, signification, and exchange. We should also note, however, Pound's continued interest, thirty-five years after his encounter with Orage's Guild Socialism, in the guild idea. In Pound's combinatory thinking, ideas were often displaced from their former significance, but were rarely wholly replaced.

The first of Pound's inclusions from Leo's edict is the single word, "Hyacinthus" (see Fig. 2). It is a beginning that typifies the function of the edict in Pound's text. "Hyacinthus" was the attempt of translator Jules Nicole to find a Latin equivalent for the Greek word *megalozelon*. Pound's next line jokingly suggested an alternative that would be just as good—or bad, "why not fake purple." His larger point was not to pick at Nicole's translation, or even, as some critics have suggested, at the inadequacy of dictionary translation in general. Pound's constructions in Canto 96 do these things, but they attempt a more radical point as well. Each time that Pound quotes the Greek, he joins it either to Nicole's Latin translation, or to his own very colloquial rendition, or to both.

The key to what is going on here emerges after a break in the lines, and Pound's introduction of the word *alogistous*. For the next seven lines Pound's text forms three simultaneous columns. The left column comprises single words which Pound isolated from the Greek of Leo's edict. The middle column is made up of, not translations of those words, but a running commentary upon them, offered once again in a deliberately colloquial or "yankee" dialect—an intersection of the verbal discourse of common men with the formal record of the law. And, on the right, are Chinese ideograms from the *Analects* of Confucius. What Pound does here is present the Greek words in the same manner as the Chinese ideograms, setting them up in a vertical column and treating them as so many discrete points of attention.

One effect of this practice has been to produce the incomprehension and frustration on the part of readers that has led reasonably enough to charges of ellipticality or aridity. Critics have attempted to explain this canto by importing long summaries, paraphrases, or quotations from *Eparchikon Biblion* to explain the meaning of Pound's words. Although Pound was unquestionably interested in his source texts, this was not the kind of reading he sought to produce. These words and elements have ceased to function primarily as part of a larger narrative and have become signs in a semiotic system over which Pound continually struggled to assert sovereignty. He endeavored in these late cantos to treat words as though they were *nomisma*:

and the idea of just price is somewhere,
    the haggling, somewhere,
also
    ἀλογίστους quite beautifully used
        tho' utopian  tzu³

καπηλεύων   or   chih¹

στομύλος   that is "mouthy"
ἀγοραῖος   forensic  to²⁻⁵

λάλος   babbler   chu¹

ταραχώδης   as on the East bank from Beaucaire
μὴ τῇ τοῦ ἐπάρχου ἐσφραγισμένον
not stamped with the prefect's seal βούλλῃ
καμπανὸν νενοθευμένον
Ducange: στατήρ
Here, surely, is a refinement of language

> *If we never write anything save what is already understood, the field of understanding will never be extended. One demands the right, now and again, to write for a few people with special interests and whose curiosity reaches into greater detail.*

Fig. 2. From Canto XCVI.

objects of inherent value upon which he could impress his own emblems and among which he could establish relations.

Pound's running commentary on Leo's Greek gives new form to an older Poundian equation—that equation between verbal precision and moral or political discrimination so vividly described by Vincent Sherry.[25] Drawing from a section of Leo's edict that specifies which kinds of vulgar behavior would cause a merchant to be expelled from his guild, Pound's inclusion plays out its fascination with Leo's inscription of his own authority. The process proves self-reflexive, for in admiring Leo's ability to make verbal precision a basis for moral discrimination, Pound makes the manner of his inclusion his poetic subject. Particular examples, well or ill-conceived, here matter less for Pound than the pursuit of precision and the registration of authority.

Pound's columnar arrangement strives to reproduce Leo's method on the basis of an essentially visual discrimination. But this same columnar arrangement, this creation of vertical axes on the page, in itself provides overt comment on Leo's language: overt because his selection of words from the edict, and his joining of the lot to the Confucian ideograms, are also "commentaries." Pound wrote of *alogistous* that it is "beautifully used," but "utopian." It is well to prohibit "silly" or "unreasonable" (*alogistous*) behavior, but more difficult to establish a basis for determining which deeds are reasonable and which are not. Pound worried, therefore, that Leo's fine discrimination was only "utopian," merely a rhetorical gesture. But Pound's worry does not take shape as a judgment, because he interrupts this vertical axis with a horizontal axis upon which "mouthy" is but a translation of *stomulos,* and "forensic" a translation of *agoraious.*

Neither of these "axes" supplants the other, and neither carries perfectly across the page. Pound's construction presents us with multiple intersections that function to foreground the very process of interpretation. Indeed, his commentary on Leo's edict is in general a kind of metacommentary on the historical project of *Thrones,* and which culminates in the prose apology at the bottom of the page. But just above the apology is Leo's use of the word *stater,* and Pound's reaction to it helps clarify its multiple functions. After consulting the lexicographer Charles du Cange, Pound learned that *stater* referred not only to a weight, but to the scale on which that weight was measured. The word evoked Pound's complete approval: "Here, surely, is a

---

25. Vincent Sherry, *Ezra Pound, Wyndham Lewis, and Radical Modernism* (New York: Oxford University Press, 1993).

refinement of language." For Pound, this word presented a near perfect image for his own use of language in *Thrones*: a use that I am calling "numismatic" as a way of explaining the manner of Pound's inclusion not only of Del Mar, but of texts like *Eparchikon Biblion* as well. By "numismatic" I mean primarily a specific notion of the way value inheres within and between words. Pound himself used the word infrequently, though often portentiously, as with his judgment on the language of Act 51 of King Henry III: "that is grammar/nummulary moving toward prosody" (Canto 97/685). His equally infrequent attempts to explain the model of value he saw in Del Mar's numismatics are elliptical—perhaps because he was unsure of himself, but certainly because, as in the case of the epistolary gloss he sent to Robert Creeley, the explanations already employed the method:

semantically the moneta also a greenback by nature.

COIN is the antithesis BOTH of NOMISMATIC   NUM
                                             and moneta: advice.
                       advice as to what is due the bearer in
                       the market.
                                     no matter what it is stamped or
printed on.
Del very good on pt. EP been makin for years/metal coin
all in barter belt . . .[26]

The isolation and emphasis upon unglossed words like "NUM" is left to exemplify the otherwise ill-explained point. Written only a year after his first encounter with Del Mar, it is interesting to see that Pound's rhetoric already presented his Victorian predecessor as the newcomer. The correspondence with Creeley is interesting too in that, for all the lessons on economics which it drew from Pound, it had been initiated like so many others to inquire about "poetic quality"—as Pound put it in the last sentence of the last of the excerpts that Creeley published.

Pound's concern with the interplay between intrinsic value and a value fixed and measured within a system of public exchange figures prominently in the Del Mar cantos. Still, the celebration in Canto 96 of the equivocal reference of *stater* to both a weight and the scale on which that weight was measured merits further attention. More precisely, the four ideograms from

26. Creeley, "Selections," 20.

the *Analects* that immediately precede that reference suggest the implications of this interest in linguistic "refinement." As Wilhelm explains, these ideograms present Confucius's complaint that "the vulgarity of purple spoils our appreciation of vermilion."[27] In this way, the ideograms return us to Pound's jest at Nicole's literary or "purple" translation of *megalozelon*. Pound saw in the edict an attempt to achieve the most elevated of ends with common ordinary language. While this perception probably bears out Nicholls's Marxist charge that Pound's populism was "reactionary" and inseparable from "an activist, elitist philosophy," it typifies Pound's later attempts to loosen "aesthetic" limitations.[28] Pound was working here to find poetry, if not in the language of the marketplace, at least in the language in which wise men (Leo, Confucius) attempt to curb the corruptions of moral relations by mercantile practice.

Nevertheless, if this is poetry that strives for nummulary currency, it is like numisma in a less fortunate sense as well, or at least less fortunate for Pound's populist ambitions. Although all poetry can be said to resist paraphrase, this poetry depends not only on the sound of individual words but also on the physical configuration of those words on the page. Whatever its popularizing or didactic aims, Pound's text requires immediate, firsthand perception.

The prose paragraph that follows Pound's remark on a "refinement of language" further exemplifies his visual-perceptual innovations. It functions analogously with Leo's concern (of Pound's following line) that "*e kai nomismata xeei*"—that coins not be filed or polished. Pound carefully included this paragraph as a prose statement. He not only made no effort to accommodate the prose to his poetic line, but, by reproducing it in a different typographical font, called attention to it as a distinct semiotic unit. It is present in Canto 96 as language whose value is tied ineluctably to its physical presentation—upon its edges not being filed, or its prose texture polished. This kind of inclusion is uncommon in the *Cantos*, and most instances of it date from this period. Canto 88, for example, contains as a prose paragraph an edict of Edward IV of England; but in this example the prose has obviously been edited, and is marked by Pound's colloquial translation, abbreviations, and omissions. The most similar example is also found in Canto 96. It is a passage quoted in Paulus Diaconus's Latin, which relates the same incident with which the opening lines of Canto 97 are concerned: Melik's "devilish" payment of the Roman tribute with his own coinage. In this case, Pound did

27. James J. Wilhelm, *The Later Cantos of Ezra Pound* (New York: Walker, 1977), 122.
28. Nicholls, *Politics, Economics, and Writing*, 52.

not include the original prose "whole," but instead used ellipses and multiple hyphenations to underscore his condensation. While not typographically distinguished from the rest of the canto, this inclusion betrays the same iconographic view of language found in the prose apology: it is an inclusion premised by the supposition that to change the physical properties of words, aural or visual, is to change their meaning.

This manner of inclusion is not in itself absolutely new to Pound's practice. But the contrary tendencies of, on the one hand, cultivating the sound of words and, on the other, generating meaning at least in part by visual presentation, here become incompatible with the other familiar features of the *Cantos*. Pound's didactic subject matter and his ideogrammic means of ordering his subject matter are both affected by these changes in his means of presenting that ordering. Consider, for instance, what happens to his interest in "the sacerdotal nature of coinage"—a "theme" that has been the subject of most critical examinations of these cantos (a notion like "the sacerdotal" lends itself to discussions of Pound's "vision"). In appropriating this theme from Del Mar, Pound included a great many raw statistics—names of coins, the ratios between coins, or even the weights of coins:

> 371 ¼ grains silver in Del's time
> as I have seen them by shovels full
>   lit by gas flares.
>   One wd/ suppose Theresa's 390,
>   but were, apparently, 353 and a fraction,
> at Salzburg 5 more, or supposedly 361, or
> "Window-dressing" as Bryan admitted to Kitson.
>   (Canto 97/687)

The very inclusion of statistics like these alters the texture of Pound's poem: they not only create distinct points of attention, but refer to "things" relatively free from metaphoric association. Even when mixed with imagery as resonant as the rather underworld-like scene of coins being shoveled into counting machines at the Philadelphia mint, the statistics check the mythopoeic. It was not, however, that Pound had suddenly developed the archivist's passion. Such inclusions are symptomatic of the programmatic changes attempted in *Thrones*. These were not extraneous importations, but amplifications of tendencies already present in Pound's work.

The Akkadian hieroglyph ("Sargon") of Canto 97 is a case in point (see Fig. 3). Following the Fenollosan procedures Pound had long applied in the

The temple is holy  because it is not for sale

From Sargon of Agade

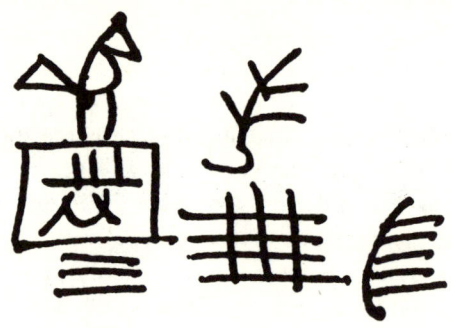

        a thousand years before T'ang,
gothic arch out of India,
    from Multan 700 *li*,
      torchlight, at Multan, offer perfume,
Son of Herakles, Napat son of Waters,
    Panch, that is Phoenician, Tyanu

 lion head

Came then autumn in April and
    "By Knoch Many now King Minos lies",
From Sargon to Tyana
        no blood on the altar stone.

Fig. 3. From Canto XCVII.

"interpretation" (rather than translation) of Chinese ideograms, several exegetes have offered to explain its meaning by breaking it down into component features, and so into thematic units. In fact, strictly formal criticism can in this case do little more. Not only did Pound follow the misreading of his source, Waddell's *Indo-Summerian Seals Deciphered*, he combined that hieroglyph with other figures that neither Terrell nor any other critic has been able to identify. Considered in the broader terms of generic innovation, however, the hieroglyph becomes a most interesting way into the perplexing mixtures of generic features characteristic of the Del Mar cantos.

In keeping with his practice throughout these cantos, Pound offered later in the canto a "translation" of the hieroglyph, but did not use it to replace the "artifact" itself:

> Flowers, incense, in the temple enclosure,
> no blood in that TEMENOS
> when crocus is over and the rose is beginning.
> (Canto 97/695)

Among the most "lyric" elements of the canto, these lines are nevertheless something very different from the hieroglyph that, we might say, inspired them. They translate a visual symbol into words that can be spoken, into words associated with other elements of the *Cantos*—such as "the rose," which Pound connects eight lines later with the song of Alcamo. Moreover, these lines only translate a part of the hieroglyph, and are but one translation among several others which Pound offers. "The temple is holy [hieroglyph] because it is not for sale" is an "interpretation" of the element directly underneath what Waddell called "the falcon." But the hieroglyph itself remains an undeciphered artifact, a stubborn block of nonmeaning in the midst of a very didactic canto. Pound's translations quite explicitly render it only in part, leaving before us a "chunk" of "the record" which we can only imperfectly comprehend. Terrell's surmise that the two figures to the right of the Sargon hieroglyph are Pound's addition is then only an additional confirmation how the hieroglyph exemplifies Pound's combinatory procedures: it mixes heterogeneous elements; it combines the same element or parts of that element in different contexts (generic mixtures); it treats what was a part of another text as a "concrete" thing in the world.

As a part of Pound's text, the Sargon hieroglyph functions rather like the lines from Leo's edict examined earlier, or like the Chinese ideograms throughout the *Cantos*. It arrests the eye and presents a configuration of discrete elements that make a strictly linear reading problematic. The effect of this technique recalls the declaration in Guillaume Apollinaire's manifesto that "our minds must learn to understand things synthetico-ideographically instead of analytico-discursively."[29] But the immediate source of this innovation was not analogies with painting, but Pound's didactic drive to write a history free from narrative limitations. By the time of his work on *Thrones*, Pound was treating semantic value as though it were nummulary value. The ideograms and hieroglyphs of the late cantos function like a semiotic legend to that design: they are not merely elements added to an otherwise consistent poem, but models of larger processes. Pound wanted to write a poem—a history—of discrete elements with indiscrete predications.

The increasing focus on individual words and phrases, throughout *Rock-Drill* and *Thrones*, was a deliberate gambit and developed out of his absorption in the work of Del Mar. In both his critical discussion of words and music, and in his manner of treating prose narrative history, Pound showed an interest in slowing down the poetic line, and "restoring" to each word distinct physical qualities. These interests continue to play a part in *Thrones*. In the opening lines for Canto 97, to return to our earlier example, we might observe Pound's introduction of the verbal anecdote from "Princess A." into the surrounding material from Del Mar. But, in that same sequence, the words "Emir el Moumenin" also appear between quotation marks and suggest a different although related kind of generic transformation. The words, which mean "commander of the faithful," were the motto struck on the coins minted by Habdimelich. Their inclusion here points to one of the salient procedures of these cantos.

By treating the coin motto as though it were a verbal phase popularly attributed to Melik, Pound may have been attempting to convey the sense in which, throughout antiquity, the striking of coins remained the surest way of disseminating news. As Del Mar argued in his *History of Monetary Systems:* "Where printing was uncommon and the newspaper unknown, a new gold or silver coinage was the most effective means of proclaiming the accession of a new ruler or the era of a new religion. . . . In the absence of felted paper and printing ink, it was the only means the ancients had of printing and disseminating the most important intelligence and opinions. Addison correctly regarded the Roman coinage as a sort of 'State Gazette,' in which all

---

29. From an article Apollinaire published under the pseudonym Gabriel Arboin, "Devant l'idéogramme d'Apollinaire," in the journal *Les Soirees* (July–August 1914); quoted in David Seaman, *Concrete Poetry in France* (Ann Arbor: UMI Research Press, 1981), 171.

the great events of the Empire were periodically published" (66–67). "It had," Del Mar concluded, introducing an idea that impressed Pound deeply, "this advantage over any other kind of monument: it could not be successfully mutilated, forged, or suppressed." Del Mar's commentary points up the particular combinatory qualities of coinage that made his subject of such interest to Pound. Besides being an object of both inherent and conventional value (coins are struck of precious metals, the ratios between which are determined as a matter of state policy), a coin is a kind of monument that combines elements of sculpture or relief with inscribed linguistic or semiotic messages. Del Mar's equation of real power with the sovereignty to coin metal would make a statement such as "Emir el Moumenin" self-evidently true. Moreover, the record of this truth would be proof from antagonistic machinations.

Pound readily appreciated each of these characteristics that marked Del Mar's interest in numismatics. As we have seen, he already tended to conceive of the historical record in "monumental" terms, speaking of "whole slabs" or "chunks" of "the record." He had furthermore been given to believe, with a kind of brash, Ruskinian confidence that would be shared by few archaeologists, that we can read or reconstruct from these fragments their "whole" context. Del Mar's work therefore seemed to confirm his own historical method. It offered new evidence for his long-held belief that economic studies offered a fundamental perspective from which to evaluate social relations.

Del Mar presented his case in his preface to *History of the Precious Metals*:

> So long as Individuals in place of government retain control of the Monetary Measure, there can be no real Religion, there can be no real Liberty, there can be no real National Life. The bases of Religion are Love and Fraternity. There can be no Fraternity whilst an Unjust Measure is permitted to introduce discontent and strife into all the transactions of social life. The basis of Liberty is Justice. There can be no Justice whilst an Unjust Measure continues to nullify the lessons of wisdom and experience. The basis of National Life is Political Equality. There can be no Equality so long as an Unjust Measure continues to rob the many for the benefit of the few.[30]

30. Alexander Del Mar, *History of the Precious Metals: From the Earliest Times to the Present* (New York: Cambridge Encyclopedia Co., 1902), ix.

Del Mar moves from thesis to fundamental definitions, to an attempt to transform those terms into relations that involve a near totality of cultural experience, and which in each case reveal its basis to be "the Monetary Measure." He insisted that "value is a relation and not an attribute," and "that money is a measure or measurer of value" which "to work equitably . . . should, like other measures, be defined and limited by law with precision" (viii).

In their insistent association of economics with ethics, Del Mar's arguments about "value" had great appeal for Pound. But Pound showed himself still more impressed by Del Mar's method, and it is on the level of method that we can see another way in which the monetary historian confirmed Pound's own procedures. We should, given Nicholls's insight that Pound tended to translate most important issues into problems of method, expect this "confirmation" to become an important source of change within the *Thrones* cantos.

For all the difference of his concerns, Del Mar resembled most of Pound's other models—Agassiz, or Fenollosa, Frobenius, Ruskin, or Gourmont—in one crucial respect: he believed it possible for the historian to reconstruct complex totalities from the most fragmentary evidence. Del Mar's most sweeping claims for his numismatic studies move well beyond justifying the archaeological examination of coins. As though forgetting his often repeated insistence that numismatic study is indispensable to the historian precisely because it deals with unfalsifiable, hard facts, Del Mar proposes—in the chapter on Muslim moneys so important to Pound—a transcendental positivism:

> To those to whom the ratio of value between the precious metals appears due to any other circumstance than the arbitrary laws of national mints, or to those whose attention to the history of this recondite subject has now been drawn for the first time, the ratio may seem a strange or inadequate criterion of political or religious domination; but it is precisely in such obscure relations between great and little things that an all-wise Creator has sheltered the truth of history from man's destructive powers. The forgery of books, the defacement of monuments, the perversion of evidences, the extermination of nonconformists, the invention of fabulous cosmogonies and superstitious fictions—all are made in vain to conceal or crush the truth so long as a blade of grass or a breath of air remains on earth to reveal it; for all Nature is united in a mysterious harmony, and to even

approximately master one branch of science is to gain a key which, with patience and industry, may eventually unlock for us all the others. (140–41)

Here Del Mar's claims about the "indestructible" evidence of coins are really secondary to broad confidence that "truth" itself is indestructible. That truth is to be identified with the "mysterious harmony" of all nature, and provides a stable and unchanging basis for "the" history of human changes. From this argument it is clear why Pound identified Del Mar with such naturalists as von Humboldt or Agassiz, or the anthropologist Frobenius (see Canto 89/612, for example). Indeed, Del Mar's writing probably struck Pound as a nearly ideal exemplar of his "'new' historical method." To invoke Pound's terms: Del Mar moved from "bits and chunks of real history" (coins) to "main principles" that were overtly "economic and moral" (the responsibility of government to control monetary issue). Del Mar connected "apparently disjunct phenomena" by seizing on a single principle and observing "the leaves and/or fruits of causation."

But although Del Mar's thematic and methodological appeal to Pound is readily explainable, it remains puzzling that Pound continually described him as a model of "style." Two selections from Del Mar's work, one of them the section from *History of Monetary Systems* most relevant to *Thrones*, were included among the titles which Pound published with John Kasper and T. David Horton as "The Square Dollar Series." A jacket blurb to these books numbered Del Mar among those few "American writers who can hold their own, either as stylists or historians, against any foreign competition whatsoever." A second notice declared Del Mar to be "America's greatest historian." Pound's conflation of traditionally aesthetic terms ("stylist") with didactic ones ("historian") explains much of his meaning. But from his praise of Del Mar as "stylist," one might expect the *Cantos* to include passages from Del Mar's work long enough to demonstrate stylistic superiority. In fact, however, Pound quotes Del Mar only in short fragments, or in a few words, or sometimes merely in a few statistical figures. Although Pound's inclusions from Benton (another writer numbered among the "Square Dollar" few) were also heavily elided, at several junctures in Cantos 88 and 89 Pound nevertheless endeavored to include the "sense of" and "force" of Benton's narrative. When working with Del Mar's book, which like *Thirty Years' View* was a predominantly narrative history, Pound did not do so.

Instead, Pound focused on generic features in it that Del Mar had subordinated to narrative. The coin mottoes offer a paradigmatic example of the kinds of materials in which Pound was interested: epigrammatic materials and factual evidence like dates and ratios. What Pound sought to emulate, as I have suggested, was the method of Del Mar's numismatic study. He sought to use Del Mar's text to produce details as "hard and fast" as the coins with which Del Mar originally worked, much as he elsewhere sought to "recover" from written texts the immediacy of oral discourse. In *Section: Rock-Drill* Pound's treatment of Benton raised narrative expectations in order to exploit them, but in his work on *Thrones* Pound abandoned such expectations altogether. His interest had moved away from a unifying narrative structure to the discrete individual elements that ordinarily comprised it. Pound's poetic process in *Thrones* was a literalization of Del Mar's claim that "truth" could be found in a single "blade of grass," as it was a radicalization of Del Mar's numismatic studies.

What Pound thereafter created had very little to do with Del Mar's actual text. As the passage describing Abd-el-Melik exemplifies, Del Mar's was a principally narrative work, and the bulk of his commentary was devoted to articulating the relations among the coin values of any one system, and among the larger valuations of competing systems. Moreover, despite his talk about the "truth" contained in the hard evidence of coins, Del Mar's deductions were not solely based on numismatic evidence, but depended too on a wide reading of other sources. Pound himself knew this, and even took to describing one of Del Mar's major contributions as his having "corrected and emended Mommsen on Roman history, and debunked Thorold Rogers."[31]

Nevertheless, as his association of Del Mar with Agassiz and Frobenius indicates, Pound was most interested in *Systems* as a methodological model. Pound's investment in numismatics manifested the historiographical drive described by Harper and Furia. But it was not so much a reality "behind" words that Pound pursued, as a reality that inhered within them. Thus even in the cantos where features of economic discourse figure in major ways, Pound altered their function to fit historiographical ends. In this way, we can see his late practice conforming to earlier pattern.

Without denying Pound's very real interest in the nature of money, numismatics functions in Cantos 96 and 97 less as a thematic argument than as a way of handling detail. Even, as in the first lines of Cantos 97, when these

31. Pound, in a note printed on the front cover of the Square Dollar Series edition of Del Mar's *Roman and Moslem Moneys* (1955), which was itself an excerpt from *History of Monetary Systems*.

cantos endeavor to reproduce Del Mar's arguments, they do so in ways that would have puzzled the economist. Del Mar's argument was precisely that coins provide a check on the written word. Pound's procedures contradicted that premise even as they paid it homage. Pound sought to treat the word as the thing itself, the coin motto as the very sword of the Prophet. He sought to extend his totalitarian method to the production of main and basic relations from the citations of individual words. Quite often, as when drawing on words or phrases with associations established earlier in the *Cantos*, he produced remarkable results. But Pound's quotations of Del Mar's "statistics" frequently do not immediately produce meaning. They stand as evidence for all that we do not yet know, for all that could not be included in the poem. Like the indecipherable hieroglyphs surrounding "Sargon," they serve as "legendary" material to guide our reading. In this sense, Pound has "aestheticized" the raw data of history even in his attempt to reconstitute the aesthetic from the historical. His "profounder didacticism" never entirely differentiated itself from his "literary" concerns; his handling of numismatic discourse remained in emphasis a "nummulary moving toward prosody."

8
E Basta

        in
            discourse
                      what matters is
to get it across e poi basta
                (Canto 79/500)

To communicate and then stop, that is the
    law of discourse
               (Canto 80/508)

to take the sheep out to pasture
to bring your g.r. to the nutriment
    gentle reader   to the gist of the discourse
                (Canto 80/513–14)

Get the meaning across and then quit.
                (Canto 88/595)

                              e basta
                (Canto 99/715)

Until recently, critics were given to assuming that the silence of Pound's final years was a self-imposed penance. Pound himself claimed otherwise: "I did not enter into silence; silence captured me."[1] That this terrible silence should prove after all to be medical, as Carpenter, Torrey, and others have argued, makes problematic that comforting notion that Pound came to recognize his political and even poetic errors. Yet although one might speak of a predominantly—although perhaps not strictly—medical condition after the early sixties, the evidence of Pound's published work does not, on the other hand, support the equally comforting assumption of clinical madness after the forties. Pound's reiterated insistence that "what matters" in discourse is to "get the meaning across" submits an adamantine purpose, inexorable and by the end ineluctably tied to his very ability to write. Considered together, Pound's medical captivity and his sense of what was needful in order to "quit" invite new speculation about his poetic failures.

    1. See Henry Kamm, "Pound, in Silence, Returns to Paris," *New York Times*, 30 October 1965, 38.

His sense of closure depended at last, not on the organic unity of his poem, but on the organic integrity of "culture": the assumption that human relations constitute a totality, wherein all forms of activity are profoundly interrelated. For Pound, the perfectly realized poem would leave its trace on a more perfectly realized society. It was the ultimate development of Ruskinian creed: the text that set out merely to include history came in the author's mind to embody history. Poetic closure could come only with the revitalization of culture to which the poem was dedicated. All of this might be seen in the grim determination of *Thrones*. For as long as he could, Pound struggled under an impossibly demanding sense of mission. It could not be enough for him merely to present the truth, he had to see that he had gotten it across: he wanted to be able to verify the impact of his work on the sensibility of an entire culture. As the interview with Pasolini and Ronsisvalle indicates, although Pound admitted failure, he limited that failure to his actual work; he never renounced the ideal, totalizing vision. For us, however, it is crucial to make that extension. At the risk of reproducing the Ruskinian organicism of Pound's own discourse, we might say that the poet's strength shares one life with his weakness; the fullness of his vision nurtured the failure of his ventures.

In "An Introduction to the Economic Nature of the United States" (1944), Pound had explained that "for forty years I have schooled myself, not to write an economic history of the U.S., or of any other country, but to write an epic poem which begins 'In the Dark Forest' crosses the Purgatory of human error, and ends in the light, and '*fra i maestri di color che sanno*.' For this reason I have had to understand the NATURE of error" (*SP*, 167).[2] Understanding the "nature" of error did not, he continued, imply the necessity of knowing "each particular case of error." This book too has respected necessity—discussing only some of Pound's diverse generic combinations—but without Pound's compensatory vision of a single, ahistorical cause. Whereas Pound juxtaposed heterogeneous blocks of materials and expected formal fragmentation to be sublated by an essential, total, coherence, I have engaged in generic analysis in order to allow for the manifold relations within and among individual texts, and between texts and the discourses in which they participate—to show how features and parts of a text construct different models of wholeness, and how these wholes

---

2. For sustained insight into what the notion of "error" meant to Pound, see Christine Froula, *To Write Paradise: Style and Error in Pound's Cantos* (New Haven: Yale University Press, 1984), esp. 139–70.

become parts of sequences or larger wholes, including generic traditions. The explanations offered here thus part from Pound's own practice in order to understand culture not as a matter of received ideas but as a cluster of related and historically contingent discourses.

For Pound the discourse of culture implied arguments about the superiority of literature to history. Some more recent critical models have reversed that relation; in the last decades of the twentieth century literary history has frequently been construed as a narrow subset of "cultural studies." In insisting on the historicity of "culture," I propose that both models are limited. Treating discourse generically, I have submitted both "literature" and "culture" to the same historical scrutiny. Pound scholarship (including this book) is dotted with titles of the "Pound and . . ." variety. That this is so suggests the importance to critics of isolating some thematically coherent aspect from the heterogeneous welter Pound so deliberately developed. Generic analysis, by contrast—and unlike the analysis of genres—lends itself to the discussion of unstable relations, and can stage Pound's work in a context that includes the popular and the popularized as well as the polite, the political as well as the literary.

Whether in economics, history, primers, music, or poetry, the discourse of "culture" informed Pound's experiments in genre; at the same time each of these genres further mediated the manner in which "culture" shaped his conception of epic. But it is not only in the *Cantos* that one encounters the (modernist) mutual inclusiveness of "epic" and "culture." Indeed, it is striking how frequently important twentieth-century critics, particularly Marxist critics, have used epic as a template upon which to hammer arguments about culture. Consider Pound's difference from critical theorists like the Hungarian Georg Lukács (1885–1971), the Russian Mikhail Bakhtin (1895–1975), or such key members of the Frankfurt school as Walter Benjamin (1892–1940), Max Horkheimer (1895–1973), and Theodor W. Adorno (1903–69): all Pound's precise contemporaries.

In *Theory of the Novel* (1920), Lukács celebrated the historical privilege of epic verse to "sing of the blessedly existent totality of life."[3] Significantly, and like the Anglo-American Victorian translators and paraphrasers of Homer before him, Lukács also argued that "verse is not an ultimate constituent either of the epic or of tragedy" and submitted that "the novel is the epic of an age in which the extensive totality of life is no longer directly given" (56).

---

3. Georg Lukács, *The Theory of the Novel: A Historico-Philosophical Essay on the Forms of Great Epic Literature* (1920), trans. Anna Bostock (Cambridge: MIT Press, 1971), 58.

Of course, to regard the novel as the modern epic establishes a different relation to the past than does reconceiving Homeric epic in terms of the modern novel. But for us it is important to see, first, that Lukács's Marxism, like Ruskin's aestheticism or Pound's, quests after totality and, second—as Terence Des Pres has noted—that Lukács also consequently conceived of epic as addressing "a totality which might be entered at any point."[4]

Like Lukács, Horkheimer and Adorno regarded the novel as heir to epic and, in *Dialectic of Enlightenment* (1944), they posited epic as a necessary first stage in the disenchantment of the world. But for Horkheimer and Adorno, Homeric epic meant Homeric "narrative," the value of which had been its ability to effect "a universality of language."[5] Bakhtin too theorized the displacement of epic by novel without seeing that displacement as a historical misfortune.[6] For Bakhtin, one might say, Lukács's "blessedly existent totality" was only an ideological totalization. Bakhtin was suspicious of such universality, and he discerned the historical value of the novel to lie in what he saw as its unique capacity for "dialogism": its ability to contain conflicting class attempts to establish an "absolute" language. And so, albeit for different reasons, Lukács, Horkheimer and Adorno, and Bakhtin all theorized epic as a necessary step in the development of culture, but a step that having been taken could not be repeated.

Of the major critical theorists of Pound's generation, only Benjamin perceived the relation of epic to cultural totality in terms approximate to Pound's. In "What Is Epic Theatre?" (1939), Benjamin identified the aims of Bertolt Brecht's "epic theatre" as the filling in of "the abyss which separates the players from the audience." "The didactic play and the epic theatre are," he concluded, "attempts to sit down on a dais."[7] The principal feature in Brecht that Benjamin identified as "epic" was, in other words, the attempt to close the distance between the aesthetic and the didactic, between art and lived experience. Benjamin's sense of epic was thus distinctive, at least in the realm of critical theory, in that it did not identity epic in primarily narrative terms. For Pound and for the critical theorists alike, the lost possibility of

---

4. Terence Des Pres, *Writing into the World: Essays 1973–1987* (New York: Viking, 1991), 158.

5. Max Horkheimer and Theodor W. Adorno, *Dialectic of Enlightenment* (1944), trans. John Cumming (New York: Continuum, 1982), 43–44.

6. See Mikhail Bakhtin's essays "Epic and Novel" and "Discourse in the Novel," trans. Caryl Emerson and Michael Holquist, in *The Dialogic Imagination* (Austin: University of Texas Press, 1981).

7. Walter Benjamin, *Illuminations: Essays and Reflections* (1955), trans. Harry Zohn (New York: Schocken Books, 1969), 154.

"epic" marked the absence of any true totality in modern experience. But however much Bakhtin retained inclusiveness as a literary value, or however much Benjamin valued art capable of immediate participation in lived experience, for them these values were no longer to be found in epic.

Once again out of step with the "advanced" thinking of his time, Pound remained convinced that the ancient form of epic could be made new. And however much Lukács, or Bakhtin, or the theorists of the Frankfurt school are to be associated with the hermeneutics of suspicion, none showed so sustained a distrust of narrative as Pound. Undoubtedly, Pound's tenaciously held faith in "the folk," in "the mind of the people," survived because he never really understood the formation of mass culture—whether as theorized by Benjamin, or even by Wyndham Lewis. Nevertheless, despite the enormity of his political errors, Pound's work provides a distinct historiographical model. His choice of epic as form was neither idiosyncratic nor inevitable, but a response to historical pressures that were making themselves felt everywhere from popular trade publications to serious critical and philosophical debate.

Reconstructing the various historical contexts within which Pound's generic experiments developed, and the interaction between those contexts, is one important step toward recovering that singularity. The conclusions I have drawn are by no means exhaustive, and from the point of view of generic analysis represent only one kind of beginning for historical revisions. Pound's work will continue to be refigured in different ways as the features and provenance of literary criticism continue to change. All criticism reforms its object, recasting its subject and effecting generic transformations. Such transformations follow inescapably from the necessity of using words different from those in the texts being addressed, or of using the same words in different ways. Criticism has its own objects; it too includes changing generic traditions that themselves include a plenitude of subgenres. In discussing the impact of Eliot's critical ordering and Pound's work, and on subsequent criticism of Pound's work, my aim was historical and critical, and in no way designed to discredit or impugn a powerful and sensitive critic. Eliot's criticism was addressed to the coherence of a "tradition"; he was not concerned with history, either in Pound's sense, or the sense that I have been developing here. It follows then that Eliot was not concerned with Pound's generic heterogeneity, or with the relations of high modernism to the low and even vulgar discourses of popular culture against which it often identified itself. I have found these relations to be of compelling interest because I am concerned, as was Pound, with the increasing isolation and marginalization of the arts. Despite the fragmentation of such of his own earlier poems as "Gerontion" or "The Waste Land," Eliot could and did assume a public of readers. From our point of view, the catholicity of taste which Eliot encouraged can seem a very self-conscious attempt to secure something that could no longer be assumed; his was a most singular, if not quite personal, success. Pound's experience was utterly different, and his failure to hold a popular audience can be seen in light of Eliot's success as a failure to imagine and make one. For readers at the end of the twentieth century, Pound's often histrionic but nevertheless genuine straining after an audience becomes an instructive lesson about the limits of "culture" as an ideal.

By examining its impact on generic configurations, I have sought to establish "culture" as a discourse, a syntax for the ordering of history and society. In this recognition begins a response to Virginia Dominguez's asking "what is being accomplished socially, politically, discursively" when "culture" is invoked to describe, analyze, justify and theorize."[8] The discourse of culture shaped Pound's writing even in its most popularizing ventures, and even where he attacked its nominal values. "Culture" informs Pound's relation of elements within and among particular genres, as it continues syntactically to shape the evaluations of his critics.

---

8. Virginia R. Dominguez, "Invoking Culture: The Messy Side of 'Cultural Politics,'" *South Atlantic Quarterly* 91, no. 1 (winter 1992): 19–42.

Index

Abd-el-Melik, or Habdimelich, 222–24, 230, 234, 238
Abercrombie, Lascelles, 104
Action, 43 n. 12
Adams, Henry, 116, 118
Adams, John, 4, 30, 105–8, 110–12, 114, 116, 118, 138, 184
Adams, John Quincy, 187
Adams, Stephen J., 171 n. 28, 172 n. 29
Addison, Joseph, 234–35
Adorno, Theodor W., 243–45
aestheticism, and the aesthetic, 5, 10, 21, 29 n. 27, 42, 45, 47, 64, 119, 121, 123, 134, 143, 156, 159, 237–39, 244
Agassiz, Louis, 194 n. 8, 236–38
Aldington, Richard, 75
Alexander, Michael, 41, 80 n. 2
allusion, or allusiveness in poetry, 1, 158–59, 165, 171, 209
Anderson, David, 149–50
Anderson, Margaret, 81 n. 2
Angell, Norman, 133
Antheil, George, 167, 194
anti-Semitism, 6, 177, 213 n. 4
Apollinaire, Guillaume, 170 n. 26, 195, 234
Apter, Ronnie, 80 n. 2, 88
Aquinas, Thomas, 2 n. 1
Arac, Jonathan, 213 n. 4
Aripert (of Lombardy), 225
Aristotle, 2 n. 1, 81–83, 202, 217
Arnaut, Daniel, 15 n. 8, 170
Arnold, Matthew, 21, 38 n. 4, 41, 52, 55 n. 30, 63, 68, 70, 75–76, 88–91, 95–96, 146
Athenaeum, 43 n. 11, 156–57
Atkins, Frederick A., 48 n. 21
Atlantic Monthly, 58 n. 36
Auden, W. H., 5
audience: for Bertolt Brecht, 244; for T. S. Eliot, 24, 246; Arthur Griffith's perceptions of, 211; for Homeric poems, 83; for Charles Lamb and prose paraphrases, 88; questions of, 18, 96, 153, 157, 164, 171–72, 192–93, 211–12, 216, 220–21, 246; for W.H.D. Rouse, 94; for Ruskin, 49
Augustan literature, 85
Austen, Jane, 17
Avison, Charles, 154

Babbitt, Irving, 75
Bach, Johann Sebastian, 174
Bacigalupo, Massimo, 177
Baker, Augustus, 133
Bakhtin, Mikhail, 89 n. 14, 243–45
Balzac, Honoré de, 13, 116
Barnard, Mary, 166
Baumann, Walter, 80 n. 2, 177 n. 38
Becker, Karl Friedrich, 87
Belanger, Terry, 128 n. 16
Bell, C. M., 89 n. 15
Bell, Ian F. A., 118–19 n. 37, 194 n. 8, 213 n. 3
Belloc, Hilaire, 130
Benjamin, Walter, 243–45
Bennett, Arnold, 6, 74–76
Bennett, Tony, 3 n. 3, 7–8
Bentham, Jeremy, 41, 68
Benton, Thomas Hart, 10, 185–91 passim, 198–99, 203–5, 237–38; *Thirty Years' View,* 185–91 passim, 200–204, 237; *Autobiography,* 188
Bercovitch, Sacvan, 44 n. 14
Bergson, Henri, 54, 160, 162
Berkman, Alexander, 130
Bernstein, Michael André, 2–3, 80 n. 2, 97
Berryman, John, 80 n. 2, 152
Bird, William, 81 n. 2
Blackstone's Commentaries, 199
Blake, William, 70, 174 n. 32
Bloom, Allan, 38–39
Bloom, Harold, 33, 61, 198
Boccaccio, Giovanni, 123 n. 5
Bonaparte, Napoleon, 118
Bookman, 23 n. 20

Index

Booth, Marcella, 211 n. 1
Bosanquet, Bernard, 41, 45, 75
Bowker, Richard Rogers, 132
Brecht, Bertolt, 244
Breit, William, 213 n. 4
Breslin, James, 21 n. 17, 26 n. 24
Bridges, Robert, 68, 70
British-Italian Bulletin, 131 n. 20
Brooke-Rose, Christine, 169
Brooks, Edward, 89 n. 15
Browning, Robert, 38 n. 4, 100–101, 153–54, 170 n. 26; and Ruskin, 143
Bryan, William Jennings, 231
Bryant, William Cullen, 90
Bukharin, Nikolai, 130
Burckhardt, Jacob, 123
Butchart, Montgomery, 54, 60
Butcher, Samuel Henry, 89–91, 93
Butler, Samuel, 89–94
Butor, Michel, 149, 217
Buxtehude, Dietrich, 176–79
Byron, Lord (George Gordon), 61

Campion, Thomas, 156–57
Cange, Charles du, 228–29
Carlyle, Thomas, 18, 25, 41, 45–48, 50, 52, 55 n. 30, 59, 68, 74, 76, 85–86, 107, 115, 117, 123, 137–38; "Characteristics," 47–48; *Sartor Resartus,* 33 n. 31, 50, 52; "Signs of the Times," 46
Carnegie, Andrew, 129
Carne-Ross, D. S., 177
Carpenter, Edward, 57
Carpenter, Humphrey, 14 n. 8, 65–66, 99, 100 n. 27, 124 n. 11, 126 n. 13, 145 n. 31, 174 n. 32, 214, 216, 241
Cary, Henry, 88
Casillo, Robert, 6, 213 n. 4
Caufield, Francis, 93
Cavalcanti, Guido, 102
Chapman, George, 87, 95
Charles I (of England), 113, 221
Chaytor, Henry John, 122
Child, A. B., 128 n. 16
Childs, John, 104 n. 33
Chilesotti, Oscar, 170
Church, Alfred John, 89 n. 15
Church of England, Society for Promoting Christian Knowledge, 128
Clare, George, 131

Clarke, Michael, 89 n. 15
Clay, Henry, 187, 190–91, 198–201, 203–5, 209
Clubbe, John, 85 n. 8
Coburn, Alvin Langdon, 174 n. 32
Coffin, George, 129
Cohen, Ralph, ix, 3–4, 11 n. 1, 26 n. 24
Coke, Edward, 113, 218
Cole, G.D.H., 131
Coleridge, Samuel Taylor, 24, 37–38, 41, 52, 63, 74, 98, 137; "Kubla Khan," 38, 74; *On the Constitution of Church and State,* 37, 52; *Table-Talk,* 137
Collins, W. Lucas, 90
Columbus, Christopher, 55, 60
Commonweal, 57 n. 33
Comstock, Anthony, 32
Confucius, 65, 74, 135, 142, 185, 194, 202, 224, 226, 228, 230
Connolly, Cyril, 16
Conrad, Joseph, 73
Constantine (of Rome), 30
Cook, Agnes Spofford, 89 n. 15
Cook, Albert, 93
Cookson, William, 25 n. 22, 54 n. 29, 80 n. 2, 217 n. 14
Coolidge, Calvin, 117
Cory, Daniel, 149
Cotterill, Henry Bernard, 93
Courtés, Joseph, 8 n. 15
Cowper, William, 90
Crashaw, Richard, 157
Creeley, Robert, 214, 229
Crevel, René, 28 n. 25
Criterion, 27, 28 n. 25, 126 n. 14, 132, 161 n. 17
criticism, literary, 11–34 passim, 70–71, 81, 124–25, 168, 176, 217–20, 243–46
cubism, 165
Culler, A. Dwight, 196 n. 10
culture, discourse of, 5, 7–8, 19, 23, 30, 38–39, 43–46, 51–52, 60, 64, 68, 74, 79, 116, 136–42, 144, 170, 183, 243, 246
Cuningpert (of Lombardy), 225

dada, 171
Daily Mail, 75
Dane, Alan, 132
Dante (Alighieri), v, 22, 47, 79, 81 n. 2, 84, 115–16, 175–76, 242
Darwin, Charles, 90

Dasenbrock, Reed Way, 165 n. 20
Davenport, Guy, 41
Davie, Donald, 12–13, 15 n. 8, 17, 31, 33, 41–42, 44, 54 n. 29, 214 n. 9, 216
Davis, Earl, 213 n. 4
Dawson, Christopher, 19
Debussy, Claude, 164
Dekker, George, 80 n. 2, 121–22, 124
DeLaura, David, 38 n. 4
Delcroix, Carlo D., 202
Del Mar, Alexander, 10, 213–19, 223–24, 226, 231–39; *History of Monetary Systems,* 213–15, 223–24, 234, 237–38; *History of the Precious Metals,* 235–36
Demant, Vigo Auguste, 133
Derrida, Jacques, 3–4, 6, 39
Des Pres, Terence, 244
Diaconus, Paulus, 225 n. 24, 230
Dial, 34 n. 33, 36 n. 1, 80 n. 1, 64 n. 43, 80
didacticism, 47, 50, 63, 85, 98, 102, 121, 126, 139–40, 219, 221–24, 244; antididactic criteria, 218
Dionysius, 152
Divus, Andreas, 98–99
Dolmetsch, Arnold, 174
Dominguez, Virginia, 246
Donne, John, 157–58
Doob, Leonard, 29 n. 26
Doolittle, Hilda (H. D.), 78
Doughty, Charles Montagu, 136
Douglas, Clifford Hugh, 44, 55, 58–59, 62, 71, 129, 131, 133 n. 21, 135, 212, 219
Dudek, Louis, 169, 173
Dylan, Bob, 138

Eagleton, Terry, 4 n. 6, 7–8, 38 n. 4, 143
Eastham, Scott, 216, 221
Eastman, Barbara, 184
Eco, Umberto, 168
economics, 29–30, 40, 55–56, 60–64, 127–34 passim, 187, 211–15, 219–23
Edward III (of England), 223
Egoist, 69 n. 49, 69 n. 50, 95 n. 19
Eliot, T. S., 9, 11–34 passim, 35–36, 40, 42, 46, 52, 72, 75, 78, 85, 98, 116, 132–33, 135, 152, 197, 245–46; *After Strange Gods,* 19; "Charles Whibley: A Memoir," 75 n. 52; *Criterion* "Commentary" for January 1932, 132; *Criterion* "Commentary" for January 1935, 19; *Criterion* "Commentary" for July 1937, 16; *Criterion* "Commentary" for 27 April 1939, 23; "Experiment in Criticism," 22–23; "Ezra Pound," 12; *For Lancelot Andrewes,* 157–58; *Four Quartets,* 158; "The Frontiers of Criticism," 18, 20–25; "The Function of Criticism," 20–21; "Gerontion," 11, 246; "Goethe as the Sage," 22; *The Idea of a Christian Society,* 19; ideas about music and poetry, 156–60, 166–67; introduction to *Ezra Pound: Selected Poems,* 13; introduction to G. Wilson Knight's *The Wheel of Fire,* 13; "John Donne," 11; "John Dryden," 79; "Kipling Redivivus," 156–57; *Literary Essays of Ezra Pound,* 9, 11–34 passim, 85; "The Music of Poetry," 158; "Notes Towards a Definition of Culture," 19; *Notes Towards the Definition of Culture,* 19–20; *On Poetry and Poets,* 21–22, 24, 158; "Poetry and Propaganda," 22; "The Problem of Education," 19; "Reflections on the Unity of European Culture," 23; "The Responsibility of the Man of Letters in the Cultural Restoration of Europe," 23; review of Edward Garnett's *Turgenev,* 13; *Selected Essays,* 73 n. 53; "Thinking in Verse," 157–58; "The Three Voices of Poetry," 22; "To Criticize the Critic," 20; "Ulysses, Order and Myth," 34 n. 33; *The Waste Land,* 11–12, 34, 126, 246
Ellman, Richard, 11 n. 1
Elzinga, Kenneth, ix, 213 n. 4
Emery, Clarke, 165–66
Empedocles, 85
encyclopédists, the French, 154
Enemy, 159
Enlightenment, 37–39, 43, 89, 107, 141, 180, 186
Eparchikon Biblion, 218, 225–26, 229
epic, form and nature of, 80–86, 95–96, 135, 139, 146–47, 177, 243–45
Epicurus, 139
Exile, 193 n. 7

Fabian Arts Group, 55
Fabian Society, and Fabian socialism, 32, 55–57, 59, 64, 68, 130
Farnell, Ida, 123
fascism, 6, 31, 44
Fenollosa, Ernest Francisco, 185, 236
Fielding, Henry, 85

Finlay, John L., 48 n. 21, 59–62
Fitzgerald, Edward, 47
Fitzgerald, Robert, 93, 125–26
Flaubert, Gustave, 32, 98, 113, 116, 119, 145, 156
Fletcher, Alfred Ewen, 48 n. 21
Flint, F. S., 131, 153
Flory, Wendy Stallard, 65, 113 n. 35, 168
Foerster, Donald, 82 n. 4
folklore, ideas of the folk, 135–36, 140–44, 180, 245
Ford, Ford Madox, 45, 73, 122
formalism, 6, 24, 80, 161, 168–71
Foucault, Michel, ix, 39, 44
Fowler, Alastair, 84 n. 6, 85
France, Anatole, 206–7
Frankfurt School, 243–45
Frazer, James, 136
Freadman, Ann, 3 n. 3
Frobenius, Leo, 118, 136, 140–44, 170, 214, 228, 230, 236–38
Froula, Christine, 81 n. 2, 199, 242 n. 2
Fuller, Buckminster, 2 n. 1
Furia, Philip, 5, 96, 109, 172, 238
futurism, 174 n. 32

Gadamer, Hans Georg, 66
Gallup, Donald, 58 n. 35, 75 n. 53
Gardner, Helen, 11 n. 1
Garnett, Edward, 13
Gay, Penelope, 153–54
genre: experiments in and transformations of, 2, 13–14, 18, 26, 56–57, 64, 107–8, 116, 125, 127, 138, 162, 180–81, 186, 198–210 passim, 215, 233–34, 242; theory of, 2–4, 7–10, 16, 32, 82, 242–43
Georgian Anthology, 104, 164
Germ, 154
Gesell, Silvio, 29, 115, 129, 212, 219
Gibbon, Edward, 135
Gilds Restoration League, 54–55
Giles, John Allen, 90
Godden, Richard, 212 n. 3
Godwin, William, 43–44
Goethe, Johann Wolfgang von, 22
Gombrich, E. H., 38 n. 4
Gosse, Edmund, 6, 32
Gosson, Stephen, 68
Gould, Joe, 104
Gourmont, Remy de, 44, 49, 236

Graham, Cunninghame, 57
Grant, Ulysses S., 117
Graves, Robert, 29
Greimas, A. J., 8 n. 15
Griffith, Arthur, 211–12
Griffs, William Elliot, 207
guild socialism, 29 n. 27, 55–56, 59, 65–66, 226
Gurdjieff, G. I., 55, 58

Hale, William Gardner, 6, 86–87
Half Hour Series, 130 n. 18
Hanson, Charles Henry, 89 n. 15
Hardie, Keir, 57
Harding, Warren G., 117
Hardy, Thomas, 164
Harper, Michael, 202 n. 14, 238
H. D. *See* Doolittle, Hilda
Hecht, Ben, 113
Hegel, Georg Wilhelm Friedrich, 154
Heidegger, Martin, 39, 40 n. 7
Henley, W. E., 76
Henry, Patrick, 105
Henry III (of England), 229
Herodotus, 137, 141
Hesse, Eva, 177 n. 37
Hewison, Robert, 49 n. 23
Heymann, C. David, 14, 216
history, the writing of, 51, 97, 192–98 passim, 215–16
Hobhouse, John, 116
Hobson, John Atkinson, 45–46, 60, 129, 133–34, 141
Hocking, Joseph, 32
Hollander, John, 153, 159
Holquist, Michael, 89 n. 14
Holter, Elisabeth Sage, 131–32, 134–35
Home Universal Library, 129
Homer, 5, 47, 79–80, 82–99 passim, 174–75, 243–44
Hoover, Herbert, 117
Horkheimer, Max, 243–44
Horton, T. David, 237
Hudson Review, 217
Hueffer, Ford Madox. *See* Ford, Ford Madox
Hueffer, Francis, 122–24
Hulme, T. E., 54, 57
Humbolt, Alexander von, 237
Hunt, William Homan, 45

Huxley, Thomas Henry, 126
Hynes, Samuel, 56–57

ideogrammic method, 10, 132, 143, 166, 168–69, 227–28
ideology, 6–8, 144, 180, 192, 244
Image, Selwyn, 42
imagism and the doctrine of "the image," 54, 67, 110, 164
inclusiveness, 14, 36, 100, 104, 110, 242–43

Jackson, Holbrook, 55
James, Henry, 1, 13, 113, 116–17, 205–6
Janequin, Clement, 170, 172–74, 176–78
Jefferson, Thomas, 30, 105, 110–12, 118, 134, 138
jeremiad, 44, 49, 71
Jevons, William Stanley, 129
Johnson, Lionel, 153
Johnson, Samuel, 24, 146
journalism, 1, 42, 71–75, 126; Benton's comments on, 189
Joyce, James, 13, 32–33, 78, 98, 113, 116, 170 n. 26
Justinian (of the Byzantine Empire), 30, 223
Justinian II (of the Byzantine Empire), 223

Kamm, Henry, 241 n. 1
Kant, Immanuel, 23
Kasper, John, 237
Kearns, George, 217–18
Keats, John, 85, 157, 180
Kemmerer, E. W., 129
Kennedy, J. M., 6
Kenner, Hugh, 2, 11 n. 1, 92, 122, 143, 169–71
Kermode, Frank, 34 n. 33
Khayyám, Omar, 47
Kipling, Rudyard, 130, 156–57
Kitson, Arthur K., 231
Klages, Ludwig, 176–78
Klinck, Dennis, 213 n. 4
Knight, G. Wilson, 13
Korn, Marianne, 65, 81, 98, 124
Kristeva, Julia, 44
Kroeber, A. L., 183, 192
kultur, 73, 115, 118, 145
Kyd, Thomas, 42 n. 10

LaCapra, Dominick, 5
Lacharmés, Pére, 142

Laclau, Ernesto, 7
Lamb, Charles, 87–88
Landor, Walter S., 61
Lang, Andrew, 89–91, 93, 95
Langbaum, Robert, 38 n. 4, 46, 103
Lattimore, Richmond, 93
Lawrence, T. E., 93
Leaf, Walter, 95
Leavis, F. R., 42
Lebenthal, Louis, 131
Leopardi, Giacomo, 67
Leo the Wise, 225–26, 233
Levenson, Michael, 47
Levin, Harry, 33, 38 n. 4
Lewalski, Barbara, 84
Lewis, Wyndham, 29, 113, 116, 124 n. 7, 174 n. 32, 179, 245; ideas of music, 159–62, 167–68; *Tyro,* 198
Lindberg, Kathryne V., 5–6, 39–40
literature: Benton on question of the social power of the written word, 188–91; the idea of, 4–5, 8–9, 19, 30, 35–37, 39, 66, 79, 85–86, 114–17, 144, 243; on its power to effect social change, 5, 12–13, 110–16, 192–93, 136–39, 217
Little Review, 126 n. 14
Litz, A. Walton, 11 n. 1, 58 n. 35
Livi, Grazia, 149
Locke, John, 189
Longenbach, James, 47, 80 n. 2, 126
Louis XIV (of France), 77
Lowell, Robert, 152
Lucretius, 85
Lukcás, Georg, 243–45
Luke, Gospel of, 55, 59
Lyotard, François, 136 n. 24

Macaulay, Thomas Babington, 188
Machiavelli, Niccolò, 74
Mackail, John William, 93, 96, 124
MacLeod, Fiona, 164
Mairet, Philip, 55, 131
Makin, Peter, 122, 216
Mallarmé, Stéphane, 75, 153
Marcet, Jane Haldimand, 128
marginalism, economic theory of, 129
Marinetti, Filippo Tommaso, 174–75
Marshall, Alfred, 128
Martin, L. C., 157
Martin, Wallace, 54, 55 n. 30, 57, 63, 212

Martineau, Harriet, 126, 128
Marvin, Francis Sydney, 89 n. 15
Marx, Karl, and marxism, 8, 44, 57, 108–9, 130, 220, 230, 243–44
mass culture, 160–61, 245
McAdam, Graham, 129
McCarthy, Dermot Robert, 58 n. 35, 67 n. 47
McCullough, John Ramsey, 128
McFarland, Thomas, 98 n. 25, 204 n. 16
McGann, Jerome, ix, 50
McKinley, William, 117
McLuhan, Marshall, 11 n. 1
Megill, Alan, 39–40, 48, 63
Menger, Carl, 129
menippean satire, 3
microphotography, 170–72
Migne, Jacques Paul, 218, 225
Milano, Francesco da, 170, 173–74, 177
Mill, James, 41
Mill, John Stuart, 32, 46, 126
Milton, John, 17, 84–85, 99, 174 n. 32
Minturno, Antonio Sebastiano, 85
Mistral, Frédéric, 122
modernism, and modernist writing, 8–10, 12, 18, 32, 34, 47 n. 19, 66, 68, 72, 78, 121, 162, 174 n. 32, 243–46
Mommsen, Theodor M., 238
Mongan, Roscoe, 89 n. 15
Monroe, Harriet, 70, 221 n. 19
Monroe Doctrine, 190
Montfort, Simon de, 76
Morris, William, 29 n. 27, 35, 41, 43, 45, 53, 55, 57, 59, 63, 70, 89 n. 15, 90, 123
Morson, Gary Saul, 3 n. 3
Mouffe, Chantal, 7
Moyer, Harvey, 130
Münch, Gerhart, 168, 170–80
Munson, Gorham, 58, 103, 132
Murray, David, 213 n. 4
music, ideas of, 153–65
Mussolini, Benito, 118, 152, 185

Nänny, Max, 2–3
narrative order, 80–99 passim, 114, 119, 122 n. 3, 175–76, 183, 189, 192, 196–98, 202, 207, 215, 237–38, 244–45
Nassar, Eugene Paul, 168
Nation, 101, 137 n. 26
National Observer, 76

New Age, 1, 6, 28, 29 n. 27, 42, 48, 55–59, 62, 65–67, 125, 131, 175 n. 34
Newcomb, Simon, 129
New Criticism, 17, 24, 26, 33, 196, 217–18. *See also* formalism
New Democracy, 101, 103–4, 110
New English Weekly, 55, 60, 131 n. 20
New Freewoman, 68
new historical method, 1, 109–10, 192–98, 216, 237
Newman, Francis W., 88–90
Newsome, Albert, 131
New Yorker, 17
Nicholls, Peter, 185 n. 4, 192, 212, 213 n. 4, 216, 218 n. 16, 219–22, 230, 236
Nicole, Jules, 226, 230
Nietzsche, Friedrich, 6, 39–40, 63, 73
Norman, Charles, 18
North American Review, 114
Northcliffe, Alfred C.W. Harmsworth, 75
numismatics, 210, 213, 215–22, 225, 227–29, 238–39

Oakes, Loisann, 169 n. 24
Odysseus, 80–81, 91, 196
Olson, Charles, 206 n. 19
Orage, A. R., 1, 6, 19, 29 n. 27, 42, 44–46, 48, 53–67 passim, 71–72, 131, 212, 225–26; *An Alphabet of Economics*, 55–56, 60–62, 129; "Current Cant," 1; *Economic Democracy* (with C. H. Douglas), 62; "An Editor's Progress," 54, 57–58; "New Standards in Art and Literature," 58; *Orage as Critic*, 54, 63 nn. 40, 41; "Perfecting English Prose," 63 n. 41; *Political and Economic Writings*, 54; *Selected Essays and Critical Writings*, 54; "Press Cuttings," 1; "Profiteering in Literature," 35; "Readers and Writers," 54, 63 n. 40
oral history and narrative, 42 n. 10, 83–84, 137, 142–43, 162, 202, 238
organicism, 6, 23, 27, 30, 33, 41, 45, 46 n. 18, 50, 56, 72, 98, 115, 119, 141, 162 n. 19, 186, 238, 242
orient, the, and orientalism, 184–85, 196–97, 217; Pound's parody of "oriental" mystique, 145–46

Pagany, 99–101, 110–11, 115–16, 138
paideuma, or "the new learning," 118, 141, 145, 217, 220

Palmer, George Herbert, 89
Panama Mission, 190
Parker, Andrew, 213 n. 4
Partisan Review, 80 n. 1
Pasolini, Pier Paolo, 149–52, 159–61, 171–72, 206 n. 19, 242
Pater, Walter, 21, 123–24, 146, 153–55, 158, 164–65, 167–68
Patey, Douglas Lane, 38 n. 4, 84 n. 6, 143
Patrizi, Francesco, 85
Pauthier, M. Guillaume, 74
Pearlman, Daniel D., 169–70
Penty, Arthur J., 55
Perloff, Marjorie, 107
Perry, Oliver Hazard, 206–7
Petrarch, Francesco, 123 n. 5
Philpotts, Eden, 58 n. 35
Pickthall, Marmaduke, 72
Plato, 54, 57, 61, 119 n. 37
Poetry, 67 n. 48, 70
Pope, Alexander, 90
popularized knowledge, and popularizing genres, 6, 8, 10, 30, 60, 121–34 passim, 143, 171–72, 184, 212, 217–18
postmodernism, 33
poststructuralism, 6
Pound, Ezra: and the Bollingen Prize for 1948, 25, 33 n. 32, 151; combinatory procedures of, 9, 92, 95, 127, 140, 149–52, 165, 172, 184, 195–96, 233; and critical theory, 243–45; and T. S. Eliot, 11–12, 23–27, 30–34, 99, 197, 245; and elitism, 1–2, 47, 126, 145–46, 230; generic experiments of, 2, 40–41, 72, 143, 146–47, 162, 199, 209–10, 233, 243; his idea of "a profounder didacticism," 48, 63–64, 66, 102, 125, 127, 135, 144, 239; his interest in placing poetry in the agora, 5, 36, 66, 96, 193; historicism of, 29; inclusive poetics of, 9, 36–37, 100, 104, 110, 165–66, 186, 192–98, 209, 214, 230–31, 242; and Wyndham Lewis, 159–62; Orage's mediation of Ruskin for, 54–64, 72 n. 51, 129; popularizing activities of, 10, 36, 47, 63, 123 n. 5, 124–25, 171–72, 184, 212, 230; prejudice against philosophy, 139; radio broadcasts, 28, 45; silence of final years, 216–17, 241; and the vision of totality, 7, 32–33, 40, 44–45, 50–52, 67, 70–71, 97–98, 105, 117–20, 135–38, 145, 181, 186, 192–93, 197, 203, 206, 208–9, 214, 224, 242

POETRY: *Active Anthology,* 54, 127; "Homage to Sextus Propertius," 72, 86, 88; *Hugh Selwyn Mauberley (Life and Contacts),* 29, 40, 42, 44, 72, 86, 101–2; *Lustra,* 101; "Mesmerism," 162; "Moeurs Contemporaines," 72; "Near Perigord," 72; *Ripostes,* 101; *Translations,* 54 n. 29

CANTOS: Benton cantos, 42, 184, 198–210, 238; *Cantos* in general, 2–5, 9–10, 14, 36, 43–44, 64, 77, 79–82, 87, 95–98, 106–7, 120, 125–26, 137–39, 146–49, 161–64, 179–81, 184, 192, 195–96, 212–14, 221–22, 231, 239; *Cantos LII–LXXI,* 71, 102, 119, 127, 146, 184, 216; Del Mar cantos, 215–39 passim; *A Draft of Cantos 17–27,* 48, 71, 99, 184; *A Draft of XVI Cantos,* 58, 184; *A Draft of XXX Cantos,* 71, 100–101, 127, 137 n. 26, 186; *Eleven New Cantos XXXI–XLI,* 9, 71, 83, 99–103, 109, 112–13, 115–20, 142, 162, 165; *The Fifth Decad of Cantos,* 71, 109, 180, 184; Italian cantos (72 and 73), 147, 151; Malatesta cantos, 58, 99, 100 n. 27, 139, 177; *Pagany* cantos, 99–113 passim, 138; *Pisan Cantos,* 10, 33 n. 32, 151, 168–69, 180–81, 198, 215, 219; *Section: Rock-Drill de los Cantares LXXXV–XCV,* 10, 42, 48, 100, 185, 204 n. 15, 216, 221, 234, 238; *Selected Cantos,* 195; *Thrones,* 7, 100, 207, 215–19, 221–22, 228–29, 231, 234, 236–38, 242; "Ur" or canceled cantos, 72, 77; I, 80, 98–99, 109, 186; IX, 100; XIX, 211 n. 1; XXIV, 99; XXV, 100, 184; XXVIII, 219; XXX, 101; XXXI, 104–5; XXXII, 105; XXXIII, 9, 104–14, 116; XXXIV, 101 n. 28; XXXVI, 102; XXXVIII, 166, 219; XXXIX, 102; XLIV, 102; XLV, 35, 102, 219; LI, 219; LXI, 183; LXXII, 152, 174 n. 32; LXXIV, 34, 152, 175; LXXV, 10, 149–82 passim; LXXVI, 151, 180; LXXVIII, 211 n. 1; LXXIX, 169 n. 24, 171, 176, 241; LXXX, 151, 194, 241; LXXXI, 151, 162, 176; LXXXII, 169, 171, 176; LXXXIII, 171 n. 27; LXXXV, 185; LXXXVI, 185; LXXXVII, 185; LXXXVIII, 10, 185–87, 193, 198–210 passim, 230, 237, 241; LXXXIX, 42, 185, 196, 237; XCI, 162; XCVI, 204 n. 15, 222, 225, 229–30; XCVII, 211 n. 1, 213, 215–17, 222–39 passim; XCIX, 241; CII, 29, 211 n. 1; CIII, 207; CVII, 113, 213; CXVI, 110, 199 n. 11, 238; CXVII, 114, 213, 238–39

PROSE: *ABC of Economics,* 9, 71, 127, 211 n. 1; *ABC of Reading,* 32, 71, 81 n. 3, 113, 127, 139, 173, 192, 194; "Affirmations," 48, 175, 180; "America: Chances and Remedies," 72 n. 51; "Another Chance," 171; "The Approach to Paris," 72 n. 51; "Arthur Symons," 136; "The Central Problem," 211; "Child's Guide to Economics," 127; "The City," 43; "Dam Nigger and the Banana Tree," 132; "Date Line," 15 n. 8, 31; "Dr. Williams' Position," 80 n. 1, 83; "The Drama as a Means of Education," 42–43; "Early Translators of Homer," 69, 95–96; "L'economia Ortologica," 127; "E. E. Cummings Examined," 205–6; "Ezra's Easy Economics," 127; *Ezra Pound and Music,* 54 n. 29, 162–68; *Ezra Pound and the Visual Arts,* 54 n. 29; *Ezra Pound Speaking: Radio Speeches of World War II,* 29 n. 26, 205–6; "Fungus, Twilight, or Dry Rot," 116; "George Antheil (Retrospect)," 161, 167; *Guide to Kulchur,* 1–2, 9, 15, 28, 29 n. 27, 32, 50, 65, 71–72, 74, 77, 96 n. 20, 97–98, 107, 109, 120, 125–27, 136–39, 141, 145–46, 164, 170, 175, 178, 180, 184–85, 192–95, 197, 204, 209 n. 20, 217; "Hands Off Alberta," 110; "Henry James," 126; "How to Read," 31, 127; *If This Be Treason . . . ,* 14; "I Gather the Limbs of Osiris," 66–67, 72 n. 51; *Impact: Essays on Ignorance and the Decline of American Civilization,* 54 n. 29, 217, 224 n. 23; "Inconsiderable Imbecilities," 1; "Indiscretions: or, Une Revue de Deux Mondes," 72 n. 51; "The Individual in His Milieu: A Study of Relations and Gesell," v, 115, 224; *Instigations,* 15, 95 n. 19; "An Introduction to the Economic Nature of the United States," 242; *Introductory Textbook,* 127; "The Jefferson-Adams Letters as a Shrine and a Monument," 114–17, 140, 142, 144–45; *Jefferson and/or Mussolini: Volitionist Economics,* 127, 161, 211 n. 1; "Ligurian View of a Venetian Festival," 173; *Literary Essays of Ezra Pound,* 9, 11–36 passim, 52; "Loeb Report (A Refresher)," 131 n. 20; *Make It New,* 14, 15, 31; "Man vs. Merchandise: Fascism in Action," 131 n. 20; *A Memoir of Gaudier-Brzeska,* 47 n. 20, 48 n. 21, 175 n. 34; "Mr. Pound on Prizes," 113; "Moneta Fascista," 127; "More on Economics," 121; "Murder by Capital," 126 n. 14; "On Technique," 29; "Paris Letter" of January 1922, 36, 63–64, 98; "Paris Letter" of April 1922, 104; "Pastiche: the Regional," 72–78, 141; "Patria Mia," 72 n. 51; *Pavannes and Divagations,* 16 n. 9; *Pavannes and Divisions,* 15, 16 n. 9; "A Place for English Writers: Definition of a Usurer," 43; *Polite Essays,* 14–15; *Profile,* 127, 134–35; "Prolegomena," 51, 193, 200 n. 13; "Provincialism the Enemy," 72 n. 51, 113, 121, 125; "Raphaelite Latin," 124; "Ren Crevel," 27–31, 85; "Revelations," 1; "The Revolt of Intelligence," 64, 72 n. 51; "Revolutionary Maxims," 1; *Selected Prose,* 25 n. 22, 54 n. 29; "The Serious Artist," 31, 68–69, 73, 157 n. 10; *Social Credit: An Impact,* 127, 134–35, 139; *The Spirit of Romance,* 3, 15, 32, 46–47, 121–24; "Status Rerum," 159; "A Stray Document," 15 n. 8; "Studies in Contemporary Mentality," 72; "Through Alien Eyes," 67 n. 47; "Vorticism," 47; *What is Money For,* 127; "The Wisdom of Poetry," 119 n. 37; "Writers! (as Joe Gould says) 'Ignite!'" 104

ANTHOLOGIES, EDITIONS AND TRANSLATIONS: *Passages from the Letters of John Butler Yeats,* 195; *Profile,* 127, 134–35, 195; *Ta Hio,* 127

REVIEWS: "Jules Romains's *Odes et Prières,*" 67–69, 96; "Robert Bridge's New Book," 68, 70, 76; "Swinburne's Letters," 42 n. 10; William Carlos Williams's *Voyage to Pagany,* 80

LETTERS: to Margaret Anderson, 81 n. 2; to Mary Barnard, 166; to William Bird, 81 n. 2; to John Lackay Brown, 126 n. 15; to Huntington Cairns, 26; to Robert Creeley, 214, 229; to Louis Dudek, 169–70, 173; to T. S. Eliot, 171 n. 28; to Harriet Monroe, 221 n. 19; to Frank Morley, 126; to Homer Pound, 99; to W.H.D. Rouse, 94–95; to Felix Schelling, 47, 64; to W. C. Wilson, 162, 164

INTERVIEWS: with Thomas Cole, 171 n. 27; with David Cory, 149; with Donald Hall, 221; with Grazia Livi, 149; with Wallace Martin, 212; with Michael Reck, 179; with Vanni Ronsisvalle and Pier Paolo Pasolini, 149–52, 161, 242

Pre-Raphaelite, 122–23
Price, John Valdimir, 128 n. 16
Proust, Marcel, 28–29
Putnam's Popular Manuals, 130 n. 18
Pythagoras, 139

Rabaté, Jean-Michel, 2 n. 1, 40 n. 7, 213 n. 4
Rainey, Lawrence S., 100 n. 27
Raleigh, Sir Walter, 42 n. 10
Randolph, John, 187, 190–91, 198–200, 203–5, 209
Ransom, John Crowe, 17
Read, Forrest, 80 n. 2, 169 n. 26, 171 n. 28
Read, Herbert, 53–54
Reck, Michael, 179
Redman, Tim, 133 n. 21, 174 n. 32
Ricardo, David, 127–28
Rice, Philip Blair, 101
Richelieu, Cardinal Armand Jean du Plessis, 77
Rivers, Isabel, 128 n. 16
Rogers, Pat, 128 n. 16
Rogers, Thorold, 238
Romains, Jules, 67–69, 96
romanticism, or romantic assumptions about literature and poetry, 5, 24, 34, 36, 39, 50, 63–64, 97, 105, 140
Ronsisvalle, Vanni, 149–50, 242
Roosevelt, Franklin Delano, 112
Rossetti, Dante Gabriel, 123, 154
Rossetti, William Michael, 154–55
Rouse, W.H.D., 89, 93–96
Rousseau, Jean–Jacques, 37
Rudge, Olga, 14, 150, 171–72
Ruskin, John, 6, 25, 29–30, 32, 38 n. 4, 41–46, 48–61 passim, 63, 68–72, 74, 76, 104, 115, 123, 126, 128, 133–34, 138, 141, 160, 181; and Browning, 143, 186, 214, 224, 235–36, 242, 244; *Ethics of the Dust,* 49; *Fors Clavigera,* 36, 48–51, 74, 107, 134, 141, 204; *A Joy Forever,* 128; *Modern Painters,* 31, 119 n. 37; *Munera Pulveris,* 49, 128; *The Seven Lamps of Architecture,* 52; *The Two Paths,* 35; *Unto This Last,* 31, 128
Rutherford, John, 122 n. 3

Sachs, Hans, 176–78
Said, Edward, 184 n. 1
Saint Ambrose, 202
St. Elizabeths Hospital, 14, 112, 113 n. 35, 179, 206 n. 19, 211 n. 1, 215–16, 221
Salel, Hugues, 95
Salmasius, Claudius, 109
Salomon, Louis B., 41 n. 9, 44 n. 16
Sandburg, Carl, 113
Scaliger, Julius-Caesar, 84–85
Schafer, R. Murray, 162–64, 173

Schelling, Felix, 47, 64
Schlegel, August Wilhelm von, 154
Schomberg, George Augustus, 89 n. 15
Schopenhauer, Arthur, 154
Schwartz, Delmore, 26
Schwartz, Sanford, 9 n. 16, 119 n. 38
Scots Observer, 76
Scott, Sir Walter, 13, 85
Seaman, David, 234 n. 29
Seneca the Younger, 4
Sextus Propertius, v, 115
Shakespeare, William, 22, 32, 90 n. 16, 113, 221
Sharp, William. *See* MacLeod, Fiona
Shaw, George Bernard, 17, 53, 57–58, 61, 74–76, 104, 126, 130
Shell, Marc, 219–20
Shelley, Percy Bysshe, 43–44, 61, 67, 97, 156–57
Sherry, Vincent, 162, 228
Shu Ching, 185, 196
Sicari, Stephen, 81 n. 2
Sidney, Sir Philip, 31, 68, 84
Sieburth, Richard, 49 n. 24, 165, 213
Sieg, Harvey, 131
Sinn Fein, 211
Siskin, Clifford, 3, 4 n. 4, 26 n. 24, 50, 143
Smith, Elbert, 187 n. 5
Smith, Justin, 122 n. 3
Snodgrass, W. D., 152
social credit economics, 29 n. 27, 55, 59, 71, 103, 131–35, 138, 212
socialism, 42, 46, 55–58, 64–65
Southey, Robert, 85
Spectator, 17, 75
Spengler, Oswald, 46 n. 18
Spenser, Edmund, 84
spirit of the age, or *zeitgeist,* idea of, 39, 46–47, 48 n. 21
Square Dollar Series, 237, 238 n. 31
Stein, Gertrude, 18, 135
Stock, Noel, 54 n. 29, 149 n. 1, 219
subject rhymes, Pound's notion of, 97
Sullivan, J. P., 88, 177 n. 35
Surette, Leon, 81 n. 2, 165, 222
Sutton, Walter, 12 n. 3
Swedenberg, H. T., 82 n. 4
Swinburne, A. C., 32, 61, 156–57
symbolism, 47–48, 75–76, 153, 159
Symonds, John Addington, 123–24

Symons, Arthur William, 136, 153, 155, 158–59
Symposium, 104
symptomatic, the perception of, 28–29, 48–51, 55, 68, 72, 74, 77, 86, 199, 215, 231
syndicalism, 57

Tasso, 42 n. 10
Tate, Allen, 2 n. 1, 137 n. 26
Tennyson, Alfred Lord, 101, 159
Terrell, Carroll F., and the *Companion to the Cantos of Ezra Pound,* 114, 116, 209, 225 n. 24, 233
Thatcher, David, 6 n. 10, 63
Theosophical Society, 54
Tocqueville, Alexis Charles de, 208
Tomlinson, Charles, 17, 31, 43
Torrey, E. Fuller, 113 n. 35, 241
Townsman, 172 n. 29
translation, 47, 86–99 passim, 225–26
Trollope, Anthony, 116, 199
Tucker, George, 199 n. 11
Tyro, 98

Upton, George P., 87 n. 10
Upward, Allen, 44, 48, 220
usura and usury, 30, 43, 185
utilitarianism, or the principle of utility, 38, 41, 50, 52, 59, 63–64, 68, 70, 104, 126, 133–34, 137, 139, 144

Valéry, Paul, 159
Vega, Lope de, v, 115
Vergil, 79, 84
Verhaeren, Emile, 67
Verlaine, Paul, 76, 153, 155, 159
Victorian literature and culture, 40, 47, 60, 67, 71, 90–91, 96, 118, 121, 123, 154–56, 196, 199, 243

Villon, François, 47
Vining, Edward Payson, 90 n. 16
vorticism, 36, 47, 110, 164, 165 n. 20, 189, 202

Waddell, Laurence Austine, 218, 233
Walras, Leon, 129
Wardlaw-Milne, John Sydney, 131
Way, Arthur Sanders, 89 n. 15
Webb, Sidney and Beatrice, 69, 130
Webster, Daniel, 188
Weintraub, Karl, 38 n. 4
Wells, H. G., 32
Whately, Richard, 128
Whibley, Charles, 6, 75–77
Whistler, James McNeill, 76
Whitman, Walt, 67–68
Wicksteed, Phillip Henry, 129–30, 132
Wilde, Oscar, 153
Wilhelm, James J., 230
Williams, Raymond, ix, 7, 38–39, 62
Williams, William Carlos, 195 n. 9
Wimsatt, W. K., Jr., 196
Woodward, Anthony, 168
Wordsworth, William, 85, 154–55, 180
Worsley, Philip Stanhope, 92
Wright, Harold, 133

Yeats, John Butler, 195
Yeats, William Butler, 13, 29–30, 34, 46–47, 72, 130
Young, Edward, "The Complaint, or Night Thoughts on Life, Death and Immortality," 67
Younghusband, Frances, 89 n. 15

Zeno, 138–39
Zola, Émile, 73
Zukofsky, Louis, 79, 170